Language and
Thought

Language and Thought

John L. Pollock

Princeton University Press
Princeton, New Jersey

*TO MY PARENTS, WHO WEREN'T
QUITE SURE WHAT I WAS UP TO,
BUT ENCOURAGED ME ANYWAY.*

Contents

Preface

A philosophical theory of language can aim for completeness in either of two senses. It may strive for "horizontal completeness", which would require it to give an account of all parts of language—singular terms, predicates, verbs, adverbs, adjectives, nondeclarative sentences, speech acts, etc. Alternatively, it may strive for "vertical completeness", analysing some linguistic notions in terms of others, but ultimately providing an analysis of language which does not take any semantical or linguistic notions as primitive. Vertical completeness requires that the theory not presuppose notions of meaning, reference, semantical rules, etc., but instead provides analyses for these notions in terms of nonlinguistic and nonsemantical notions. The theory of this book aims at vertical completeness. The objective is to start with nonlinguistic notions and build up a complete theory of language out of them. To assess the extent to which this goal has been achieved, the reader is referred to the final section of the appendix where the path of the analysis is reviewed. The book also attempts to achieve a certain amount of horizontal completeness, but that is more of a task for linguistics than philosphy, and no claim is made to real horizontal completeness in this book.

I first began thinking about this material in 1965 in response to the attack on analyticity by Quine and Putnam. The orientation of the work has changed over the years, and it now touches on analyticity only peripherally. Nevertheless, in my mind it lays to rest the ghost of those early concerns. I began serious work on the book in 1975, and a first draft was completed in 1977. The book has subsequently gone through two complete rewritings and several somewhat less extensive revisions, but the philosophical content has remained roughly constant. The changes have been mainly concerned with style of presentation.

This book reflects my feeling that is a lamentable lack of precision in most contemporary work in the philosophy of language. This is true even of those works that give the appearance of precision by making heavy use of logic and formal semantics. Such works have tended to ignore the question of how formal semantics is supposed to bear upon more fundamental philosophical questions. I have tried to achieve a much greater degree of precision in the current work. But there is a problem inherent in such a goal. Precision and readability are to some extent incompatible with one another. Readers of early versions of this book were unanimous in their opinion that the book was too hard to read. Thus the bulk of the revisions which the book has undergone have been concerned with striking a reasonable balance between precision and readability. No doubt many will complain that the book is still too hard to read, but I feel that it would be a mistake to sacrifice further precision in the interest of readability.

Because the philosophical content of the book was substantially completed four years ago, I have not been able to keep the references entirely up to date. I am sure that there are some highly relevant recent publications that have been overlooked in the bibliography, and I apologize to those authors for my oversight.

While I am on the topic of the bibliography, let me confess to another habit which may or may not be a bad one. I frequently develop my own position in response to criticisms of other views which I term 'traditional views' or 'the received view', but I rarely accompany the description of such views with extensive bibliographical citation. These are always views that I feel are or have been current, but it is not always easy to pin them on individual philosophers. It may even be that no one has ever held them. This does not really make any difference. They are views that I think are worth discussing regardless of who has held them. The ultimate business of the philosopher is to get at the truth on various issues, and not to say who said what. Although insofar as possible one should give credit where credit is due, in the last analysis it is the business of the historian rather than the philospher to trace views to their originators.

Very little of the material in this book has been published in the form of articles. This is partly because the presentation is highly systematic and the material does not lend itself to being split into article length portions. It is also partly because I kept thinking that I was about ready to publish the material in book form and did not wish to put the effort into writing separate articles on the material. There are, however, two exceptions to this. Much of the first chapter was published in an article entitled "Propositions and statements" in *The Pacific Philosophical Quarterly*. The material on *de re* belief in Chapter Three was published in almost its present form in an article entitled "Thinking about an object" in *Midwest Studies in Philosophy*. I wish to thank these publications for permission to reprint the material here.

I have received helpful comments from many philosophers. I would particularly like to thank Diana Ackerman, Rolf Eberle, Richard Feldman, Brian Loar, Nathan Salmon, and John Tienson. I would also like to thank the numerous graduate students who have labored through various portions of this material in my seminars, and I would like to thank the philosophy departments around the country who graciously invited me to present portions of this material at their colloquia.

Tucson, Arizona
May, 1981

Language and
Thought

I
The Statemental Theory of Meaning

1. The Traditional Theory of Language

Most philosophical theories of language fit into a tradition which attempts to explain various aspects of language by relating language to thought. This tradition is represented by a number of theories which differ in their details but agree in general outline. I will refer to all of these theories as 'versions of the traditional theory of language'. The theory takes its main impetus from Frege, but other proponents of the theory have included Bertrand Russell, G. E. Moore, C. I. Lewis, J. L. Austin, P. F. Strawson, Ludwig Wittgenstein, Richard Montague, John Searle, David Lewis, David Kaplan, and others. The views of these philosophers differ from one another in important respects, but there is enough of a family resemblance to regard them as endorsing variants of a common theory. Perhaps no philosopher, however, has ever endorsed all of the tenets of the theory I will now describe.

The key to the putative relationship between language and thought which this theory espouses is the notion of a proposition. Propositions have been supposed to play a dual role. On the one hand, propositions are supposed to be objects of belief and vehicles of thought (and presumably objects of other propositional attitudes as well). On the other hand, propositions are supposed to be products of assertion. According to this tradition, when a speaker assertively utters a sentence, what he asserts is a proposition. Thus one can assert what one believes and believe what one asserts.

We can draw at least a formal distinction between objects of belief and products of assertion. Let us, provisionally, define prop-

1

ositions to be objects or potential objects of belief or disbelief.[1] We can define *statements* to be products or potential products of assertion.[2] In ordinary philosophical parlance the term 'statement' is used ambiguously, on the one hand to refer to the speech act of making a statement, and on the other hand to refer to the statement made. In order to avoid confusion, I will only use the term in the latter way. The speech act of making a statement will be called a 'stating'. 'state' will also be used as a transitive verb so that we can talk about 'stating a statement'.

The central thesis of the traditional theory of language can now be formulated as the view that statements and propositions are the same things. This dual role of propositions provides the basis around which the rest of the theory is built. It is the conceptual role of propositions as objects of belief or vehicles of thought which enables them to provide content for linguistic assertions—what gets asserted is something which can be believed or otherwise entertained in thought. Furthermore, be reflecting upon the nature of thought, one can apparently acquire knowledge about linguistic assertions and hence about language. Conversely, by examining language, one can, it seems, acquire knowledge about the structure of thought. Thus traditional theories of language are simultaneously theories of thought.

The traditional view of propositions is that they have constituents, notably concepts and logical operators. Concepts are what can be believed or disbelieved of objects. If I believe that my typewriter is brown, then there is something which I believe of my typewriter, viz., that it is brown. More generally, we can talk about relational concepts, which are what we can believe or disbelieve of *n*-tuples of objects. We talk about objects *exemplifying* concepts. To say that my typewriter exemplifies the concept of being brown is just to say that my typewriter is brown. The extension of a concept is the set of all objects exemplifying it.

Concepts are supposed to be constituents of propositions, but the general notion of a propositional constituent is a problematic

---

[1] The reason for putting the definition in this way is that it is not obvious that all propositions can be believed. For example, can one believe an explicit contradiction? I am indebted to Jose Benardete for this way of avoiding the problem. The present definition will be refined still further in section two.

[2] It is unfortunate that we talk about *making* a statement. I have given lip service to this way of talking by saying that statements are products of assertion, but it is not to be supposed that we literally bring a statement into existence by stating it.

one and there is no generally accepted theory about this. The leading assumption is that propositions can be individuated in terms of their structure and constituents, and thus that they have however much structure this requires. Equivalently, there is as much propositional structure, and there are as many categories of propositional constituents, as are required for describing the contents of those cognitive states (like belief) which have propositions as objects. The inventory of propositional constituents is presumed to include at least concepts and logical operators. Does it include anything else? It is probably fair to take the traditional theory as claiming that it does not, although there have been differences of opinion on this. Some philosophers, most notably Russell, have taken physical objects to be constituents of propositions, and recent philosophers have talked in the same vein about "directly referential propositions". I will say more about this in section two.

The traditional view that there are no propositional constituents other than concepts and logical operators has an important implication which many philosophers have recently come to doubt. This is that it is only possible to think of a particular object *under a description*, where the description in question is a concept uniquely exemplified by that object. On the supposition that thinking about an object involves at least entertaining a proposition about that object, this implication results from the fact that given the preceding inventory of propositional constituents, the only way a proposition could select a particular object as its subject is by containing a concept uniquely exemplified by that object. There would be no other kind of propositional constituent which could select the subject of the proposition and accordingly determine what object one is thinking about. This has pervasive consequences for the theory of reference.

The putative dual role of propositions leads naturally to a theory of meaning, which I will call *The Propositional Theory of Meaning*.[3] The most fundamental part of the propositional theory of meaning is a theory of meaning for declarative sentences.[4] It is supposed that

---

[3] There is really more than one theory here, but I will regard them all as variants of a common theory.

[4] Throughout this book, by 'sentence' I mean 'declarative sentence' unless I say otherwise. I assume that the meaning of an interrogative sentence, imperative sentence, etc., is ultimately to be explained in terms of the meaning of related declarative sentences. This will be defended in Chapter Twelve.

when a speaker assertively utters[5] a sentence he thereby asserts a proposition. Presumably it is the meaning of the sentence which determines which proposition is thereby asserted, so the historically earliest versions of the propositional theory identified the meaning of the sentence with the proposition asserted. Sentences were supposed to "express" propositions, and the proposition expressed by a sentence was supposed to be its meaning. This theory of sentence meaning was embellished with a theory of lexical meaning. Sentences are constructed out of various meaningful elements—words and phrases—and the meaning of the whole sentence is a function of the meanings of those elements and the way they are combined. This seems to parallel the way in which propositions are constructed out of concepts and logical operators, so it was proposed that words and phrases express concepts and logical operators, and that the latter are the meanings of those linguistic items.

This simple version of the propositional theory of meaning is subject to an immediate difficulty which, although obvious once pointed out, was overlooked for many years.[6] Consider a sentence containing indexical expressions:

He is here.

Clearly, there is no one proposition which is always expressed by this sentence. If there were, we could ask whether this sentence, all by itself and independent of context, is true (i.e., expresses a true proposition). But that is absurd. The sentence 'He is here', all by itself, is neither true nor false. Rather, the sentence can be used to express many different propositions regarding the locations of different people and some of those propositions are true and others false. We might reasonably say of this sentence that instead of *its* expressing a proposition, a speaker using this sentence expresses a proposition. Which proposition the speaker expresses is a function not merely of what sentence he uses, but also various contextual elements. Does this mean that the sentence changes meaning from one occasion to the next? Some philosophers have thought so, but we must be careful here to distinguish between what the sentence

---

[5] I am following the customary procedure of using 'speaker', 'utterance', etc., in talking about all verbal behavior, be it written or spoken.

[6] The difficulty seems to have been discovered independently by a number of philosophers including at least Richard Cartwright, P. F. Strawson, Richard Montague, and David Kaplan.

means and what the speaker means. What the speaker means is the statement he is trying to make. What the speaker means does change from one occasion to the next. But the *sentence* does not change meaning. Talk about the meaning of a sentence is independent of any context. For example, without saying anything about context, we can say that the English sentence 'He is here' has the same meaning as the German sentence 'Er ist hier'. Thus the meaning of a sentence cannot be identified with the proposition expressed by the speaker. This fundamental tenet of the original version of the propositional theory of meaning is false.

It is worth noting just how widespread the phenomenon of indexicality is. It is most obvious in sentences containing explicitly indexical words like 'here' and 'he'. But it must not be overlooked that most sentences make implicit reference to a time—the time of utterance. When I utter the sentence 'There is a red book on the table', I mean that there is *now* a red book on the table. To believe that there is a red book on the table at one time is to believe a different proposition than to believe that there is a red book on the table at another time. Thus the proposition asserted by uttering the sentence 'There is a red book on the table' depends upon when it is uttered. This source of indexicality is present in most sentences.

Predicates and singular terms are also subject to indexicality. The words 'he' and 'is here' do not express fixed concepts. On the assumption that they do express concepts, these words must be regarded as expressing different concepts on different occasions. Thus what the simplest version of the propositional theory says about lexical meaning is also false.

In light of these kinds of difficulties, the original propositional theory of meaning has given way to what may be called 'the indexical propositional theory of meaning', and this theory is generally accepted by a large portion of the philosophical community. The indexical theory adopts the common-sensical position that the meaning of a declarative sentence determines, and is in turn determined by, what propositions are expressed by a speaker using the sentence under various circumstances. On this theory, the meaning of a sentence could be regarded, roughly, as a function mapping circumstances into propositions. Applied to any appropriate set of circumstances, the function gives us the proposition which would be expressed by a speaker using the sentence under those circumstances. A more conventional way of putting this would be that the meaning consists of or is constituted by the rules which determine what

5

proposition is expressed by an utterance of the sentence. I think it is fair to say that this view of meaning is widely accepted.

The indexical propositional theory of meaning can be regarded as having two components. Let us say that *the statemental theory of meaning* is the theory which takes the meaning of a declarative sentence to be constituted by the function which determines what statement would be made by uttering the sentence under various circumstances. The propositional theory of meaning can then be regarded as affirming the statemental theory of meaning and identifying statements with propositions. The advantage of formulating the theory in this way is that we can retain the statemental theory of meaning even if we reject the identification of statements with propositions.

It is convenient to distinguish between the meaning of a sentence and the *sense* of the sentence as used on a particular occasion. The sense of the sentence, as used on a particular occasion, is the statement made by using the sentence on that occasion. The sense of the sentence 'He is here' varies from occasion to occasion while the meaning remains fixed. According to the statemental theory of meaning, the meaning of a declarative sentence is determined by that function determining the sense of the sentence in various circumstances in which it might be used.

It is not quite accurate to identify the meaning of a sentence with a function from circumstances to statements. The difficulty is that under a single set of circumstances, one and the same nonambiguous sentence can be used simultaneously by two different speakers to make two different statements. For example, both speakers might utter the sentence 'I am here'. Each is making a statement about himself, and hence a different statement from the other speaker, but these statements are stated by uttering the same sentence in a single set of circumstances. The reason two different statements are made is, of course, that the single set of circumstances treats the two different utterances differently. To see how the circumstances of utterance treat a particular utterance made under those circumstances, we must examine what we might call 'the semantically relevant properties' which the utterance itself has under those circumstances. These will typically include such things as the time and place of the utterance, the identity of the speaker, perhaps various intentions of the speaker, etc. Following something like the current usage of the term 'pragmatics', let us call these *the pragmatic parameters of the utterance.*[7] The pragmatic parameters of an utterance are those parameters which are relevant to the determination of what statement is made or whether a statement is made. Which parameters will be the pragmatic parameters of an utterance is determined by what sentence is being uttered. For example, the identity of the speaker is one of the pragmatic parameters of an utterance of the sentence 'I am here' but not of an utterance of the sentence 'There is a book on the table'. Thus we can also call these *the pragmatic parameters of the sentence.* The meaning of the sentence is then determined by that function which, when applied to the pragmatic parameters of its utterance, determines what statement is made by that utterance of the sentence. Under some circumstances no statement will be made, so the function will be undefined for some combinations of values of the pragmatic parameters. Let us call this function the *S-intension* of the sentence ('*S*' for '*statement*'). This is the function which determines the sense of the sentence on each occasion of its being uttered.

The statemental theory of meaning proposes that the meaning of a declarative sentence is constituted by its *S*-intension in the sense that, necessarily, two declarative sentences have the same meaning iff they have the same *S*-intensions.[8] This claim is, I think, practically a truism. It seems just obvious, on the one hand, that the meaning of a sentence determines what statements are made by using the sentence under different circumstances, and hence generates the *S*-intension. It seems equally obvious, on the other hand, that the *S*-intension is sufficient to determine the meaning of the sentence. This is to say that if two sentences have different meanings, then there must be some circumstances under which it is possible to make different statements with them despite their pragmatic parameters having the same values (insofar as they overlap), which is just to say that the *S*-intensions of the two sentences are distinct. Thus I feel that we can safely assume the statemental theory of meaning for declarative sentences. This does not commit us to saying that the statements made are propositions, so to endorse the statemental

[7] Pragmatics is supposed to be concerned with what proposition is asserted when a sentence is uttered. For a good discussion of recent philosophical work in pragmatics, see van Fraassen [1977].

[8] I talk about '*the* meaning' and '*the S*-intension' of *P*, but if *P* is ambiguous it has more than one meaning and more than one *S*-intension.

theory of meaning is not yet to endorse the propositional theory of meaning.

The indexical propositional theory of meaning also embodies a modified theory of lexical meaning. We saw that words all by themselves cannot generally be regarded as expressing concepts, but it seems reasonable to suppose that in asserting a proposition by uttering a sentence, a speaker is using the constituent words and phrases to express the constituents of the proposition. A proposition is supposed to be built out of concepts and logical operators, so it seems reasonable to propose that when a speaker utters a meaningful word or phrase in the course of asserting a proposition, he is using it to express a concept or logical operator. We can regard the latter as the *sense* of the lexical item on that occasion of its use. Then we can regard the meaning of the lexical item as being constituted by the rule which determines what concept or logical operator is expressed by it in a given set of circumstances. More precisely, we can talk about the pragmatic parameters of the lexical item, and take its meaning to be determined by that function which when applied to specific values of the pragmatic parameters gives us the sense of the item as used in circumstances in which the pragmatic parameters have those values.

The propositional theory of lexical meaning is more plausible for certain linguistic items than for others. It is most plausible for predicates, and I think it is mainly because it has seemed to work so well for predicates that philosophers have felt that it must work for other parts of speech as well. Unfortunately, it has proven very difficult to force certain parts of speech into the mold which appears to fit predicates so well. Proper names have long been an annoyance to the traditional theory because we seem unable to find appropriate concepts for them to express. But before we condemn the traditional theory on this score, we should take note of just how strong the traditional reasons are for supposing that proper names must express concepts. When one entertains a proposition about a particular object, it seems that one must be thinking about the object in terms of some description of it. You cannot get the object itself into your head, so the only way to think of it is under a description. This mental description is a concept. Thus it seems that a singular proposition can be about a particular object only via a concept which picks out that object. Hence, singular terms *must* express concepts. This is a compelling argument, despite the fact that its conclusion is not very plausible.

8

We distinguished between the propositional and statemental theories of sentence meaning and endorsed the latter. It seems that we should make a similar distinction between a propositional and statemental theory of lexical meaning. If sentences are used to make statements, then it seems reasonable that lexical items should be used to express constituents of statements. A statemental theory of lexical meaning would take the sense of a lexical item to be a statemental constituent rather than a propositional constituent. Such a theory, however, is much more contentious than the statemental theory of sentence meaning. It presupposes a doctrine of statemental structure and constituents which may seem problematic, particularly if statements are different from propositions. Although I will ultimately endorse such a theory, I will not try to foist it upon the reader at this time.

2. Propositions

I have endorsed the statemental theory of meaning. In this section and the next I will explore the statement/proposition distinction and use it, first, to argue against the propositional theory of meaning, and second, to propose embellishments to the statemental theory of meaning which will suit it for an assault on a number of problems which have proven recalcitrant within the more restrictive propositional theory.

Let us begin by focusing upon an important obscurity in the traditional account of propositions. Propositions are supposed to be *what* we believe or disbelieve, but under different circumstances we employ different criteria for deciding whether one believes the same thing on two occasions. Suppose that yesterday I believed that there was a book on the table and today I believe that there is a book on the table. On this basis we could correctly report that I believe the same thing today as I did yesterday. On the other hand, we could also insist that what I believe today is *not* the same thing as what I believed yesterday, because what I believed yesterday might have been false while that I believe today is true.

We can avoid the preceding difficulty by distinguishing between believing something *of a time* and believing something *simpliciter*. The sense in which I believed the same thing yesterday as I believe today is that I believed the same thing *of a time* yesterday as I believe of a time today. On the other hand, what I believe *simpliciter* is *itself* about a particular time—I don't believe it *of* a time, I just believe it. Now we have a choice regarding how we are going to use the term 'proposition'. We could take propositions to be either what we believe or disbelieve simpliciter or what we believe or disbelieve of times. Let us call these *nontransient* and *transient propositions*, respectively. The term 'proposition' has occasionally been used to refer to transient propositions, but I think it is more common to restrict it to nontransient propositions.

The distinction between transient and nontransient propositions is just the tip of the iceberg. For example, we frequently judge two people to believe the same thing if they believe the same thing of the same object, even if they are thinking of the object in two different ways (e.g., under two different descriptions). At other times, we would insist that in order for them to believe the same thing they must be thinking of the object in the same way. Objects of belief of the former sort might be called 'directly referential propositions'. They have figured prominently in recent theories of proper names, although many traditional theorists would have denied that there can be such propositions.

What we are finding is that under different circumstances, more or less stringent conditions are required for believing the same thing. These different conditions lead to finer- or coarser-grained objects of belief. This phenomenon was largely overlooked or ignored by traditional theories of thought. Insofar as such theories pronounced on the matter, they would probably have favored restricting 'proposition' to maximally fine-grained objects of belief or disbelief, but the situation is far from clear and is mainly a matter of terminology.

At this point one might begin to wonder whether there really are all these different objects of belief of varying graininess. For present purposes the best response to such skepticism is that we need not take propositions very seriously in the philosophy of language. At a crude level, the narrative function of language is to convey thoughts. Talk of propositions is just a convenient way to describe the contents of our thoughts. To say that there is a proposition of a certain sort is to say that it is possible for one to have a belief of a corresponding sort. At the expense of additional complexity, we could dispense with talk of propositions in the current investigation and talk instead of types of belief states individuated in terms of sameness of content. Different criteria for sameness of content generate different types of belief states and correspondingly different objects of belief.

There are two kinds of considerations which are involved in content-comparisons of belief states. First, the belief states can be compared introspectively. An introspective difference in the way one is thinking of an object is relevant to the fine-grained object of one's belief, but less relevant to what directly referential proposition one believes. Different criteria for sameness of content result from taking different introspective differences to make a difference to what is believed. The finest-grained criterion will require there to be no introspective differences. For example, in thinking x to be F, there must be no introspectively discernible difference either in the way one is thinking of x or in the way one is thinking of the property attributed to x. If there is no introspectively discernible difference between belief states, I will say that they are *phenomenologically indistinguishable*.

Even phenomenological indistinguishability is not sufficient to guarantee that two belief states have the same content. There is also a kind of indexicality involved in belief. For example, the time at which one is in the belief state is generally relevant to what one believes. This underlies the transient/nontransient distinction. But a variation in the time of belief is not reflected by an introspectible difference in the belief states. And there may be other indexical considerations which might be involved in comparisons of content. Maximally fine-grained objects of belief result from maximally fine-grained criteria for sameness of content. The latter must require not only phenomenological indistinguishability of the belief states, but also that all the relevant indexical parameters be the same.

Coarse-grained objects of belief can always be described in terms of maximally fine-grained objects of belief. This is because a coarse-grained object of belief ϕ can be described by describing the circumstances under which one can be said to believe it, i.e., by describing the range of belief states which are states of believing ϕ. Every belief state can be regarded as having a maximally fine-grained object of belief, so an equivalent description of ϕ proceeds by describing the maximally fine-grained objects of belief by believing which one can believe ϕ. If we wished, we might simply identify the coarse-grained object of belief with the corresponding set of maximally fine-grained objects of belief. For example, we might identify a transient proposition with the set of all nontransient propositions belief in which would constitute believing the same thing of different times. Similarly, we might identify the directly referential proposition that x is F with the set of all maximally fine-grained objects of belief wherein x is thought of in different ways and believed to be F.

Objects of belief of varying degrees of graininess are all equally respectable philosophically. But maximally fine-grained objects of belief are in various ways philosophically central. First, there is reason to believe that a number of traditional theses about propositions were only intended to apply to maximally fine-grained objects of belief. For example, whether it is true or not that maximally fine-grained objects of belief are all constructed exclusively out of concepts and logical operators, that is certainly not true of coarse-grained objects of belief. Second, as we have seen, coarse-grained objects of belief can be described in terms of maximally fine-grained objects of belief, and hence are theoretically dispensable. We lose nothing by formulating a theory of language entirely in terms of maximally fine-grained objects of belief. Third, a theory which takes coarse-grained objects of belief as primitive and does not explain them in terms of maximally fine-grained objects of belief is basically incomplete. Without an account of what it is to believe a particular coarse-grained object of belief, we don't really know what object of belief we are talking about, and so the theory is correspondingly vague.[9] But an account of what it is to believe the coarse-grained object of belief has the effect of describing it in terms of maximally fine-grained objects of belief. Thus any satisfactorily complete semantical theory which proceeds in terms of objects of belief must appeal ultimately to maximally fine-grained objects of belief. For these reasons, I will confine my use of the term 'proposition' to maximally fine-grained objects of belief. It should be emphasized that this is not to imply that there is anything wrong with coarse-grained objects of belief. This restriction on the use of the term 'proposition' is intended primarily to avoid senseless disputes about, e.g., whether there are "really" such things as directly referential propositions. The answer to the latter question is, "It depends upon what you mean by 'proposition'."

Having decided how we are going to use the term 'proposition', next consider how we are to understand talk about the structure of propositions. The traditional assumption was that propositions are individuated by their structure and constituents. If two propositions are distinct, they must either have different constituents, or their

---

[9] For example, some philosophers might want to identify belief in a directly referential proposition with *de re* belief. Then the dispute over what is required for *de re* belief would automatically infect the question of what objects of belief we are talking about when we talk about directly referential propositions.

constituents must be put together differently. Having announced that I do not take propositions seriously, I cannot very well take propositional structure seriously either. It cannot be that propositions "really have" a certain kind of structure (like atoms) which we are setting out to discover. If talk of propositions is just a convenient way of talking about sameness of content for belief states, then talk of propositional structure must be just a convenient way of describing propositions (or the corresponding belief states). The individuation of propositions is parallel to sameness of content, and the latter is determined jointly by phenomenological indistinguishability and indexical parameters. Thought has a certain amount of introspectible structure. We can tell by introspection, for example, that we are thinking of an object in a certain way and thinking some particular thing about it. Thus if propositions are to be individuated by structure and constituents, that structure must mirror to some extent the structure of the corresponding belief states, and propositions must contain constituents corresponding to the introspectively simple elements of the belief states and also constituents corresponding to the indexical parameters. It must at this point be an open question whether we can really give useful descriptions of this sort for propositions, but at least for the purposes of this book it will turn out that we can.

3. Statements

The central assumption of the traditional theory of language is that statements and propositions are the same things. The central thesis of this book will be that they are not. It will be contended that traditional theories of language have taken a simplistic view of the relationship between language and thought, and that there is a real distinction to be made between propositions and statements. It will not even be quite true to say that statements are coarse-grained objects of belief. Statements have a different function than propositions and this results in their having different characteristics. To be sure, some statements are propositions, but that is only a kind of limiting case. Most statements fail to be propositions and many propositions fail to be statements.

The full defense of the claim that statements and propositions are distinct will be scattered throughout this book. It will be argued in Chapter Three that the propositions we entertain when we think about particular objects are generally not statements, and on that

13

basis it will be argued that singular statements about particular objects are rarely propositions. In Chapter Six the analogous conclusion will be urged for most general statements and general propositions. Both of these conclusions will require considerable preliminary development. However, even at this early point, by looking at statements made by uttering sentences containing the first-person pronoun 'I' and the corresponding beliefs that one may have about oneself, we can exhibit considerations which appear to indicate that there must be a distinction between statements and propositions. Unfortunately, when we proceed in this way, the considerations which we must adduce are rather contentious, and although I find the arguments in their favor compelling, there are others who do not. Thus I would not want to leave the impression that the statement/proposition distinction in any way depends upon these considerations regarding first-person statements and propositions. The appeal to these considerations is just the quickest way to motivate the distinction. If the reader finds these considerations unconvincing, he is referred to the discussions of proper names and synthetic predicates where the same conclusions about statements and propositions can be generated from entirely different bases.

Now let us turn to first-person beliefs. We can talk a bit loosely about 'ways of thinking of objects'. As we have seen, the traditional theory of thought alleges that we can only think of objects under descriptions. In opposition to that, it will be argued in Chapter Three that it is actually rather unusual to think of objects under descriptions. But we need not pursue that general conclusion in order to see that the traditional view is false. Consider how we think of ourselves. I propose that each person has a way of thinking of himself which he alone can employ.[10] Let us separate this claim into two parts. First, I claim that there is a special way of thinking of oneself which is ordinarily reflected by the use of the first-person pronoun 'I'. When one has a belief about himself which he can properly report by saying ⌜I am F⌝, he is thinking of himself in this special way. Second, I claim that no one else can think of me in that same way.

Let us begin with the first claim. That there is this special way of thinking of oneself is best seen by contrasting it with other ways

---

[10] John Perry [1977] has recently argued against what he regards as the linguistic reasons in Frege [1965] for holding this same view, so it should be emphasized that the reasons advanced here are epistemological—not linguistic.

of thinking of oneself. I can, for example, think of myself under a description; or I might see myself in a mirror and think of myself in whatever way we normally think of objects we are perceiving. These are ways in which other people can also think of me. But notice that these ways of thinking all have the characteristic that I can be mistaken about whether they are ways of thinking of myself. If I see myself in a mirror, I may not realize that it is I that I am seeing; and I may correspondingly think to myself 'That is not I'. In doing so I must be using 'I' to express a way of thinking of myself which is distinct from the perceptual way of thinking of myself. Similarly, given any other way of thinking of myself, I may sensibly believe that the person I am thinking about in that way is not I, from which it follows that in that belief I am thinking about myself in two different ways. My use of 'I' reflects a special way of thinking of myself which is distinct from all of the descriptive or perceptual ways of thinking of myself. But it seems that another person can only think of me in those descriptive or perceptual ways, so he cannot think of me in this privileged way.[11]

If we confine ourselves to logical considerations, it is apt to seem puzzling that we have this special way of thinking of ourselves. A possible explanation is epistemological. Anything we know about some object other than ourself must presuppose some descriptive characterization of that object. There is no way to get into epistemic contact with another object except in terms of facts about it. However, the same thing cannot be true of oneself. All of our knowledge arises ultimately from epistemologically basic propositions, and epistemologically basic propositions are always first-person propositions.[12] They are propositions like 'I am appeared to redly', 'I am in pain', 'I recall having eggs for breakfast', etc. Unless we could know the truth of these propositions without first acquiring descriptive knowledge of ourselves, all knowledge would be impossible. Thus epistemological necessity requires us to have a nondescriptive way of thinking of ourselves.

If no one else can think of me in my privileged way, then the propositions I believe when I think of myself in this way are

[11] This must be hedged. In Chapter Three it will be urged that there are other ways of thinking of people besides the descriptive and perceptual ways considered here. But that will not affect the present argument because they are still distinct from my privileged way of thinking of myself.

[12] Some philosophers will deny this, but I have defended it at length in Pollock [1974].

propositions only I can believe. They are, in this sense, "logically idiosyncratic". Let us define:

(3.1) ϕ is *logically idiosyncratic relative to* S iff $\Diamond(S$ believes $\phi)$ & $\Box(\forall S^*)(S^* \neq S \supset S^*$ does not believe $\phi)$.

Is it really clear that no one else can think of me in the same non-descriptive way as I can think of myself? If someone else is thinking of me, his cognitive state cannot just miraculously come to be about me. There must be something about his state which makes me its object. For example, another person's state could be a state of thinking of me by virtue of being descriptively or perceptually connected with me. But then it would not be a matter of thinking of me in my privileged way. Is there anything which could make another person's cognitive state a state of thinking of me in the same way I think of myself when I think of myself in my privileged way? The only possibility that comes to mind is that his state might be phenomenologically the same as mine. I am not sure that such interpersonal judgments of phenomenological sameness make sense, but even if they do another person's cognitive state being phenomenologically the same as mine would, if anything, make it a state of thinking of *him*self in his privileged way—not a state of thinking of me in that way. So it seems to make no sense to talk about someone else thinking of me in my privileged way. There is no conceivable circumstance which could make that true. Hence my beliefs about myself wherein I think of myself in my privileged way are logically idiosyncratic.

It should be emphasized that there is a difference between entertaining a proposition and thinking about that proposition. Although I cannot entertain someone else's first-person proposition, I can think about it (and have just been doing so). I know what it is to have first-person beliefs, so I know what it is like for someone else to have first-person beliefs, and I can think of his first-person propositions as the propositions he believes when he has first-person beliefs. Note, however, that I can only think of another person's first-person propositions in terms of some way of thinking of that person, and my way of thinking of that person is different from the way he thinks of himself in having those first-person beliefs.

The thesis that first-person propositions are logically idiosyncratic is apt to seem counterintuitive if one takes propositions too seriously. Logically idiosyncratic propositions may seem ontologically

16

mysterious. If propositions are "really out there", how can it be that one person can believe a proposition which no one else can believe?[13] But recall that talk of propositions is really just talk of belief. All that is being claimed here is that when I think of myself in my privileged way, no one else can think precisely the same thought. That is because there is nothing which would count as thinking the same thought. This may still be surprising, but it is not strongly counterintuitive.

The logical idiosyncrasy of first-person beliefs is essential to their playing the role they do in cognition. Perry [1977] gives the following example: "An amnesiac, Rudolf Lingens, is lost in Stanford library. He reads a number of things in the library, including a biography of himself. . . . He still won't know who he is, . . . no matter how much knowledge he piles up, until that moment when he is ready to say, . . . '*I* am Rudolf Lingens'." Perry, and more recently David Lewis [1979], take this example to show that Lingens' belief that he is Lingens (when he acquires it) cannot consist merely of believing a proposition. An essential part of their reasoning is that if Lingens' belief did consist of believing a proposition, then if someone else believed that proposition that would constitute *his* believing that he was Lingens. But, so goes the argument, as the proposition is true, other people *ought* to believe it. But it is not the case that other people ought to believe that they are Lingens, so believing that one is Lingens cannot consist of believing such a proposition. It is the next to the last step of this argument which fails. Lingens' belief that he is Lingens consists of believing a *first-person* proposition, but such propositions are logically idiosyncratic. Thus the mere fact that such a proposition is true is no reason for thinking that other people ought to believe it—they can't believe it. Thus there is no obstacle to Lingens' believing that he is Lingens consisting of believing a proposition.

Given the existence of logically idiosyncratic propositions about oneself, it follows that one can also believe logically idiosyncratic propositions about objects other than oneself. This is because one can think of those objects in terms of descriptions involving one's privileged way of thinking of oneself. For example, I can think of

[13] This sort of reasoning seems, in part, to underlie David Lewis's argument [1979] that first-person belief does not have propositional objects. What Lewis means by 'proposition' is 'set of possible worlds', and he takes a strongly realistic view of possible worlds.

my mother under the description 'the mother of me' where I think of myself in my privileged way. This is a way of thinking of my mother which no one else can employ, and hence it generates a proposition about her which is logically idiosyncratic relative to me. I can think of other objects in terms of similar *mixed descriptions* composed in part of purely qualitative logical items and in part of my privileged way of thinking of myself. I can think of my chair as the chair in which I am now sitting, Angell Hall as the building in which I am now working, etc.

Such mixed descriptions are epistemologically important. It is in principle possible to think of objects in terms of purely qualitative descriptions, but if we seriously consider how often we know that there is a unique object satisfying a purely qualitative description, the answer would seem to be 'almost never'.[14] Descriptions we can give of particular objects almost invariably relate them to other particular objects. For example, we can describe an object in terms of its spatio-temporal coordinates, but those coordinates must in turn be fixed by relating them to particular objects. Or we might describe an object in terms of its causal relation to other objects, etc. In order to provide a foundation for such a chain of descriptions, we must be able to describe or otherwise select some objects in other ways, and we frequently do this by relating them to ourselves. We describe some objects in terms of how they are related to us (for example, we may be perceiving them), other objects in terms of how they are related to the first objects, and so on. The descriptions we generate in this way are always mixed descriptions. If we were constrained to employ only purely qualitative descriptions in thinking about objects, we would virtually never be in a position to think of any individual object.

Thus far we have encountered three ways of thinking of objects: one can think of oneself in one's privileged way; one can in principle think of other objects in terms of purely qualitative descriptions; and one can more realistically think of other objects (and oneself) in terms of mixed descriptions. It will be argued in Chapter Three that it is also possible to think of objects in another way which is "phenomenologically simple" but rests upon a descriptive backing, and it will be maintained that the propositions arising from this way of thinking of objects are also logically idiosyncratic. However, for now nothing will turn upon whether this is so.

[14] I take this observation from Chisholm [1976a].

When we think of an object in a particular way in the course of believing something about it, we are believing a proposition about that object. The structure of the proposition reflects the structure of our cognitive state. Our cognitive state contains our way of thinking of the object—this is the subject constituent of our thought. Correspondingly, the proposition believed contains a subject constituent which designates that object. Let us call such constituents *propositional designators*. The most familiar propositional designators are definite descriptions, but there must be others as well. When we believe propositions about ourselves wherein we think of ourselves in our logically privileged ways, those propositions have subject constituents which are not definite descriptions. They are propositional designators of a different sort. We can call them *personal designators*. Personal designators can then be incorporated into more complicated definite descriptions which are not built exclusively from concepts. As this investigation proceeds, we will find that there are other kinds of propositional designators as well, i.e., there are other ways of thinking of objects.

Now let us reconsider the identification of propositions and statements. It has been suggested that many and perhaps most of those propositions we believe about individual objects are logically idiosyncratic. But logically idiosyncratic propositions cannot be statements. Statements must be stateable. Stating is communicating. You cannot communicate a logically idiosyncratic proposition, because two different people cannot believe or even entertain the same logically idiosyncratic proposition. Thus logically idiosyncratic propositions are not statements. Half of the traditional identification of statements with propositions fails.

To see that the other half also fails, consider the statements we make by uttering sentences containing 'I'. Suppose I say, 'I am tired'. If my statement is "in earnest"—if, as we say, I "believe what I say"— then I believe that I am tired. The proposition I thereby believe is logically idiosyncratic. Hence it is not the same thing as my statement. But surely my statement is not some other proposition. If it were then my believing what I say would consist of believing that other proposition instead. So it follows that my statement is not any proposition at all. Similarly, if I make a statement about a particular object by uttering a sentence containing a proper name, and I believe what I say, then I am thinking about that object in some particular way. But it has been suggested that the proposition I thereby believe will characteristically be logically idiosyncratic, and hence it cannot be the same thing as the statement I assert either. Once again, if believing what I say consists of believing this proposition, then my statement cannot be some other proposition; so the statement I make is not a proposition.[15]

The appeal to 'I' has been the quickest way to generate the statement/proposition distinction, but it may also be the most contentious. I do stand behind the preceding remarks and I find the arguments compelling, but it should be reiterated that the viability of the statement/proposition distinction in no way turns upon the preceding remarks. As will be seen in Chapters Three and Six, the distinction can be generated equally well by looking at the functioning of proper names or at those predicates which will be called 'synthetic predicates'. The purpose of the preceding remarks has been to motivate the distinction quickly so that it can be taken into account during the remainder of this chapter.

If I make a statement and it is not a proposition, what is it? Statements are objects of statings. The function of stating is to convey information. Without, for the moment, trying to be precise, we can say that the conveyance of information consists of the speaker having a certain proposition in mind and his audience coming to have related propositions in mind. Let us call these *the sent-proposition* and *the received-propositions* respectively. The sent-proposition is the proposition the speaker must believe if his stating is "in earnest", i.e., if he "believes what he says". The received-proposition is the proposition in terms of which a member of the audience understands the speaker. The simplest case is that in which the sent-proposition and the received-proposition are the same proposition, but that is not necessary for the conveyance of information. For example, the speaker may be attempting to convey to his audience that a certain object has a certain property. As long as his audience knows what object he is referring to and understands what property he is attributing to it, his purpose will have been achieved. It is not necessary to his purpose that the audience comes to think of

[15] A possible rejoinder at this point would be to insist that the statement made is the same as the proposition entertained, but that where the traditional theory errs is in supposing that in order to understand what a speaker says the members of the audience must come to entertain the very same proposition as the one the speaker asserts. This suggestion will differ only verbally from a special case of the theory advanced below, but it cannot be maintained in general because, as we will see in Chapter Three there are numerous cases in which the same statement can be made by "sending" different propositions (in the sense of the succeeding paragraphs).

the object in the same way as the speaker. If the audience thinks of the object in a different way than the speaker, then the received-proposition is not the same as the sent-proposition despite the conveyance of information having been successful. Thus we can say that the function of stating is to get the audience to receive a proposition related in some specified way to the sent-proposition, but perhaps not identical with the sent-proposition.

Apparently statements transcend propositions. Insofar as a proposition is communicable, it will also be a statement (in which case the sent- and received-propositions will be the same), but there are statements which are not propositions. One reason we employ such statements is that the propositions we entertain when we think about individual objects are almost invariably logically idiosyncratic, in which case it is in principle impossible for the received-proposition to be identical with the sent-proposition. The requirement that the sent- and received-propositions be identical would make almost all of our discourse about individual objects impossible. The distinction between statements and propositions arises from the necessity for language to avoid the logically idiosyncratic elements of our thought. In this connection, it will be argued in Chapter Six that logically idiosyncratic elements also arise from the consideration of concepts and predicates. In general, nonpropositional statements are devices for abstracting from the logically idiosyncratic elements of our thought and conveying just *part* of what we believe.

Although a statement may be distinct from the sent- and received-propositions, it can be characterized in terms of them. The function of a statement is to convey information. Thus the statement can be characterized by describing the information conveyed by stating it under different possible circumstances. The information conveyed in a particular case is described by describing the sent- and received-propositions. The more similar they are, the more information is conveyed. This suggests proceeding as follows. Under different circumstances, speakers can state the same statement by sending different propositions. Let us call those features of the circumstances which affect what propositions are possible sent- and acceptable received-propositions *the dynamic parameters of the statement*. Then a statement ϕ can be characterized by specifying, for each set of values of the dynamic parameters, what the possible sent- and acceptable received-propositions are for each person. This information is most easily codified by a function which we will call *the diagram* of the statement. The diagram is a function which, to each

21

set of values of the dynamic parameters, assigns the ordered pair $\langle \Sigma, \Omega \rangle$ of functions where for each person S, $\Sigma(S)$ is the set of propositions S could be sending in making the statement and $\Omega(S)$ is the set of propositions that would be acceptable received-propositions if S were a member of the audience:

> (3.2) If ϕ is a statement and $v_1, \ldots, v_n$ are the dynamic parameters of ϕ, the *diagram* of ϕ is that function ζ such that, necessarily, if $x_1, \ldots, x_n$ are particular values of the parameters $v_1, \ldots, v_n$ respectively, then $\zeta(x_1, \ldots, x_n) = \langle \Sigma, \Omega \rangle$ where Σ and Ω are functions such that for each person S, $\Sigma(S)$ is the set of possible sent-propositions for ϕ relative to $x_1, \ldots, x_n$ for S and $\Omega(S)$ is the set of acceptable received-propositions for ϕ relative to $x_1, \ldots, x_n$ for S.

The possible sent- and acceptable received-propositions may vary from person to person because, among other things, they may be logically idiosyncratic.

There must be constraints on diagrams for them to actually be the diagrams of statements. A minimal constraint is that for any particular set of values of the dynamic parameters, all possible sent-propositions and all acceptable received-propositions must have the same truth value. I suggest that there is also a modal constraint which requires that for any particular set of values of the dynamic parameters, either all of the possible sent- and acceptable received-propositions are necessary or they are all contingent. Without the modal constraint, it would be possible for one person to accept a statement by believing a necessary truth while a second person accepted the same statement by believing a contingent truth. That would be at least peculiar. However, this modal constraint will have no effect on anything until Chapter Eight, at which point it will be discussed again. In addition to the truth value constraint and modal constraint, there may be other constraints on diagrams of statements, but no attempt will be made here to say what they are.

In an important sense, the characterization of statements in terms of their diagrams constitutes an analysis of statements in terms of propositions. It would be very much in the spirit of contemporary philosophical logic to go on to identify statements with their diagrams, thus in some sense doing away with statements altogether.

There may be reasons for resisting this,[16] but at the very least it seems that all *talk* of statements is eliminable in favor of talk of their diagrams.

Our characterization of statements in terms of their diagrams enables us to understand why various logical notions are applicable to both statements and propositions. For example, we talk about propositions being true, but we also talk about statements being true. Truth for statements is definable in terms of truth for propositions, viz., a statement is true iff its possible sent- and acceptable received-propositions are true.

4. Sentence Meaning

We have followed the traditional theory in taking the meaning of a declarative sentence to be constituted by its *S*-intension, where the latter is a function determining what statement is made by uttering the sentence under various circumstances. The traditional theory goes on to identify that statement with a proposition, but I have been arguing that such an identification is incorrect and that the statement should instead be characterized in terms of its diagram. This difference will prove to be of considerable importance in dealing with problems in the philosophy of language. The logical mechanism of sent- and received-propositions provides an added level of structure which enables us to formulate linguistic theories

---

[16] The principal difficulty with such an identification is that it would preclude our saying that some statements *are* propositions. In the particularly simple case of a statement for which there is only one possible sent-proposition and it is also the only acceptable received-proposition, we want to say that the statement in question literally *is* that proposition and not the function ζ. A second obstacle to the identification is that the diagram of a statement is not unique. If ϕ has more than one dynamic parameter, then we can generate "equivalent" diagrams by simple rearranging the order of the arguments. Furthermore, the dynamic parameters themselves may not be uniquely determined. We will frequently find that the dynamic parameters must be such that certain information is obtainable from them but that there is more than one set of parameters which would accomplish this and that the only way to choose between alternative selections of the parameters is on the basis of convenience. We will encounter an example of this in section three. In such a case, it seems reasonable to say that the statement has different diagrams corresponding to different choices of the dynamic parameters. Thus it seems better to say that statements are "logically correlated with" their diagrams rather than being identical with their diagrams. In the same sense, the natural numbers are logically correlated with certain sets.

that could not be formulated within the propositional theory. For example, the theory of proper names included in the propositional theory (as developed in section one) claims that when a speaker asserts a proposition by uttering a sentence containing a proper name, that proposition contains as a constituent the propositional designator in terms of which the speaker is thinking of the referent of the name. In other words, the statement made is identified with the sent-proposition. Presumably, on this account, a member of the audience can only understand the speaker's statement by coming to entertain the same proposition as the one the speaker is asserting. If he comes to entertain a different proposition, he has misunderstood the speaker. But the way the speaker thinks of the referent of the name will ordinarily reflect his peculiar relationship to the referent, and will frequently even be logically idiosyncratic. Consequently, this theory of names seems to make it virtually impossible for the audience to ever understand a speaker who makes a statement by uttering a sentence containing a proper name. That is surely preposterous. We can avoid this embarrassing consequence by distinguishing between, on the one hand, the statement the speaker makes, and on the other hand, the proposition the speaker sends and the propositions the members of the audience receive. We need not require the members of the audience to receive the same proposition as the speaker sends in order for them to understand what he is saying. This idea will be devloped in Chapter Three.

To give a concrete illustration of the power of the logical machinery contained in our statemental theory of sentence meaning, let us consider how it might be employed in giving the meaning of simple sentences containing the first-person pronoun 'I'. Giving the meaning of such sentences proved an insurmountable task within the propositional theory of meaning. The difficulty is the one we have already noted. If a person says ⌜I am F⌝ and "believes what he is saying", he is thinking about himself in terms of his personal designator. Accordingly, his sent-proposition contains that personal designator. But that makes it logically idiosyncratic. Consequently, if the statement made were the same as the sent-proposition, no one in the speaker's audience could understand it. Frege [1956] arrived at this same conclusion, and inferred from it that although when one thinks ⌜I am F⌝ to himself he thinks of himself in terms of his personal designator, when he *says* ⌜I am F⌝, in order to make his statement comprehensible, he must change his thought and think of himself in some other way. This is an implausible conclusion at best. We can avoid it by invoking the distinction between the speaker's sent-proposition and the statement stated.

Let us suppose that F expresses a concept α. The only obvious pragmatic parameter for the sentence $\ulcorner$I am $F\urcorner$ is the identity of the speaker. For each speaker S, there is a unique statement ϕ_S which he states, under all circumstances in which he states anything, by assertively uttering $\ulcorner$I am $F\urcorner$. Thus the S-intension of $\ulcorner$I am $F\urcorner$ is that function Δ such that, for each S, $\Delta(S) = \phi_S$. It remains to describe the statements ϕ_S. That can be done in terms of their diagrams. If δ is a propositional designator, let $(\alpha:\delta)$ be the proposition which results from ascribing α to δ. For a person S, let ι_S be his personal designator. Then $(\alpha:\iota_S)$ is a possible sent-proposition for ϕ_S for S. Is $(\alpha:\iota_S)$ the only possible sent-proposition for ϕ_S? It is plausible to suppose that it is, although Kaplan [1977] has (in effect) claimed otherwise. As the present account is intended primarily for illustrative purposes, let me simply be dogmatic on this point and assert that $(\alpha:\iota_S)$ is the only possible sent-proposition for ϕ_S. This will be reconsidered with care in Chapter Four.

When S states ϕ_S and thinks of himself in terms of ι_S, the members of his audience cannot think of him in that same way. They must think of him in terms of a propositional designator, but there is no obvious basis for preferring some propositional designators to others as long as they all designate S. Thus it appears that if S^* is a member of S's audience and δ is *any* propositional designator designating S, if S^* can entertain propositions containing δ, then $(\alpha:\delta)$ is an acceptable received-proposition for ϕ_S for S^*.

Thus our description of the meaning of $\ulcorner$I am $F\urcorner$ is as follows. First, the sole pragmatic parameter of $\ulcorner$I am $F\urcorner$ is the identity of the speaker, and the S-intension of $\ulcorner$I am $F\urcorner$ is that function Δ which to each speaker S assigns ϕ_S.[17] Second, we describe ϕ_S in terms of its diagram. There is only one possible sent-proposition for ϕ_S, and it is the same on every occasion. However, the acceptable received-propositions vary from circumstance to circumstance. Whether $(\alpha:\delta)$ is an acceptable received-proposition depends upon whether δ designates S, and that in turn may depend upon contingent facts (e.g., δ might be a definite description). Thus we must adopt something as a dynamic parameter that determines which designators

---

[17] This is an oversimplification. The time of utterance must also be a pragmatic parameter and the statement stated must involve temporal reference. However, this sophistication will be systematically ignored until Chapter Four.

designate S. The simplest such parameter is the set of such designators itself: $\{\delta|\delta$ designates $S\}$. We can take this to be the sole dynamic parameter.[18] Then for a particular value of this parameter:

$$(4.1) \quad \Sigma(S^*) = \begin{cases} \{\alpha:\iota_S\} \text{ if } S^* = S; \\ \varnothing \text{ if } S^* \neq S. \end{cases}$$

$$\Omega(S^*) = \{(\alpha:\delta)|\delta \text{ designates } S \text{ and } S^* \text{ can entertain} \\ \text{propositions containing } \delta\}.[19]$$

This description of meaning could not have been given within a propositional sematics. It will be tidied up somewhat in Chapter Four, but it illustrates the power of our statemental theory of sentence meaning.

5. Lexical Meaning

Now let us turn to lexical meaning—the meaning of the words and phrases out of which sentences are constructed. As a first approximation, it seems that the meaning of a lexical item (a meaningful linguistic item smaller than a sentence) should be what determines its contribution to the meaning of a sentence containing it. However, this is a bit too strong. There are contexts in which words function in peculiar ways so that their meanings are not relevant to the meanings of the expressions containing them. One familiar example of this is a quotation text. The meaning of 'box' is not relevant to the meaning of the sentence '"box" has three letters'. Quotation contexts are not the only examples of this phenomenon. For example, the meaning of 'He is a square peg in a round hole' is not constructed, at least in the syntactically expected way, from the meanings of 'square', 'peg', etc. Let us say that an occurrence of a lexical item is *nonsemantical* when its meaning does not contribute to the meaning of the sentence containing it, or at

---

[18] Note, however, that we could choose other parameters and thereby generate different diagrams. For example, we might take the sole dynamic parameter to be the possible world that is actual.

[19] Note that this has the consequence that if $S \neq S^*$, then $\phi_S \neq \phi_{S^*}$. This is because if $S \neq S^*$, then there are no possible sent-propositions for ϕ_S for S^* but there are possible sent-propositions for ϕ_{S^*} for S^*. Note also that although the sent-propositions for ϕ_S are logically idiosyncratic, ϕ_S itself and its diagram are public objects that anyone can think about. This is because, as noted above, although I cannot entertain someone else's logically idiosyncratic propositions, I can think about them.

least not in the normal way.[20] Then the meaning of a lexical item is what determines the contribution of a semantical occurrence of that item to the meaning of a sentence containing that occurrence. As a definition, this would be circular, because the notion of a semantical occurrence was defined in terms of lexical meaning, but it is too vague to be much of a definition anyway. Despite its vagueness, however, it will prove to be a useful guide in formulating a more precise account of lexical meaning, and a precise definition will be provided in the Appendix.

A general approach for making the notion of lexical meaning more precise is illustrated by our treatment of sentence meaning. At least for many kinds of linguistic items we can make a distinction between their *senses* as used on particular occasions and their meanings (which do not vary from occasion to occasion). In the case of a sentence P, the sense of P as used on a particular occasion is that statement which it is used to state on that occasion. The meaning of P is constituted by that function which, when applied to the pragmatic parameters of an utterance of P, determines the sense of P on that occasion. For many other kinds of linguistic items we can also find logical or semantical items (e.g., concepts) which they can be regarded as expressing on specific occasions of their use. These logical or semantical items can be dubbed the 'senses' of the linguistic items on those occasions of their use. Furthermore, it will generally result that the contribution which a semantical occurrence of one of these linguistic items makes to the determination of what statement is made by uttering the whole sentence is a function of the sense of the item on that occasion. Thus if α is such an item, its meaning can be taken to be constituted by that function which, to each use of α, assigns its sense on that occasion. This is a function Δ_α which takes as arguments the values $x_1, \ldots, x_n$ of various pragmatic parameters $\pi_1, \ldots, \pi_n$ of the utterance and assigns the sense $\Delta_\alpha(x_1, \ldots, x_n)$ of α on that occasion of utterance (insofar as α has a sense under those circumstances). Thus if we can make sense of senses, we can make sense of lexical meaning in terms of senses.

It is not obvious how generally the above approach to lexical meaning can be pursued. In particular, it is not obvious whether we can always find suitable semantical items to play the role of

---

[20] In the case of an ambiguous sentence, the notion of a semantical occurrence must be relativized to the different meanings of the sentence. For example, bearing in mind that ordinary English often eschews quotation marks, the occurrence of 'John' in 'John is short' may be either semantical or nonsemantical.

senses for meaningful words and phrases. The traditional theory of language supposed that propositions are constructed out of concepts, combined by various logical operations, and then concluded that meaningful parts of sentences must express (or be used to express) either concepts or logical operators. If this were accurate, we could take the senses of words and phrases to be the concepts and logical operators they are used to express. However, if sentences are used to assert statements rather than propositions, then it is unreasonable to suppose that meaningful parts of sentences are used to express propositional constituents. If anything, they should express constituents of statements rather than of propositions. Let us examine this possibility.

It seems to make sense to talk about the structure and constituents of statements. For example, if I make a statement by saying 'Herbert is bald', my statement has a structure which might be schematized as '$(B:h)$'. My statement is *about* a particular object. It has a subject constituent h which selects an object and then the statement attributes something, B, to that object. B and h can be regarded as constituents of the statement. This talk of statemental structure can be understood in terms of the structure of the corresponding sent- and received-propositions. To illustrate this and simultaneously advance our theory of lexical meaning, we will turn to what will be called 'attributes'. Having made a distinction between propositions and statements, we should make a similar distinction between concepts and attributes. We defined a concept to be something which can be believed of an object or sequence of objects; let us define an *attribute* to be something which can be stated of an object or sequence of objects. The significance of attributes for lexical meaning is that they seem to be the senses of predicates. Predicates are used to state things of objects, so it becomes trivial to say that predicates are used to express attributes.[21] Furthermore, the identity of the attribute expressed is what determines the contribution of a semantical occurrence of a predicate to the determination of what statement is made by uttering a sentence containing it. Thus we can proceed as above and identify the meaning of a predicate F with the function Δ_F—the *A-intension* of F—taking the values of Δ_F to be the attributes expressed by F on different occasions of its use.

---

[21] An analysis of the precise sense in which a predicate can be used to "express" an attribute will be proposed in the Appendix.

The traditional theory of language identifies attributes with concepts, but it will follow from there being statements which are not propositions that there are attributes which are not concepts. For example, while watching home movies I may see a figure on the screen and exclaim, 'That is I'. In doing so, I have stated something of the person whose image I was seeing, i.e., I have ascribed an attribute to him. If I believe what I am saying, then I believe the referent of 'that' to exemplify a certain concept—the concept of of being I (wherein I think of myself in terms of my personal designator). But that cannot be what I am stating of the referent of 'that', because that would make my statement logically idiosyncratic. Thus the attribute I am ascribing to the person whose image I see is distinct from the concept I believe him to exemplify. If the attribute were some other concept, then believing him to have that attribute would consist of believing him to exemplify that other concept instead. So the attribute cannot be any concept at all.

Although the attribute cannot be identified with a concept, we can talk about sent- and received-concepts in connection with attributes just as we talked about sent- and received-propositions in connection with statements. As in the case of statements, the range of possible sent- and acceptable received-concepts is described by the diagram of the attribute:

(5.1)   If A is an attribute and $v_1, \ldots, v_n$ are the dynamic parameters of A, the *diagram* of A is that function ζ such that, if $x_1, \ldots, x_n$ are particular values of the parameters $v_1, \ldots, v_n$, then $\zeta(x_1, \ldots, x_n) = \langle \Sigma, \Omega \rangle$ where for each person S, $\Sigma(S)$ is the set of possible sent-concepts for A relative to $x_1, \ldots, x_n$ for S and $\Omega(S)$ is the set of acceptable received-concepts for A relative to $x_1, \ldots, x_n$ for S.

An obvious constraint on the diagram of an attribute is that for any particular set of values for the dynamic parameters, all of the possible sent-concepts and acceptable received-concepts must have the same extension. We will say that an object *exemplifies an attribute* when it exemplifies the possible sent- and acceptable received-concepts for the attribute, and we will take the *extension* of the attribute to be the set of objects exemplifying it.

Attributes are among the constituents of statements. We can now make it clear what that comes to, and indicate in a general way how talk of the structure of statements is to be understood. Where A and B are attributes, consider the statement that all A's are B's.

Using '$(\wedge x)$' for the universal quantifier and '$\Rightarrow$' for the material conditional, we can describe this statement as having the structure $(\wedge x)((A\!:\!x) \Rightarrow (B\!:\!x))$.[22] What that means is that the sent- and received-propositions for this statement have the corresponding structure $(\wedge x)((\alpha\!:\!x) \Rightarrow (\beta\!:\!x))$ where α and β are possible sent- or acceptable received-concepts for A and B respectively. Generalizing this, I would propose that all talk of statemental constituents or statemental structure is to be analyzed similarly in terms of talk of the constituents and structure of the sent- and received-propositions for the statements.

Attributes are one kind of statemental constituent. Attributes in statements play a role analogous to concepts in propositions. Propositional designators are another kind of propositional constituent, and we need an analogous category of statemental constituents. For example, let ϕ be the statement I make by saying 'Herbert is bald'. The sent- and received-propositions for ϕ all have the form $(\alpha\!:\!\delta)$ where α is a sent- or received-concept for the attribute A expressed by 'is bald' and δ is a propositional designator designating Herbert. For each set of values for the dynamic parameters and for each person S, let $\Sigma_\partial(S)$ be the set of these propositional designators δ which can thus be constituents of possible sent-propositions for ϕ for S, and let $\Omega_\partial(S)$ be the set of propositional designators δ which can thus be constituents of acceptable received-propositions for ϕ for S. If we take the functions Σ_∂ and Ω_∂ to comprise the diagram of a statemental constituent ∂, we can then describe ϕ as having the form $(A\!:\!\partial)$. This is just to say that for each set of values of the dynamic parameters and for each person S, the possible sent-propositions for ϕ for S are just those of the form $(\alpha\!:\!\delta)$ where α is a possible sent-concept for A for S and $\delta \in \Sigma_\partial(S)$; and similarly for the acceptable received-propositions. The function which, to each set of values for the dynamic parameters, assigns the pair of functions $\langle \Sigma_\partial, \Omega_\partial \rangle$ will be called a *statemental designator diagram*. We would like to regard this diagram as describing a statemental constituent ∂ whose role is to select propositional designators to be constituents of sent- and received-propositions. ∂ might reasonably be called a *statemental designator*. But is there any such entity as ∂? We defined statements to be 'what can be stated' and

---

[22] In describing statements and propositions in terms of their structures, I will use '$(\wedge x)$' for the universal quantifier, '$(\vee x)$' for the existential quantifier, '$\wedge$' for conjunction, '$\vee$' for disjunction, '$\Rightarrow$' for the material conditional, '$\Leftrightarrow$' for the material biconditional, '$\neg$' for negation, and '$\approx$' for identity.

attributes to be 'what can be stated of objects', but there appears to be no such convenient formula by which to introduce statemental designators. Should this make us suspicious of there being such things? I think not. If there is no natural entity of the appropriate sort, there are always made-up entities (e.g., the diagram itself, or equivalence classes of diagrams), which can play the role of statemental designators. The reason it makes no difference precisely what we take to be the statemental designator is that the only thing about the statemental designator which will be important for our purposes is its diagram. Our understanding of statemental structure is in terms of the diagram of statements, so to say that a particular statemental designator plays a certain role in the structure of a particular statement is just to say that its diagram is related to the diagram of the statement in a certain way. For example, to say that ∂ is a constituent of the statement $(B:\partial)$ ('Herbert is bald') is just to say that the sent- and received-propositions for $(B:\partial)$ are constructed in part out of the sent- and received-designators for ∂. Thus, for our purposes, it makes no difference what ∂ is so long as it has the right diagram. The entity itself is really just a convenient thing to hang the diagram onto.

Much the same thing is true of statements and attributes. For their use in semantics, only their diagrams are important. Their diagrams, in effect, give their content, and that in turn is what is required in describing the meanings of sentences and predicates. Thus the ontological commitments of our semantical theory are not as great as they might have seemed. What statements and statemental constituents actually are is not so much a mystery as an 'I don't care'. You can have them be pretty much anything you like, including all sorts of set-theoretically manufactured items.

Statemental designators are prime candidates for being the senses of proper names, definite descriptions, and other singular terms. We can reasonably propose that singular terms are used to express statemental designators, and that the meaning of a singular term τ is determined by the function Δ_τ which, to particular values of the pragmatic parameters of τ, assigns the statemental designator expressed by it under circumstances in which the pragmatic parameters have those values. Let us call Δ_τ the *D-intension of* τ. For example, a simple account of meaning for definite descriptions (not necessarily an account I wish to endorse) would take the meaning of ⌜the F⌝ to be constituted by its D-intension Δ ⌜the F⌝, and describe the latter by saying that the pragmatic parameters of ⌜the F⌝ are the pragmatic

31

parameters of F, and that if $x_1, \ldots, x_n$ are particular values of those parameters and $\Delta_F(x_1, \ldots, x_n) = A$, then $\Delta_{\ulcorner\text{the } F\urcorner}(x_1, \ldots, x_n)$ is the statemental designator which can be symbolized as $\ulcorner \imath A \urcorner$ and described in terms of its diagram as follows:

> the dynamic parameters of $\imath A$ are the same as the dynamic parameters of A, and the possible sent-designators (or acceptable received-designators) for $\imath A$ are the descriptions $\imath\alpha$ such that α is a possible sent-concept (or an acceptable received-concept) for A.

This account of definite descriptions is formulated purely for illustrative purposes. The account of definite descriptions proposed in Chapter Four will be considerably more complicated. But this account illustrates the general way in which we can give semantical accounts of singular terms within our statemental theory of meaning. We shall have to explore the extent to which such accounts are adequate, but Chapters Three and Four will muster considerable evidence in favor of the adequacy of this general approach.

Thus far we have three kinds of statemental constituents—attributes, statemental designators, and logical operators—and they can be used to describe the meanings of three kinds of lexical items—predicates, singular terms, and logical words and phrases. It is unclear whether this inventory of statemental constituents is complete. In this connection, note that we do not yet have any kind of statemental constituent which could plausibly be taken as a sense for an adverb like 'very'. Perhaps there is no such statemental constituent and the semantics of adverbs must be handled in a different way than we handle the semantics of predicates and singular terms. This question is touched upon again in the Appendix where it will be argued that the meanings of some words are to be described in a different manner. In the meantime, the scope of the investigation will be limited to singular terms and predicates.

6. Stating, Sending, Referring, and Predicating

6.1 *Stating*

A notion which will be fundamental to the theory developed in this book is that of stating. We have said something about what statements are, characterizing them in terms of their diagrams, but what is it to state a statement? An analysis of this notion will be provided in Chapter Twelve, based on the idea that to state something is to commit yourself to it. However, that analysis is a long way off, so some preliminary remarks about stating are in order here.

Languages are systems of rules. In the philosopher's technical sense, languages are institutions.[23] Among the rules of a language L are some telling us how to make statements by uttering sentences of L. It is noteworthy, however, that speakers can often make statements while violating the rules of their language. The rules of L determine what is a syntactically correct utterance of L. But in actual speech, misspeaking and ungrammaticality are quite common. Most violations of syntactical rules are not even noticed by a speaker's audience because it is perfectly clear to the audience what the speaker means. It cannot reasonably be claimed that when one is guilty of such misspeaking or ungrammaticality one must thereby fail to state.

The orthodox view of the connection between syntax and semantics is that an utterance is grammatically correct iff the semantical rules of the language enable us to make a statement with that utterance. Given that a speaker can make statements by performing ungrammatical utterances, one might be tempted to forsake this orthodox view. I think, however, that that would be a mistake. What appears to be happening here is this. Stating is communicating. Communication is successful if one is attempting to make a particular statement and one's audience knows what statement one is trying to make. It follows that in such a case one does state even if one violates the rules of his language. We have a distinction here between stating *simpliciter* and stating by conforming to all of the rules of L. Let us call the latter 'stating within L'. Stating which is not stating within L is parasitic on stating within L. If a speaker performs an ungrammatical utterance, but his utterance is a "near miss", a reasonable audience knowing the rules of L will be able to tell what statement he was trying to state within L. This is only possible because the audience knows the rules of L and the speaker's utterance came close to conforming to those rules.

I claim, then, that in cases of stating while misspeaking, one is not stating within L. The alternative would be to insist that one is stating within L but that the rules governing stating are much more complex than the orthodox view envisages. So long as we consider only cases of simple misspeaking and ungrammaticality, it might be

---

[23] The notion of an institution and its applicability to language will be investigated in detail in Chapters Ten–Twelve.

difficult to decide between these two accounts. But such simple examples quickly trail off into much more difficult examples. Consider a pair of bilingual speakers who habitually mix up German and English in a single utterance when they talk with one another. They are making statements to one another, but there is no conventional language L such that they are stating things within L. Rather, they are making use of both English and German in order to make statements, but are making statements within neither language.

In effect, linguistic institutions are tools for use in communicating. The "standard" way of using these tools is by conforming to their rules. But that is not the only way to use them in communication. If one's utterance is a sufficiently close approximation to an utterance sanctioned by the institution, or is perspicuously related to it in some other way, communication may succeed. In such a case, one is using the institution, but in a nonstandard way. There are many reasons for such nonstandard use. Grammatical rules are complicated and sometimes difficult to conform to. In oral communication particularly, one does not always have time to carefully think out his entire sentence before uttering it, with the result that the sentence may go awry before reaching the end. Alternatively, speakers may take shortcuts (perhaps most cases of misspeaking have this character). There can also be aesthetic reasons for violating the rules of one's linguistic institutions. In all such cases, one is using the institution, but in a nonstandard way, and hence one is stating without stating within L.

It should be emphasized that, as we are using it, 'stating within L' is a technical locution. Stating within English is not to be identified with the ordinary notion of *speaking English*. One is speaking English even when one misspeaks. Speaking English can be identified with the more open-ended notion of stating while trading principally upon the conventional rules of English. Perhaps our terminology would be less misleading if we were to use the locution ⌜to state$_L$⌝ in place of ⌜to state within L⌝. However, having pointed out the distinction between stating within L and speaking L, I will continue to use the more convenient locution ⌜to state within L⌝.

The distinction between stating *simpliciter* and stating within L is an important one for the systematization of language. The fact that a speaker of L can make a certain kind of statement by performing a certain kind of utterance does not have any *direct* implications for the rules of L. For example, it seems reasonable to propose that the rules of English preclude using a proper name to refer to an individual who does not bear that name. Nevertheless, if one's intended referent is clear to one's audience, one can make a statement about that intended referent (and thereby refer to it) by uttering a sentence containing a name which the referent does not bear. This does not show that English does not, after all, contain a rule precluding such a use of a proper name. Rather, one is stating but not stating within English.

6.2 Propositional Sending

We have characterized statements in terms of possible sent-propositions and acceptable received-propositions, and we will make heavy use of the notion of the sent-proposition in subsequent chapters. It is important to realize that we do not yet have a definition of that notion. A definition will be provided in Chapter Eleven, but again preliminary remarks are in order. The definition which will be proposed can be roughly sketched here. Ordinarily, when we make a statement we are "putting thoughts into words". We begin with a certain proposition—normally one we believe—and we make a statement which conveys all or part of that proposition. In other words, we make a statement for which the proposition is a possible sent-proposition. We select our statement with that purpose in mind. The proposition with which we start is the sent-proposition. There may be more than one sent-proposition because the speaker may start with several related propositions and make a statement which is intended to express each of them equally. This characterization of the sent-propositions will be made precise in Chapter Eleven.

When a speaker makes a statement, must there always be a sent-proposition? Consider a concrete example. Suppose Schmidt is an anthropologist studying a culture whose language he does not speak. He is outside a walled village and wants to get in. He observes locals approaching the gatekeeper and saying 'Oogloomoophoo', whereupon the gatekeeper admits them. Schmidt conjectures that 'Oogloomoophoo' means either 'I am a loyal subject of the king' or 'I am a devout worshipper of the local diety', but he doesn't know which. Anxious to get inside the village, Schmidt approaches the gatekeeper and says 'Oogloomoophoo', fully intending to commit himself to whatever statement the locals were making. What Schmidt lacks here is a sent-proposition. Has Schmidt made the statement the locals were making, or did he only pretend to make it? I find that people have markedly diverging intuitions on this question. Some people find it obvious that Schmidt made the statement, and

35

others find it equally obvious that he did not. My own intuitions are of the latter sort, but in light of the marked divergence of opinion and the fact that no other considerations seem to bear on this question, I am inclinded to believe that there may be no fact of the matter here. I suspect that this divergence reflects a genuine difference in idiolect whereby different people use the verb 'to state' differently.

We can accomodate both intuitions by simply defining two different notions. I will use the verb 'to weakly state' in the broader sense which does not require one to be sending a proposition. This verb will be defined in Chapter Eleven. Then we can define:

(6.1)   *S strongly states* ϕ iff *S* weakly states ϕ and in doing so is sending some proposition.

We have characterized strong stating in terms of weak stating, but in an important sense strong stating is the more basic notion, weak stating riding on its coattails. This is because statements themselves are characterized in terms of their possible sent-propositions, and hence in terms of the notion of sending a proposition, which only occurs in strong stating. For this reason, I will use 'stating' to mean 'strong stating' throughout this book. It must be emphasized, however, that the choice between weak stating and strong stating in this connection is just a convention and, with only slight modifications to our theory, we could instead use 'stating' to mean 'weak stating'.

6.3 *Predication*

We defined attributes to be what can be stated of objects. The act of stating an attribute of an object is an act of predication. However, it is reasonable to define predication a bit more broadly than this. We have seen that minor infractions of linguistic rules can lead to stating which is not stating within *L*. This happens when the infractions are sufficiently transparent that they do not prevent the audience from knowing what statement the speaker is trying to make. More substantial infractions may prevent the speaker from stating but may not block communication entirely. For example, if a speaker is grossly mistaken about the meaning of the word 'diquat', thinking it somehow descriptive of a person, the speaker might utter the sentence 'The diquat has red hair' while gesturing at Herman in such a way that it is clear that he is talking about Herman. It may be that no one knows precisely what statement the speaker is trying to make because no one knows what he thinks 'diquat' means, so the speaker fails to make a statement. But it may nevertheless be clear whom he is talking about and what he is predicating of that person. In such a case, it seems reasonable to say that predication occurs without stating.

We can capture the preceding notion of predication as follows. Let us begin by defining:

> (6.2) *S statementally predicates A* of *x* iff *S* states a statement of the form $(A:\partial)$ where ∂ designates *x*.

Statemental predication is predication that occurs in the course of stating. Then it seems that nonstatemental predication occurs when the speaker is trying to statementally predicate and his intention is clear to his audience:

> (6.3) *S predicates A* of *x* iff either (1) *S* statementally predicates *A* of *x* or (2) by performing his utterance *S* is trying to state a statement of the form $(A:\partial)$ where ∂ designates *x*, and it is clear to *S*'s intended audience that for *some* ∂ designating *x*, *S* is trying to state $(A:\partial)$.

The reason for including nonstatemental predication in our account of predication is that an important amount of communication occurs in that case even though stating is not entirely successful.

We can also define the notion of predicating *A* of *x within L*. This consists of predicating *A* of *x* by conforming to the rules of *L* and thereby making a statement about *x* within *L*. Unlike predication in general, one can only predicate *A* of *x* within *L* by making a statement within *L* because one must be conforming to the rules of *L*.

6.4 *Reference*

To refer to an object is to talk about it. Reference can occur in the context of a variety of kinds of speech acts including stating, questioning, commanding, promising, etc. One ordinarily refers *by* performing a speech act of one of these other sorts. Let us say that a kind of speech act (e.g., stating) is *complete* iff one can perform a speech act of that kind within a language *L* without doing so by performing a speech act of another kind within *L*. Stating, questioning, etc., are complete, but referring is not—one can only refer within *L* by performing another kind of speech act within *L*.

Referring can be a byproduct of the successful performance of a number of different kinds of complete speech acts, including stating, questioning, commanding, requesting, promising, etc. Accordingly, we can talk about statemental referring, interrogative referring, imperative referring, etc. Let us begin with statemental referring. We can distinguish between two notions of statemental referring. First, the strong notion:

(6.4)   *S strongly statementally refers to* x iff $(\exists A)(\exists\partial)[A$ is an attribute & ∂ is a statemental designator designating x & S states $(A:\partial)]$.

If we were to identify statemental referring with strong statemental referring, it would follow that a speaker can only statementally refer to an object by making a statement about that object. This may seem an objectionably strong requirement. We have seen that a speaker can succeed in predicating even when his attempt to state is unsuccessful. Why shouldn't the same thing be true of referring? For example, if Jones says 'Smith is xmpft', attempting to make a statement about Smith but failing to do so because there is no such word as 'xmpft', if his intended referent is clear to his audience, it does not seem unreasonable to claim that Jones has referred to Smith despite his failing to state. On the other hand, it does not seem unreasonable to insist that no reference has occurred in this case either. It is clear to whom Jones was *trying* to refer, but it is not obvious whether that should be deemed sufficient to make the reference successful. Let us define:

(6.5)   *S weakly statementally refers to* x iff either (1) S strongly statementally refers to x or (2) $(\exists U)[U$ is an utterance & it is both true and clear to S's intended audience that $(\exists A)(\exists\partial)(A$ is an attribute & ∂ is a statemental designator designating x & S is trying to state $(A:\partial)$ by uttering $U)]$.[24]

What is at issue is whether weak statemental referring is genuine referring. I am inclined to think that we can have it either way. Nothing else in the theory of language appears to turn upon this, so it is just a matter of how we are going to talk. It makes the theory a bit simpler if we identify statemental referring with strong statemental referring, so that is what I will do. However, we could just as well proceed in the opposite manner without it making any substantial difference to our overall theory of language.

[24] We count any locutionary act, written or oral, as an utterance.

In order to generalize this account of referring to other speech acts, we must observe that complete speech acts have *objects*, in the same sense as that in which the object of a stating is a statement. It will be argued in Chapter Twelve that the object of a yes/no question, a command, a request, or a promise is a statement. The object of a *wh* question is an attribute or a statemental designator. We can then define:

(6.6)   If Σ is a kind of speech act, S refers$_\Sigma$ to x iff $(\exists \partial)(\exists \xi)[S$ performs a speech act of type Σ whose object is ξ & ∂ is a statemental designator which is either a constituent of ξ or identical to ξ & ∂ designates $x]$.

II
Traditional Theories of Proper Names

1. Introduction

The basic objective of the next three chapters is to give an account of the meanings of singular terms, i.e., of singular referring expressions. We will begin our investigation of singular terms by investigating proper names. As with any meaningful lexical item, the meaning of a proper name is constituted by whatever determines its contribution to the meaning of sentences containing semantical occurrences of it. Thus the meaning of a proper name is given by giving a general account of the meanings of sentences containing proper names.

It was suggested in Chapter One that a singular term is used to express statemental designators, and that the statemental designator expressed determines the term's contribution to what statement is made. Accordingly, the statemental designator can be regarded as the sense of the term, and the meaning of a singular term will be a function which determines its sense on each occasion of use. We must now consider the extent to which we can actually find appropriate statemental designators to serve as senses for proper names and other singular terms. In this connection, note that nothing is presupposed regarding what sorts of entities can be statemental designators. The important feature of a statemental designator is simply its diagram, because that is what determines its role in the makeup of a statement containing it. Consequently, the question whether there are appropriate statemental designators is really just the question whether there are appropriate statemental designator diagrams.

The purpose of this chapter is to discuss the four main historical and current theories of proper names. These are the connotation theory, the denotation theory, Searle's theory, and the historical connection theory. Chapter Three will develop an alternative theory whose formulation is made possible by the statemental theory of meaning.

2. The Connotation Theory

The connotation theory is probably the theory that has been most popular historically, although it has fallen into recent disrepute. The connotation theory is the theory to which we are led naturally by the traditional theory of language. The basic contention of the connotation theory is that proper names are used to express concepts (or definite descriptions built out of concepts), and these concepts (their *connotations*) are their senses on different occasions of their use. The sense in which a proper name "expresses" a concept is supposed to be that the concept becomes an actual constituent of a statement made by uttering a sentence containing the name. Thus, if in uttering the sentence $\ulcorner N$ is $F\urcorner$, a speaker uses the name N to express a concept α and uses F to express an attribute β, then the statement he makes is the statement $(\beta : \imath \alpha)$, i.e., the statement that the thing which is α is β. The connotation theory must supply an account of what determines which concept is the connotation of a name as used on a particular occasion. The customary answer is that it is 'the concept in mind'. It is alleged that when a speaker uses a proper name to refer to a particular individual, he must be thinking about that individual in some way—under some description. This mental description is a concept, and it is taken to be the connotation. Alternatively, the connotation might be a concept which is somehow conventionally tied to the name.

The connotation theory is inescapable if it is maintained that the statement made by uttering $\ulcorner N$ is $F\urcorner$ is a proposition and it is agreed that the only propositional designators there are are definite descriptions of the form $\imath \alpha$ where α is a concept. As both of these are endorsed by the traditional theory of language, advocates of that theory were led directly to the connotation theory.

Ordinarily, when asked what concept a word expresses, we attempt to answer by paraphrasing the word in terms of other words which, in combination, express the same concept. Thus in describing the concept expressed by a proper name, we are naturally led to try to find some predicate not containing the proper name which expresses the same concept. Suppose that given a proper name N we could find a predicate A_N expressing the same concept. Then a sentence of the form

(2.1) N is F

would have the same sense as a sentence employing the definite description:

(2.2)   The thing which is A_N is F.

Bertrand Russell was one of the early advocates of this theory, holding that the sense of a name (its connotation) is determined conventionally and is the same on every occasion of its use, but one could equally hold that it varies from occasion to occasion, being determined by the pragmatic parameters of the utterance. To illustrate the theory, Russell proposed that the name 'Homer' expresses the same concept as that expressed by 'author of *The Iliad* and *The Odyssey*'. Hence, according to this theory, the proposition asserted by uttering

(2.3)   Homer was Greek.

is the same proposition as the one asserted by uttering

(2.4)   The author of *The Iliad* and *The Odyssey* was Greek.

The connotation theory proposes, in effect, that proper names are used as short for definite descriptions. The major difficulty for this theory lies in the unavailability of appropriate definite descriptions. Two sorts of considerations lead to this same conclusion. First, if a proper name N is used to express the same concept as some predicate A_N, then the sentence

(2.5) N, if he existed, was A_N.

expresses a necessary truth. For example, on Russell's proposal,

(2.6)   Homer, if he existed, wrote *The Iliad* and *The Odyssey*.

expresses a necessary truth. But this seems wrong. Let us tamper with history a bit and suppose that there was a blind Greek poet named 'Homer'. He was not a very good poet. However, he happened to have a scribe who, unknown to everyone else, was a brilliant poet. The scribe wrote *The Iliad* and *The Odyssey*, and brought them to Homer for his opinion. Homer, being somewhat of a scoundrel, had his scribe put to death and claimed the epic poems for himself. He circulated them under his name, and his contemporaries came to believe, and to assert, that Homer wrote *The Iliad* and *The Odyssey*. This was passed down through history to us, and on this basis we now believe that Homer wrote those poems. What we are asserting when we utter the sentence

(2.7)   Homer wrote *The Iliad* and *The Odyssey*.

is the same thing as what Homer's Greek contemporaries were asserting when they uttered a related sentence in Greek. Their statement was not a necessary truth—it was false. Thus ours is also false. It follows that when we assertively utter sentence (2.7), 'Homer' does not express the same concept as 'author of *The Iliad* and *The Odyssey*'.

In the above fable, what makes it true that our use of the name 'Homer' refers to the blind Greek poet rather than to the actual author of *The Iliad* and *The Odyssey* is the historical connection between our present use of the name and the original use of a related name by Homer's Greek contemporaries. In using the name as we do, we intend to refer to the same person they did, despite the fact that we may not be able to provide a definite description of the person to whom we are referring.

These considerations seem to indicate that the connotation theory is false. Notice that it makes no difference at all to the example what description of Homer we might propose to incorporate into the definite description. We could always propound a fable in which it would turn out that Homer, the person to whom we are actually referring, does not satisfy that description. Thus 'Homer' cannot be short for any such definite description.

We can arrive at this same conclusion from another route. Consider a teacher—Professor Jones—who knows a great deal about Leibniz. He has two students—Jacob and Rudolph. Neither student has previously heard of Leibniz. Professor Jones teaches Jacob all about Leibniz' contributions to philosophy, and he teaches Rudolph all about Leibniz' contributions to mathematics and natural science. Each student thereby acquires a fairly extensive knowledge of part of Leibniz' work (comparable to what an average undergraduate might learn in a philosophy course dealing exclusively with Leibniz), but they learn nothing in common about Leibniz. There is no description which either could give of Leibniz which the other would recognize. Now let us suppose that after they have both completed their courses of studies, Professor Jones happens to mention casually to each that Leibniz was an important political figure in his time. Each student, excited by this new bit of information, repeats it to someone else. They do this by uttering the same sentence as Professor Jones uttered:

(2.8)   Leibniz was an important political figure in his time.

Surely Jacob and Rudolph can be making the same statement as Professor Jones. After all, each student takes himself to simply be repeating Jones' statement. But then they are making the same statement as each other. However, if Jacob and Rudolph were each using the name 'Leibniz' as short for a definite description, they would have to be using it as short for different definite descriptions because they share no significant knowledge about Leibniz. But then it would follow that they were making different statements in uttering (2.8). Such a conclusion seems to be incorrect. Our untutored intuition is that Jacob and Rudolph are each making the same statement as Professor Jones, and hence the same statement as each other.

As attractive as the connotation theory seemed initially, it now appears to be false. Definite descriptions are not related to proper names in the simple way envisaged. But this leaves us with a real problem. If the sense of a proper name is not determined by some concept expressed by the name, what else can there be which does determine the sense?

3. Searle's Theory

John Searle has attempted to construct a theory which meets the preceding objections to the connotation theory.[1] Observing that it is logically possible for the referent of a name to fail to have any particular descriptive property commonly attributed to it, Searle proposes that associated with each use of a name N is a whole set $\mathscr{P}_N$ of descriptive properties. The referent of the name could fail to have any one or any small subset of these properties. But, according to Searle, it is a necessary truth that the referent of the name has at least one of these properties. More generally, Searle proposes that:

(3.1)   If $\mathscr{P}_N$ is the set of properties associated with N, the referent of N is that object which has a sufficient number of the properties in $\mathscr{P}_N$ and more of them than does any other object.

[1] Searle [1958] and [1969].

Searle's theory is intended to explain how it could turn out, for example, that Homer did not write *The Iliad* and *The Odyssey*. He explains this by proposing that these are not the only descriptive properties contained in the set of properties associated with the name 'Homer'. When we say that Homer did not write *The Iliad* and *The Odyssey*, we refer to the person who had a sufficient number of the properties associated with 'Homer', and more of them than anyone else, and state that he did not write *The Iliad* and *The Odyssey*.

As stated, Searle's theory leaves many questions unanswered. First, it is only explicitly a theory of referring—not a theory of meaning. It tells us how the referent of a proper name is secured, but it does not tell us what statement is made by uttering a sentence containing that name. One is naturally led to ask what theory of meaning could generate Searle's theory of referring. There is one obvious theory of meaning which would have this result. According to that theory, if $\mathscr{P}_N$ is the set of properties "associated with" the name N, and $\mathscr{P}_N = \{A_0, \ldots, A_k\}$, then the proposition asserted by uttering

(3.2) N is F.

is the same proposition as that asserted by uttering

(3.3)   The thing which has a sufficient number of the properties $A_0, \ldots, A_k$, and more of them than anything else, is F.

This is to reduce Searle's theory to a version of the connotation theory. Let us abbreviate ⌜has a sufficient number of the properties $A_0, \ldots, A_k$⌝ as ⌜$\mathscr{A}_N$⌝. Then what is being proposed is that the proper name N can be replaced by the definite description ⌜the thing which is $\mathscr{A}_N$⌝. On this explication of Searle's theory, it does not amount to the outright rejection of the connotation theory, but rather to the proposal that the descriptions traditionally considered in connection with proper names were unrealistically simple, and should instead be of the logically complex form of $\mathscr{A}_N$.

Searle might not accept this explication of his theory. His explicit theory is only a theory of referring. However, our interest here is in theories of meaning and this is the only obvious theory of meaning which would yield Searle's theory of referring. Furthermore, it is an interesting theory of meaning, well worth discussing. Thus I shall discuss it, under the title 'Searle's theory', despite the fact that Searle may not hold it. Many of the objections that will be raised are objections as much to the theory of referring as to the theory of meaning.

Taking Searle's theory to be a version of the connotation theory, let us reconsider the two criticisms that were made of that theory. The first was that it could happen, e.g., that Homer did not write *The Iliad* and *The Odyssey*, and hence that 'Homer' does not express the same concept as does the predicate 'wrote *The Iliad* and *The Odyssey*'. Searle's embellishment of the connotation theory was explicitly designed to meet this objection. Any particular properties in the set $\mathscr{P}_N$ could turn out not to be possessed by the bearer of N. It does follow from Searle's theory that the bearer of N could not lack *all* of the properties in $\mathscr{P}_N$, but that result is more plausible. However, in order to test this hypothesis, we must first get clear on just what set $\mathscr{P}_N$ is to be associated with a given use of the name.

There are two possibilities regarding the origin of the set $\mathscr{P}_N$: (1) membership in $\mathscr{P}_N$ might be determined by the speaker—the properties in $\mathscr{P}_N$ are those the speaker would or could provide as describing the bearer of the name; (2) membership in $\mathscr{P}_N$ might be determined conventionally, by all users of the name combined. There is reason to believe that the second alternative is Searle's view, but let us begin by considering the first. If we suppose that the properties associated with a particular utterance of a name are simply those the speaker could in some sense provide, both of the original criticisms of the connotation theory can be brought to bear. First, it could happen that the only properties I associate with 'Homer' are those of being a blind Greek poet who wrote *The Iliad* and *The Odyssey*. Despite this, it could be true that Homer did not write *The Iliad* and *The Odyssey*. To be sure, in this example there remain the properties of being a blind Greek poet, but these are not sufficient to determine the referent of 'Homer'—presumably there have been many blind Greek poets. Furthermore, it could turn out that Homer was neither blind nor Greek nor a poet. We could elaborate our fable by supposing that Homer was really a Carthaginian spy masquerading as a blind Greek, and that all the poetry attributed to him was in fact the product of his unfortunate scribe.

The second of the original objections to the connotation theory also applies to the present theory. This is that two different people could use the name to refer to the same person and make the same statement about him and yet the sets of descriptions they would supply of the bearer of the name would have no significant members in common.

These considerations indicate that we must take membership in $\mathscr{P}_N$ to be determined conventionally by all users of the name combined. But now we encounter new difficulties. If the proposition asserted by saying $\ulcorner N$ is $F \urcorner$ is (3.3), then in order for the speaker to believe what he says or for the hearer to accept what the speaker is saying, either must believe (3.3). However, on the present proposal we cannot expect all of the users of a name (or even any of the users of the name) to know all of the descriptions in $\mathscr{P}_N$. Thus it seems that no one (not even the speaker) can understand what is being said. Such a conclusion is absurd, but there is no obvious way for the present theory to avoid it.

A further problem for the present theory is that of explaining how all the members of $\mathscr{P}_N$ become associated with a particular use of the name. It is supposed that they cannot all be provided by a single user of the name, so there must be something else which ties them all together as being part of the set associated with a use of the name. What could this be? A natural response is that the different members of $\mathscr{P}_N$ are associated with one another in a single set by virtue of being the descriptions that different speakers would associate with the name N. On this account, $\mathscr{P}_N$ is the set of all descriptions for which there exists a person who would associate them with the name N. However, this proposal overlooks the obvious but insufficiently appreciated fact that proper names are often the names of many people. There have been innumerable people named 'Homer' down through history. With a particular use of the name 'Homer' to refer to a particular person, we cannot associate all of the descriptions people would have given throughout history for all of the different people named 'Homer'. The only descriptions that are appropriate are those associated with the name when it is used as it is presently being used. But what is it for the name to be used as it is presently being used? When is a name being used the same way on two different occasions?

An obvious suggestion is that a name is being used the same way on two different occasions iff it is being used to refer to the same individual on both occasions. On this proposal, the set $\mathscr{P}_N$ associated with a particular use of a name to refer to a particular individual x is the set of all descriptions for which there is a person who would associate them with the name as used to refer to the individual x. But this leads us to identify too many statements with one another.

Let us suppose that Homer, who was in fact a Carthaginian spy, was so brash as to use his own real name in his role as a blind Greek poet. It was well known to the Greeks that there was a famous Carthaginian spy named 'Homer', but they never suspected that he was the same person as their Homer. A Greek contemporary of Homer could well have assertively uttered two sentences, first uttering:

(3.4)   Homer is an evil man.

with the intention of referring to the Carthaginian spy, and then uttering:

(3.5)   Homer is not an evil man.

with the intention of referring to the putative Greek poet. On the present theory, because the two uses of 'Homer' refer to the same individual, they would have the same set of descriptions associated with them, and hence the proposition asserted by uttering (3.5) would be the negation of the proposition asserted by uttering (3.4). However, the speaker of (3.4) and (3.5) could surely have believed what he was saying in both cases without thereby believing an explicit contradiction. Thus we cannot define membership in $\mathscr{P}_N$ in the manner proposed.

In fact, it seems reasonably clear that a name is being used in the same way on two different occasions if it is being used with the same sense on both occasions, and hence that membership in $\mathscr{P}_N$ must be defined by appealing to the sense of the name. But it is precisely the notion of using a name with a particular sense that we are attempting to analyze. Thus it appears that the only way to make Searle's theory plausible will make it circular.

I can see no other way that different descriptions, provided by different people, could be combined into a single set $\mathscr{P}_N$ to be associated with a particular use of a name by a single individual. These difficulties appear to be insurmountable. Accordingly, the connotation theory must be rejected even in the sophisticated form proposed by Searle.

4. The Denotation Theory

There is an historical alternative to the connotation theory which avoids the necessity of finding connotations for proper names.

This is the denotation theory, the customary formulation of which is:

(4.1)   Proper names have a denotation but no connotation.

We can formulate the denotation theory more precisely as follows:

(4.2)   The sense of a proper name, as used on a particular occasion, is uniquely determined by its denotation (i.e., its referent) on that occasion.

In other words, the contribution which the use of the name makes to what statement is made is a function simply of the referent of the name. The way in which the speaker is thinking of that referent is irrelevant to what statement is made. Donnellan [1972] flirted with this theory, and Kaplan [1977] has firmly endorsed it.

Principle (4.2) constitutes only a partial specification of the sense of a proper name. It tells us that if a speaker utters two sentences containing two proper names which have the same referent, and the speaker thereby says the same thing about the referent of each name, he is making the same statement twice. Principle (4.2) does not, however, tell us what statement that is. I will shortly propose a strengthening of (4.2) which answers this question.

Note further that (4.2) tells us nothing about the meaning of a proper name over and above what it tells us about the sense. Advocates of the denotation theory have frequently gone on to identify the meaning with the denotation, but that has generally resulted from their failing to distinguish between meaning and sense.[2] The denotation theory is a theory about the sense of a proper name as used on different occasions, and is compatible with different theories regarding meaning. The meaning of a proper name N is constituted by that function Δ_N which determines the sense of N on each occasion of its use. We could insist, somewhat in the vein of the traditional advocates of the denotation theory, that Δ_N is a constant function assigning the same sense to N each time it is used. This would be to take the meaning of N to be constituted by its denotation, purely and simply. This necessitates regarding proper names as ambiguous when they are the names of more than one thing. Alternatively, we could regard a proper name as having a single meaning despite its being used to refer to different objects on different occasions, and take Δ_N to be the function which

---

[2] Kaplan [1977] is an obvious exception to this.

determines which referent and hence which sense it has on those different occasions. Either approach is compatible with taking the sense of a proper name to be determined by its referent.

Although the denotation theory is one of the historically familiar theories of proper names, it cannot be accomodated within the traditional theory of language. On the assumption that when we make a statement by uttering a sentence containing a proper name, that statement is a proposition, the denotation theory would seem to require the existence of "directly referential" propositions, to use the terminology of Kaplan [1977]. These are propositions which are about an object "directly", without involving a particular way of thinking of an object. The object itself would somehow be a constituent of these propositions. As we have seen, directly referential propositions are unproblematic as coarse-grained objects of belief, although they cannot be fine-grained objects of belief and hence are not propositions in our sense of the term 'proposition'. Different ways of thinking of the same object yield different (fine-grained) propositions. Given the traditional assumption that the statement made must be a (fine-grained) proposition, it cannot be a directly referential proposition.

However, given our statemental semantics, the denotation theory does not require the existence of directly referential propositions. All it requires are directly referential *statements*. The essential contention of the denotation theory is that the role played by a proper name in selecting what statement is made is a function merely of the referent of the name. How the speaker is thinking of that referent makes no difference to what statement is made. But the way in which the speaker is thinking of the referent does make a difference to what proposition he is sending. Thus I would urge that the denotation theory is best construed as denying that the statement made is the same as the sent-proposition. I propose the following as a reasonable reconstruction of the denotation theory utilizing our characterization of statements in terms of their diagrams. Consider a sentence $\ulcorner N$ is $F\urcorner$, and for simplicity let us suppose that the predicate F expresses a concept α. Then we could regard the Denotation Theory as telling us that if δ is *any* propositional designator designating the referent of N, then $(\alpha:\delta)$ is both a possible sent-proposition and an acceptable received-proposition for the statement made by uttering $\ulcorner N$ is $F\urcorner$. Generalizing this, and assuming that names are used to express statemental designators (their senses), the latter being characterized by diagrams describing the possible sent-propositional designators and acceptable received-propositional designators, we can regard the denotation theory as alleging:

(4.3)   The sense of a proper name, as used on a particular occasion, is that statemental designator ∂ which is such that $(\exists x)[x$ is the referent of the name as used on this occasion and a propositional designator δ is both a possible sent-designator for ∂ and an acceptable received-designator for ∂ iff δ designates $x]$.

Thus it becomes possible to formulate the denotation theory within our statemental semantics in a way which avoids the problems encountered in trying to formulate it within the traditional theory of language.

In my opinion, the denotation theory, as formulated in (4.3), involves an important insight. That is that the statement one makes by uttering a sentence containing a proper name is not identical with the sent-proposition. Speakers can be thinking about the same object in different ways, and thereby sending different propositions, but nevertheless be making the same statement. That is precisely where the connotation theory flounders. It will be argued in Chapter Three that this insight provides one of the fundamental keys to understanding proper names.

Although I believe that the denotation theory takes an important step in the right direction (and away from the traditional propositional theory of meaning), there seem to be compelling reasons for rejecting it. In effect, it goes too far in collecting sent-propositions together into the diagram of a single statement. There are two kinds of considerations which lead to this conclusion. These considerations arise from two consequences of the theory. The first is:

(4.4)   Given two sentences which differ only in that they contain semantical occurrences of different proper names at some point, if on some occasion the names have the same referent, and the other constituents of the sentences are used in the same way, then in assertively uttering these two sentences the speakers are making the same statement.

The second consequence concerns what happens when names are used in such a way that they have no referent. According to the denotation theory, the sense of a name is determined by its

51

referent. What statement a speaker makes by uttering a sentence containing a semantical occurrence of the name is a function of the sense of the name. Thus:

(4.5)   If a speaker uses a name in such a way that it has no referent, then it has no sense, and hence it should be impossible to make a statement by uttering a sentence containing a semantical occurrence of the name.

Let us take these two consequences in order. To test (4.4), consider a case in which you take yourself to know two people well: Jim Robinson and Jim Thompson. Imagine, however, that there is really just one person who is leading a double life and he has been fooling you with makeup, costumes, voice tricks, elevator shoes, etc. Now suppose you utter the sentence 'Jim is tall', meaning to refer to Jim Robinson. If Brown understands you to be talking about Jim Thompson, he has misunderstood you. It cannot be denied that such misunderstanding is possible. But according to the denotation theory, you would be making the same statement regardless of whether you were talking about Jim Thompson or Jim Robinson, and so Brown would not be misunderstanding you. It must be concluded that, contrary to the denotation theory, there are two different statements that can be made here by saying 'Jim is tall'.

Turning to (4.5), it should be impossible to make a statement by assertively uttering a sentence containing a semantical occurrence of a name used in such a way that it has no referent. To test this principle, let us borrow an example from Donnellan [1974]. What purported to be the diary of a real person named 'Jacob Horn' was published some years ago and many people believed it to be genuine. However, the diary was a work of fiction and Jacob Horn did not exist. Consider the negative existential sentence:

(4.6)   Jacob Horn did not exist.

I have just made a true statement by asserting (4.6). However, the denotation theory entails that that is impossible. Nor does this problem pertain uniquely to negative existentials. Suppose I believed *The Horn Papers* to be genuine, and in reporting their contents to an acquaintance I uttered the sentence:

(4.7)   Jacob Horn had a thick brown beard.

Surely I am making a statement, and I may very well believe what I say, indicating that there is a sent-proposition. Once more, the denotation theory cannot accomodate this.[3]

I believe that the denotation theory is on the right track, distinguishing as it does between the statement and the sent-proposition, but a correct theory of proper names must give a more sophisticated account of the statemental designator which is the sense of a proper name as used on a particular occasion. Such an account will be proposed in Chapter Three.

5. The Historical Connection Theory

In recent years, a new theory of referring has been proposed. This is the so-called 'causal theory' or 'historical connection theory' of Kripke [1972] and Donnellan [1972] and [1974]. This theory is best motivated by the consideration of examples. Let us pick on Homer again. We suppose that, contrary to popular belief, Homer was neither blind nor Greek nor a poet, and he did not write *The Iliad* and *The Odyssey*. In fact, Homer was a Carthaginian spy masquerading as a blind Greek, and the epic poems were actually written by Homer's scribe. Homer's Greek contemporaries were unaware of all this and believed instead that he was a blind poet, of Greek citizenship, author of *The Iliad* and *The Odyssey*. With respect to these beliefs, they were wrong on every count. However, this did not prevent them from being able to refer to Homer, because they were able to identify him in other ways, e.g., in terms of his appearance, in terms of his day-to-day affairs, as the man living at 367 Socrates Square, etc. However, these everyday beliefs they had about Homer were not considered to be the important ones, and so they are not the ones that were passed down through history. Instead Homer was written up in the *Athens Times* as 'the author of *The Iliad* and *The Odyssey*', and fathers would point him out in the street to their sons as 'the famous blind poet'. These sons repeated to their sons how they remembered seeing Homer, the

---

[3] Donnellan [1974] attempts to handle this sort of difficulty in terms of "blocks". But his analysis provides only truth conditions for statements involving nonreferring uses of names. The difficulty to which (4.5) leads is that the denotation theory gives us *nothing to think* in connection with such a statement. There would be no possible sent- or acceptable received-propositions. But that is impossible. To describe a statement it is not sufficient to give its truth conditions. We must describe its diagram, and that is what the denotation theory cannot do.

blind Greek poet who wrote *The Iliad* and *The Odyssey*, and the distant readers of the west coast edition of the *Athens Times* recounted to their acquaintances what they had read about Homer. In this way, many stories about Homer were perpetuated, but they were all false! We get an historical chain of speakers stretching all the way from Homer's Greek acquaintances to present-day classicists. Each member of the chain learned about Homer from earlier members of the chain. What makes it true that each person in the chain is referring to the original Homer is that the people from whom each person acquired his use of the name 'Homer' were themselves referring to the original Homer, and a subsequent member of the chain is referring to whomever the earlier members of the chain were referring to. Each later reference is historically connected with the earlier references, and the fact that the earlier members of the chain did succeed in referring to Homer guarantees that the later members of the chain also succeed in referring to Homer despite the fact that all of the later speakers' potentially individuating beliefs about Homer are false.

This illustrates the historical connection theory of proper names. It is important to realize that it is only a theory of referring—not a theory of meaning.[4] According to this theory, what makes a present use of the name 'Homer' refer to the original Carthaginian spy is that it is historically connected, in the appropriate way, to earlier references to Homer. But it is inadequate just to say this. The theory is formulated in terms of historical connections or causal connections, but obviously not just any connection will do. What is required is a clear account of precisely what the requisite connection is, and exponents of the theory have been unable to give an account. Without such an account, it is not possible to evaluate the theory with any confidence. What we have here is not so much a theory as a general picture waiting to be filled out. We will return to the question of just how it should be filled out several times in the course of this investigation, and will ultimately endorse some of the basic insights of this theory.

---

[4] This theory of referring is compatible with a number of different theories of meaning. Both Kaplan [1977] and Donnellan [1972] have considered coupling it with the denotation theory, and McKinsey [1978] has explored the possibility of coupling it with the connotation theory.

III
The Meaning of a Proper Name

1. Introduction

We can distinguish between three levels of theories regarding proper names: (a) a theory of referring; (b) a theory of sense; (c) a theory of meaning. If we look at a simple sentence of the form $\ulcorner N$ is $F\urcorner$ where N is a proper name: (a) a theory of referring will tell us what determines to what we are referring by using a proper name when we utter this sentence and thereby make a statement; (b) a theory of sense will tell us what statement we are making on different occasions of uttering this sentence; and (c) a theory of meaning will tell us what the S-intension of the sentence is which determines the senses on different occasions. We will develop theories of these three levels, taking them in order.

2. Referring

Let us begin by looking at referring. There is a common misconception to be dispelled. Philosophers have sometimes talked as if names denote objects all by themselves and independently of either context or the intervention of a speaker. The absurdity of such a view is manifest if we consider a proper name like 'Bill'. We can use this name to refer to many different individuals. There must be something besides the name itself which determines to which individual we are referring on any given occasion. A theory of referring must tell us what that is.

We will confine our attention to statemental referring. There is an important sense in which we do not need a separate theory of statemental referring, because an account of referring will result automatically from an analysis of stating. Suppose a speaker utters the sentence $\ulcorner N$ is $F\urcorner$, thereby making a statement and referring to an object x. He is referring to x by virtue of making a statement which is about x by virtue of containing some statemental designator which designates x. Thus it is the identity of the statement which determines the identity of the referent. We could stop here and say that this is our theory of referring. However, this theory of referring would not be useful in the subsequent construction of a theory of sense because it presupposes a theory of sense in assuming that we know what statement is made. Thus it is desirable to have a different account of referring which does not proceed in terms of stating.

If a speaker makes a statement ϕ and thereby statementally refers to x, he must be sending a proposition ψ which is a possible sent-proposition for ϕ, and furthermore ψ must be about x by virtue of containing a propositional designator designating x. Thus a plausible first proposal is that a speaker refers to an object x iff his sent-proposition is about x.[1] However, the speaker's sent-proposition being about x is not sufficient to guarantee that the statement he is making is about x. For example, S might send a proposition ψ which contains as a constituent the compound propositional designator $\imath x(S{:}x,\delta)$ (e.g., 'the sister of δ') and thereby contains the constituent δ. It may be that by sending ψ the speaker is stating ϕ, where ϕ contains a statemental designator ∂ for which $\imath x(S{:}x,\delta)$ is a possible sent-designator, and thus the speaker is statementally referring to the designatum of $\imath x(S{:}x,\delta)$. However, ϕ may not be about the designatum of δ because there may be other possible sent-designators for ∂ which do not contain δ as a constituent, and accordingly ϕ does not contain a statemental designator designating the designatum of δ. For example, I may make a statement about Martha by saying 'Martha is bald'. I may be thinking of Martha in terms of the description 'the sister of Tom', but I am not thereby making a statement about Tom despite my sent-proposition being about both Tom and Martha. Thus, despite S's sending a proposition which is about x, it does not follow that S is statementally referring to x.

Suppose S states ϕ by uttering a sentence of the form $\ulcorner R(t_1, \ldots ,t_k)\urcorner$ (where $t_1, \ldots ,t_k$ are singular terms) and thereby sends a proposition ψ. Only some of the propositional designators in ψ will designate objects to which S is statementally referring. To determine which propositional designators designate referents, we must match up the

---

[1] Note that in cases in which the speaker is referring to more than one object in the course of making his statement, this would leave unresolved the question of what determines which singular term in a sentence is being used to refer to which object.

singular terms t_i with particular designators in ψ. The speaker is using a particular term t_i to refer to a particular object x which is the designatum of a particular propositional designator δ. We might reasonably say that S is using t_i to "send" δ, and it is by virtue of this that he is using t_i to refer to x. Similarly, he is using the predicate to "send" a certain concept. In order to pursue this, we need a way of bringing parts of the sent-proposition into correspondence with parts of the sentence and saying that the lexical items are used to "send" the propositional constituents.

An obvious proposal is that it is the intentions of the speaker that determine which parts of the sentence are used to send which parts of the sent-proposition. In ordinary cases of stating, the speaker intends to be using certain lexical items to send certain propositional constituents. He designs his sentence with this in mind, choosing sentential constituents for the express purpose of sending corresponding propositional constituents. This is the normal case of stating, but a more nondifferentiated kind of stating is also possible. Someone who does not speak English well might be told the meaning of a certain English sentence without being told the meanings of its lexical parts. He could then use the sentence to send a proposition without having any intentions at all regarding what parts of the proposition are being sent by what parts of the sentence. We still want to say that the predicate is being used to send a certain concept, singular terms are being used to send certain propositional designators, and so forth. In particular this is necessary, as before, to sort out reference. Thus it cannot be the intentions of the speaker which determine this. And if the speaker's intentions do not play this role in nondifferentiated stating, then it does not seem that they can play this role in differentiated stating either.

The appeal to cases of nondifferentiated stating suggest that it must be the objective meanings of the lexical items which determine what propositional constituents they are used to send. The intentions of the speaker determine what proposition is being sent, but it is the meanings of the lexical items in the sentence he utters which determine what parts of that sent-proposition are being sent by using those lexical items. Just how do the meanings do that? A lexical item w has an intension which selects some statemental constituent α as its sense under the particular circumstances of the utterance. The statemental constituent α in turn has a diagram which selects specific propositional constituents as "possible sent-objects" for α under the circumstances of the utterance. Thus corresponding to each singular term t_i under the actual circumstances in which S states ϕ there will be the set $\Sigma(t_i)$ which includes all of the propositional designators which *could* be sent by using t_i under those circumstances. It might then seem reasonable to propose that we can match up the singular terms t_i with the propositional designators in the sent-proposition by merely appealing to the sets $\Sigma(t_i)$: the speaker is using t_i to send δ iff δ is a constituent of his sent-proposition and $\delta \in \Sigma(t_i)$. Unfortunately, this attractive proposal will not work because the semantical rules governing proper names and many other singular terms impose virtually no restrictions on $\Sigma(t_i)$. In any concrete situation, any proper name can be used to send a vast array of propositional designators. Thus the sets $\Sigma(t_i)$ are too large to determine which designator is being sent by using a particular singular term.

If we concentrate exclusively on the singular terms in the sentence uttered, there is no way of determining which singular term is used to send which propositional designator because at least many singular terms tend to be semantically interchangeable to a large degree. The solution to this difficulty lies in looking at the rest of the sentence first. We must decompose the entire sentence simultaneously into parts which are used to send parts of the sent-proposition. The semantical constraints on other sorts of lexical items tend to be much more stringent than those on singular terms, enabling us to ascertain what propositional constituents those other items are used to send, and that information can be used in turn to ascertain what propositional designators are being sent by the singular terms. To illustrate this, suppose once more that the speaker makes a statement by saying 'Martha is bald', thereby sending the proposition $(B:\imath x(S:x,\delta))$. We want to know which designator, δ or $\imath x(S:x,\delta)$, is being sent by the use of the name 'Martha'. There is no way to tell by just looking at the semantical constraints governing 'Martha'. But the matter can be resolved by looking first at the predicate 'is bald'. Our sentence is a simple subject/predicate sentence of the form $\ulcorner N$ is $F\urcorner$. The S-intension of this sentence prescribes that it can only be used to send propositions of the form $(\alpha:\tau)$ where α is a concept and τ a propositional designator. In order for 'Martha' to be used to send the propositional designator τ, it must be the case that 'is bald' is simultaneously being used to send the concept α. Thus if we can determine what concept is being sent by using 'is bald', we will be able to tell what propositional designator is being sent by using 'Martha'. There are two ways of decomposing our sent-proposition to give it the form $(\alpha:\tau)$, viz., $(B:\imath x(S:x,\delta))$ and $((B:\imath x(S:x,y)):\delta)$ (where $(B:\imath x(S:x,y))$ is the concept exemplified by an object y if the sister of y is bald). These are two ways of describing the same proposition. If 'Martha' were being used to send δ, then 'is bald' would have to be used to send the concept $(B:\imath x(S:x,y))$. But the meaning of 'is bald' precludes its being used to send the latter concept, so 'Martha' must be used instead to send $\imath x(S:x,\delta)$. This requires using 'is bald' to send the concept B, but that is precisely what the intension of 'is bald' permits.

The preceding example illustrates that it is by appealing to the meaning of the predicate that we are able to determine which designators are being sent by using the singular terms in the sentence the speaker utters. Although the semantical constraints on what propositional designators can be sent by using a singular terms are often very minimal, the constraints on what concepts can be sent by using a given predicate tend to be quite stringent. As we must simultaneously bring all of the parts of the decomposition of the sent-proposition into correspondence with lexical parts of the sentence, the meaning of the predicate indirectly imposes severe restrictions on what designators can be taken to be sent by the use of the singular terms. We can employ this observation to generate a precise definition of the notion of using a singular term to send a particular propositional designator. Given a predicate R and a concrete circumstance of utterance to determine the values of the pragmatic parameters, let $\Sigma(R)$ be the set of possible sent-concepts for the speaker for the attribute expressed by R under those circumstances. Then we can define:

(2.1) If S utters a sentence $\ulcorner R(t_1, \ldots, t_k)\urcorner$ where $t_1, \ldots, t_k$ are singular terms and R is a predicate, and S thereby makes a statement and sends a proposition ψ, S is using t_i to *send* a propositional designator δ_i iff $\delta_i \in \Sigma(t_i)$ and there is a concept α in $\Sigma(R)$ and there are propositional designators $\delta_1, \ldots, \delta_{i-1}, \delta_{i+1}, \ldots, \delta_k$ in $\Sigma(t_1), \ldots, \Sigma(t_{i-1})$, $\Sigma(t_{i+1}), \ldots, \Sigma(t_k)$ respectively, such that $\psi = (\alpha:\delta_1, \ldots, \delta_k)$.[2]

This definition presupposes that when a statement is made there will be a unique decomposition of the sent-proposition which satisfies these conditions. If, by uttering the sentence, the speaker intends to be sending a proposition for which there is more than one

---

[2] This definition will be generalized and made more precise in the Appendix.

such decomposition, it appears that there is nothing to determine precisely what statement is to be made (there would be different equally viable candidates), and thus no statement is made.

Our analysis of statemental referring now becomes:

> (2.2)   In uttering a sentence P, S is using the singular term t to statementally refer to x iff t is a constituent of P and S is making a statement by uttering P and thereby using t to send some propositional designator designating x.

In statemental referring, the referent is determined by the propositional designator which the speaker is using the singular term to send. We might say that the speaker is "thinking of the referent in terms of the sent-designator". However, a disclaimer is in order here. Philosophers customarily use the term 'thinking' only in talking about occurrent thought. One can be in various cognitive states involving beliefs, intentions, etc., without indulging in occurrent thought and hence without thinking in this sense. And it seems reasonably clear that we can make statements and statementally refer without occurrently thinking about our referent. All that is required is that one be in "cognitive contact" with the referent via an appropriate sent-designator. We could avoid the locution 'thinking about the object' altogether in discussions of reference, but that would involve complicated circumlocution which would often obscure the points being made. Consequently, I shall persist in talking about "how the speaker is thinking of the referent" for want of any other convenient terminology, but one should not construe this as requiring the speaker to have occurrent thoughts about the referent. It is just a more colloquial way of talking about what propositional designator the speaker is sending.

3. *De Re* Propositions

I have argued that the referent of a singular term is determined by what propositional designator the speaker is sending by using it, or more loosely, by the way in which the speaker is thinking of the referent. This general sort of principle has been endorsed by many traditional theories of referring.[3] Coupled with the allegation that it is only possible to think of a particular object by thinking of it

---

[3] See Strawson [1950] and Searle [1969].

under a description, this has led philosophers to endorse variants of what Donnellan [1972] has called 'the principle of identifying descriptions', according to which a speaker can only refer to an object if he is in a position to supply some description which uniquely characterizes that object. Donnellan and Kripke [1972] have both argued against this principle, and on that basis theories of referring which proceed in terms of how the speaker is thinking of the referent have been deemed suspect. Notice, however, that we are only committed to the principle of identifying descriptions if we endorse the view that you can only think about an object under a description. That is a view which we have already rejected at least in the case of thinking about oneself. Furthermore, as I will urge, the arguments given by Donnellan and Kripke seem to be best understood as directed against the traditional picture of thinking about an object, and have nothing directly to do with reference.

The purpose of this section is to argue that the most common way of thinking about an object does not consist of thinking of it under a description. A particular nondescriptive way of thinking about an object will be described, and beliefs wherein one does think of an object in that way will be called '*de re* beliefs'. The propositions believed will be called '*de re* propositions'. By way of contrast, beliefs in which one only thinks of objects in terms of (conceptual) descriptions will be called 'purely *de dicto*'. In arguing that there are these nondescriptive ways of thinking of objects, I take myself to be agreeing with Donnellan and Kripke, although the upshot of this is to make the preceding account of referring in terms of sent-designators immune to objections of the sort they have advanced against traditional accounts of referring.

3.1 *The Existence of* De Re *Propositions*

The orthodox claim that you can only think about an object under a description is the claim that to have a belief about an object is to believe a proposition containing such a description. Thus a necessary condition for thinking of an object under a description is given by:

(3.1)   In believing ψ, S is thinking of x under the description α only if, necessarily, in believing ψ, S is thinking about whatever object uniquely exemplifies α.

This principle provides a useful test for whether one is thinking of an object under a description.

The clearest examples in which you are not thinking of an object under a description seem to me to be cases in which you are thinking of an object about which you know a great deal. In such cases, although you have many descriptions available to you, you are frequently not thinking of the object *under* any of those descriptions. For example, I might be thinking about my wife, Carol. According to the orthodox view, I must be thinking of Carol under some description. What description might that be? It might first be suggested that I am using some description involving the name 'Carol'. That I am not follows, by principle (3.1), from the fact that I would still be thinking of the same individual even if it were to turn out that I am operating under a posthypnotic suggestion and my wife's name is not 'Carol' after all. Perhaps, then, I am thinking about her under the description 'my wife'. But this cannot be right either. If it turned out that the supposed minister who married us was an imposter, and hence that our marriage is not legal, this would not have the result that I was not thinking about her, despite its having the consequence that Carol is not my wife. Once again, the proposed description fails the test of principle (3.1). It seems that similar tales will establish that I am not thinking of my wife under any simple description.[4] This is reminiscent of the circumstances that led Searle to his theory of proper names, and so it might be suggested that the proper description is of the sort discussed by Searle. I have a great many beliefs about my wife. These beliefs provide many descriptions which I associate together in my mind as being descriptions of a common individual. Suppose these descriptions are $\alpha_1, \ldots, \alpha_n$. Then perhaps I am thinking of Carol under the Searle-type description 'the thing which satisfies sufficiently many of $\alpha_1, \ldots, \alpha_n$ and more of them than anything else'.

It is not implausible to suppose that the Searle-type description passes the test of principle (3.1). But it, and any other complicated description, fails another test. As propositions are fine-grained objects of belief, occurrently believing a proposition ϕ is a different phenomenological state than occurrently believing ψ, then $\phi \neq \psi$.

---

[4] Notice that we cannot, without regress, appeal to "doxastic" descriptions like 'the person I believe to be my wife'. That description does pick her out, because she is the unique person I believe to be my wife. But according to the theory under consideration, in order for it to be true that I believe her to be my wife, I must think of her under some other description, and it is the existence of that other description which is in doubt.

Applying this to my belief that Carol has red hair, it is phenomeno-logically unrealistic to suppose that the proposition I believe actually contains a Searle-type description as a constituent. I am not mentally surveying all of the vast number of descriptions I could give of Carol and collecting them together into a single thought. In fact, I could not even enumerate all of those descriptions without considerable mental effort. If I have to search a description out, it is not part of my actual thought. The belief I have when I occurrently believe Carol to have red hair is phenomenologically distinguishable from the belief I would have if I employed such a complex Searle-type description, and hence the propositions are distinct.

It must be concluded that in a case like this in which I know a great deal about the object of which I am thinking, I do not ordinarily think of it under a description. If I do not think of my wife under a description, how does my belief pick out its subject? It is a bit tempting to suppose that when I think about my wife in this way, she herself is a constituent of my thought. I just *think of the woman*, I do not think of her under a description. According to this proposal, some propositions contain objects themselves as constituents, rather than descriptions which pick out the objects, and then in thinking about an object we entertain these directly referential propositions. This is to claim that directly referential propositions are, after all, fine-grained objects of belief.

It would be hard to imagine how the object itself could somehow be a constituent of our belief, but a little reflection indicates that that is an incorrect picture of the situation anyway. Recall again the case of Robinson and Thompson who are really one and the same person leading a double life. You could know "each person" well and think of each nondescriptively without knowing that they were one and the same person. If you occurrently believed that Robinson was tall and you occurrently believed that Thompson was tall, you were certainly having two different thoughts. Your two states of occurrent believing were phenomenologically distinguishable, so you were believing two different propositions, despite the fact that you were believing the same thing about the same object and you were not thinking about the object under a description in either case. This indicates that even though your thoughts about Robinson and Thompson were not mediated by descriptions, they involved some kind of mental representation. If your belief that Robinson is tall was different from your belief that Thompson is tall, then you must have been thinking about Robinson and Thompson in different ways, and hence the man himself was not a literal constituent of your thought.

There is some kind of mental representation involved in beliefs like the foregoing, but it does not consist of thinking of the object under a description. Cases of the sort we have been discussing have a unique phenomenological character. They involve thinking of objects in special ways. I propose to call these '*de re* ways of thinking of objects', or more briefly, '*de re* representations'. Belief wherein one employs *de re* representations will be called '*de re* belief'. I will say that a *de re* representation *represents* the object about which it is a way of thinking. That object will be called the *representatum* of the representation. If a belief involves a particular representation, then the representatum of that representation is the (or a) subject of the belief.

One of the most important characteristics of *de re* ways of thinking of objects is that they do not involve thinking of the objects under descriptions, but they cannot be defined in that way. There are other nondescriptive ways of thinking of objects which must be distinguished from *de re* ways. For example, I urged in Chapter One that everyone has a special nondescriptive way of thinking of himself. Thinking of oneself in that way is phenomenologically distinguishable from thinking of someone else (or oneself) in a *de re* way. And it will be urged below that there are other nondescriptive ways of thinking of at least certain kinds of objects. I propose that we define '*de re* belief' to be belief that works the way I say it does (below). Our substantive claim is then that we have *de re* beliefs, so defined.

Frequently, the objects about which we think in *de re* ways are objects with which we are perceptually acquainted, and it might initially be suspected that this is necessary for our being able to think of an object in a *de re* way. However, I also think of Aristotle and George Washington in *de re* ways. That I do not think of them under descriptions follows from precisely the same sort of argument as was employed in demonstrating that I do not think of my wife under a description. Thus it must be possible to come to think of an object in a *de re* way as a result of being either perceptually or descriptively connected with it. Just what beyond our initial acquaintance with an object is required for our coming to think of it in a *de re* way is a psychological question about which *a priori* philosophy can say little, but it does not seem that the psychological constraints can be very severe.

64

3.2 *The Subject of a* De Re *Belief*

Numerous questions arise concerning *de re* beliefs and *de re* representations, some logical and some psychological. The most important for our purposes seems to be this: Given a *de re* representation, what determines its representatum? It seems initially reasonable to suppose that the representatum must be determined in some way by the *de re* beliefs one has involving that representation. Such an account is more plausible for some cases than for others. There seem to be essentially two ways in which we come to employ *de re* representations: (1) we may begin with the *de dicto* belief that there is a unique object exemplifying some concept α (α is normally a long conjunction), and we subsequently come to think of that object in a *de re* way; (2) we may simply perceive the object and immediately come to think of it in a *de re* way. In the latter case, it is unclear whether we must originally have any beliefs at all involving the *de re* representation, and even if we do, they would seem to be irrelevant to determining the representatum. The perception itself determines the representatum. When we acquire a *de re* representation perceptually, then we are thinking about whatever we are perceiving.

Perhaps we should split the account of *de re* representation in two, giving separate accounts of *de re* representations acquired perceptually and *de re* representations derived from antecedent *de dicto* beliefs. It seems initially plausible to suppose, in the latter case, that if we begin with the *de dicto* belief that there is a unique thing exemplifying α, and there is such a unique object x, then if we move from the *de dicto* belief to a *de re* representation, we are automatically thinking about x. This is the *belief satisfaction* account of *de re* representation. However, an example suffices to show that more is required than just belief satisfaction. Suppose my friend Richard tells me a story about a putative ancient Greek named 'Dilapides' whose philosophical view was that everything is broken. Richard is just making the story up, but I believe him and so come to believe that there was a unique individual having all the characteristics attributed to Dilapides in the story. Suppose that at this point I do not think of Dilapides in a *de re* way but merely have the *de dicto* belief that there was a unique individual with all those characteristics. Among the characteristics I attribute to Dilapides may be that of being the person about whom Richard was telling me, but we can suppose that after a bit I forget where I heard the story and simply retain the *de dicto* belief that there was a unique individual having all of the characteristics enumerated in the story. Suppose that at that point I come to think of the putative Dilapides in a *de re* way. Suppose further that, purely by chance and unknown to Richard, there was a unique individual having all of those characteristics. It would follow from the belief-satisfaction theory that in thinking about Dilapides I am thinking about that individual. But that seems false. A necessary condition for my beliefs to be about a specific individual is that in telling me the story, Richard was telling me about that individual. As Richard was not in fact talking about any individual, it follows that when I think of Dilapides in a *de re* way I am not thinking about anyone, regardless of whether there is someone satisfying all of my beliefs about Dilapides.

Consider another example. Suppose that I am in charge of a maximum security building which is protected by all sorts of electronic sensors which will indicate the presence of anything moving in its immediate vicinity. The sensors indicate the presence of a small animal on the roof, and upon hearing a 'meow' transmitted from the roof I conclude that there is a cat on the roof. I come to think of this putative cat in a *de re* way, draw more conclusions about it on the basis of the information conveyed by the sensors, etc. Suppose further that there is a cat on the roof, but it has somehow escaped detection by the sensors which are in fact sensing the presence of a misguided squirrel (who meows). Although there is a cat on the roof, I am not thinking of *that* cat when I think in a *de re* way about the putative cat on the roof. There is no connection between my thought and the cat that just happens to be there. A necessary condition for me to be thinking about that cat is that it be the cat about which the sensors are giving me information. Nor am I thinking about the squirrel. My *de re* belief is derived from the *de dicto* belief that there is a cat on the roof, and as such must be about a cat if it is about anything. If this is not obvious, suppose instead that what the sensors detected was a branch blowing onto the roof and that the 'meow' was the sound of the branch scraping against something. I am clearly not thinking about the branch when I think in a *de re* way about the putative cat.

When I acquire a *de re* representation on the basis of an initial *de dicto* belief, I begin with the *de dicto* belief that there is a unique α (for some concept α). But the preceding examples indicate that when I come to think in a *de re* way I am not automatically thinking about the unique α (even if there is one). I am not thinking about the unique α *whatever* it is; rather, I am thinking about a particular object (the object Richard told me about, or the object detected by the sensors) as the unique α. A necessary condition for me to think about the object in this way is that it be the unique α, but that is not a sufficient condition. I suggest that what more is required is that I have epistemic contact with the unique α.[5] This epistemic contact takes the form of a good reason for thinking that there is a unique α.[6] If that epistemic contact relates me to a particular object (e.g., the object Richard was talking about, or the object detected by the sensors), then my *de re* way of thinking can only be a way of thinking about that particular object.

In defense of this suggestion, first note that in order for one to come to think of the α in a *de re* way, it does seem to be required that he have a good reason for thinking that there is a unique α. For example, suppose the unsupported belief that there is a unique eleven-toed English mathematician named 'Charlie' is implanted directly in Louis' brain through neurological manipulation, and this leads Louis to think in a *de re* way about this putative individual. It turns out to everyone's surprise that there really is a unique eleven-toed English mathematician named 'Charlie'. As there is no connection between this fact and Louis' belief, we would not agree that Louis has all along been thinking of Charlie.

If epistemic contact with the unique α is required, in what does that consist? In the Dilapides example, I had a good reason for believing that there was a unique individual possessing all of the attributes enumerated in the story, but that reason was defeasible and would be defeated by the discovery that the unique individual possessing all of those attributes was not the individual Richard was telling me about. I also had a defeasible reason for believing there to be a unique cat on the roof, and that reason would be defeated by the discovery that the unique cat on the roof was not being detected by the sensors. I suggest in general that a necessary condition for me to come to think of the unique α in a *de re* way is that I have a good reason for believing there to be a unique α, and that reason would not be defeated by knowledge of the actual facts of the matter. Knowledge of the actual facts might give you a different reason for believing there to be a unique α, but if your

[5] This is reminiscent of some remarks in Kim [1977].

[6] By 'good reason' here I mean 'reason which supplies at least some justification'. The justification may be less than is required for knowledge.

original reason were not sustained then you would not have been thinking of the unique α. If your reason would not be defeated by knowledge of all the relevant facts let us describe it as *nondefective*. Thus a necessary condition for me to come to think of the unique α in a *de re* way is that I have a good nondefective reason for believing there to be a unique α.

I might, however, have a good nondefective reason for believing there to be a unique α, but ignore it and instead believe there to be a unique α for a different reason which either is not a good reason or is defective. For example, if in the Dilapides case I had independent evident for the existence of Dilapides but ignored it and instead believed in the existence of Dilapides simply because Richard told me that he existed, I would not then be thinking in a *de re* way about the real Dilapides. For epistemic contact we must insist, then, that one not only *have* a good nondefective reason for believing there to be a unique α, but also that one believe it *for* a good nondefective reason.

The notion of a good reason requires elaboration. There is a distinction between a reason being a good reason by itself, and its being a good reason given everything else that one believes. If one not only believes the reason, but also believes various propositions which are defeaters for the reason, then the reason may be a good reason by itself, but not a good reason given one's other beliefs. The claim that one proposition ψ by itself is a good reason for believing another proposition θ affirms a logical relationship between ψ and θ. It is to say that ψ is what I have elsewhere[7] called a *logically good reason* for θ. The preceding observation is then the observation that the justification arising from a logically good reason may be destroyed by one's believing various defeaters for the logically good reason.

Defeaters may prevent one's logically good reason from giving one knowledge in either of two ways. On the one hand, if one *believes* defeaters, this may destroy one's justification and thereby prevent one from having knowledge. On the other hand, there may be defeaters which are true without one believing them. In that case one's reason is defective, in the sense defined above, and although one's justification remains intact, one still does not have knowledge.

[7] See Pollock [1974], Chapter Two.

Turning to epistemic contact, we have required that one's reason for believing there to be a unique α be a logically good reason, and that it not be defective. We have not, however, said whether epistemic contact requires that one's reason not be defeated by other beliefs one has. In other words, does epistemic contact require merely a logically good reason, or a reason that is good in the context of everything else that one believes? One would naturally suppose the latter to be required, but somewhat surprisingly, it seems that only the former is required. For example, suppose that Jones tells me that there is a unique individual of a certain description α, and on that basis I come to believe that there is such an individual and I come to think of that putative individual in a *de re* way. Suppose further that Jones knows that there is such an individual and is telling the truth. However, I have independent overwhelming evidence to the effect that Jones is a liar and not to be trusted in such matters. Despite this evidence, I believe Jones (perhaps he is my father, and various psychological forces are involved in this irrational behavior). Under the circumstances, I am not justified in believing that there is a unique α. I believe that for a logically good reason, viz., Jones told me that there is a unique α and what people tell me tends to be true, but I also believe defeaters for that reason. Given that Jones really was talking knowingly about a particular individual and I believed him, it seems that I am subsequently thinking about that individual despite the fact that I am not justified in believing him to exist. This illustrates that epistemic contact requires my reason only to be a logically good one, not that it be undefeated by my other beliefs. Summing up then, epistemic contact consists of my believing there to be a unique α for a nondefective logically good reason.

The way in which my epistemic contact with the unique α may relate me to a *specific* object is that there is a relation R such that my reason for believing there to be a unique α would be defeated by the discovery that it is false that the thing standing in the relation R to me is the unique α. In the Dilapides example, R is the relation in which I stand to an object iff it is the object Richard was telling me about; and in the cat-on-the-roof example, R is the relation in which I stand to an object iff it is the object detected by the sensors. When my reason for believing that there is a unique α is defeasible in this way, then a necessary condition for me to think of the unique α in a *de re* way (starting from the *de dicto* belief that there is a unique α) is that I stand in the relation R to a unique object and that object is the unique α. That this is a necessary condition follows from the requirement that my reason be nondefective. This explains the sense in which my epistemic contact may select a specific object for my *de re* representation to represent. Let us call a reason which is defeasible in this manner a *specific reason* for thinking that there is a unique α. It is a reason for thinking that a specific thing is the unique α.

It is also possible to have a nonspecific reason for believing that there is a unique α. For example, I have reason to believe that each person has a unique (biological) father, and on that basis I may believe that Jones has a unique father without having any idea who Jones' father is. Despite the fact that I have only a nonspecific reason for believing this, I can come to think of Jones' father in a *de re* way. Thus specific reasons are not required for epistemic contact.

I propose then that we adopt the following as our account of *de re* representation for those cases in which the representation is derived from a *de dicto* belief:

(3.2)   If τ is a *de re* representation derived from S's (earlier) belief that there is a unique α, τ represents x iff: (1) x is the unique α, and (2) at the time of the derivation, S believed there to be a unique α for a nondefective logically good reason.

According to (3.2), *de re* representations are devices for thinking about objects about whose existence we have found out in particular ways. You have not found out that an object exists if your reasons are defective. The cases in which there is a unique α but you are not thinking about it are cases in which you have not found out that there is a unique α, either because your reason for believing there to be a unique α was not a logically good reason or it was defective.

Superficial consideration of (3.2) suggests that it makes representation a peculiar admixture of description satisfaction and epistemic contact. However, that is misleading. In order to find out that a certain object exists, you must be thinking about it in some way. Principle (3.2) just deals with the case in which, in finding out that the object exists, you were thinking of it under a description. The belief-satisfaction part of (3.2) is an artifact of this restriction to cases in which we begin by thinking of the object under a description.

There are other ways of thinking of objects, i.e., other representations. For example, in thinking about an object we are perceiving, we do not normally think of it under a description. Given any representation v, it seems that we should be able to begin with the belief that there is a unique thing which is v, and then derive a *de re* representation from that. When we speak of "the belief that there is a unique thing which is v",[8] we mean a belief about a certain object (or putative object), where that object is represented in your belief by v, to the effect that there is a unique thing which is that object. It then appears that we can generalize (3.2) to:

(3.3)   If v is a representation and τ is a *de re* representation derived from S's belief that there is a unique thing which is v, τ represents x iff: (1) v represents x, and (2) at the time of the derivation, S believed there to be a unique thing which is v for a nondefective logically good reason.

To illustrate (3.3), consider *de re* representations that are derived from perception. We have a basically simple account of representation in this case:

(3.4)   If τ is a *de re* representation derived from S's perception of x, then τ represents x.

I suggest that (3.4) can be derived from (3.3) together with some facts about perception. You perceive an object by being "perceptually presented with" a percept, where a percept is a mental item (in the same sense that an afterimage or a pain is a mental item). There is a vast philosophical literature about the relationship between the percept and the object of which it is a percept, but I propose that we can think of percepts as ways of thinking of objects, i.e., representations. As such, they fall into the same category as *de re* representations and the representations which consist of thinking of objects under descriptions. Percepts represent perceived objects in precisely the same sense that other representations represent objects. This might suggest that the *de re* representations which are derived from perception are the percepts themselves. However, once we have perceived an object, we do not continue to think of that object in terms of the percept after the perception, for two reasons. First, we may continue to think of the object while forgetting what it looked

[8] To dispel possible confusion, note that the 'is' here is the 'is' of identity, not the 'is' of predication.

71

like, so clearly we are not thinking of it in terms of the percept. Second, the percept (which is a repeatable thing) must be available for perceiving (and hence thinking about) another object which looks the same way at a later time. Thus the *de re* representation is in some sense derived from the operation of the percept without being identical with the percept. Given that the percept is a representation, it makes sense to talk about one having the belief that there is a unique thing which is "that object", wherein you think of "that object" in terms of the percept. This is presumably a belief which you have in an ordinary case of perception in which you do not take yourself to be hallucinating. The suggestion is then that your *de re* representation is derived from this existential belief, and that the representation proceeds in accordance with (3.3). In order for this to be correct (and assuming (3.4)), it must be the case that whenever your reason for holding the existential belief is defective, you are not really perceiving anything. Your (defeasible) reason for holding the existential belief is simply that you are presented with that percept.[9] Is it true that whenever the relevant facts of the case are such that knowledge of them would defeat this reason, you are not perceiving anything in terms of that percept? To evaluate this, we must consider what facts can defeat this reason. There seem to be only two kinds of facts which can do this: (1) there not being any object suitably placed for you to be perceiving it with this percept; (2) your perceptual apparatus being abnormal so that even if there is a suitable object to be perceived, your percept is not caused in the normal way by the presence of that object. If either of these is the case, then you do not perceive anything with your percept. If this is correct, then your reason being defective does entail that you are not perceiving anything with the percept. Hence (3.4) becomes derivable from (3.3), suggesting once again that (3.3) is the basic principle governing *de re* representation.

We arrived at our notion of a *de re* belief by examining cases in which, despite a person's having a number of descriptions available to him of the object about which he is thinking, he is not thinking about that object *under* any of those descriptions. Our analysis of representations now enables us to see that there can also be cases in which a person thinks about an object without being able to give *any* description which uniquely characterizes it. If a *de re* representation is derived from an initial *de dicto* belief to the effect

---

[9] This is defended at length in Pollock [1974].

that there is a unique thing which is α, then initially one can provide the description 'the thing which is α' for the object. But once one has the use of the *de re* representation for thinking about the object, there is no reason one must remember any longer that the object was the thing which was α. If one forgets this, one's *de re* beliefs about the object may no longer contain sufficient descriptive material to uniquely characterize the object. Donnellan [1972] gives an example which might be construed as having this form:

> Suppose a child is gotten up from sleep at a party and introduced to someone as 'Tom', who then says a few words to the child. Later the child says to his parents, 'Tom is a nice man'. The only thing he can say about 'Tom' is that Tom was at the party. Moreover, he is unable to recognize anyone as 'Tom' on subsequent occasions. His parents give lots of parties and they have numerous friends named 'Tom'. The case could be built up, I think, so that nothing the child possesses in the way of descriptions, dispositions to recognize, serves to pick out in the standard way anybody uniquely.

In such a case, upon meeting the man at the party, the child might have acquired a *de re* way of thinking of him. Initially, he may have had descriptions which were sufficient to pick the man out (e.g., 'the man I am now looking at'), and by virtue of those descriptions his representation had a well-determined representatum. He no longer recalls those descriptions, but that does not incapacitate his representation.

There remain many puzzling questions about *de re* belief, both logical and psychological. *A priori* philosophy cannot be expected to resolve the psychological questions, but a few words regarding some of them may nevertheless help to clarify the way in which *de re* belief works. The basic psychological question concerns what it takes to acquire a *de re* representation and begin thinking of an object in a *de re* way. *Logically*, there are no restrictions to thinking about an individual in a *de re* way beyond the requirement that one can initially think of the object in some other way in order to get things started. Presumably there are some psychological restrictions to the acquisition of *de re* representations, but they do not appear to be very stringent. In particular, it is illuminating to note that one can knowingly think of the same individual in more than one *de re* way. This is nicely illustrated by another of

Donnellan's examples:

> A student meets a man he takes to be the famous philosopher,
> J. L. Aston-Martin. . . . The meeting takes place at a party and
> the student engages the man in a somewhat lengthy discussion. . . .
> In fact, however, although the student never suspects it, the man
> at the party is not the famous philosopher, but someone who
> leads the student to have that impression.
>
> Imagine, then, a subsequent conversation with his friends in
> which the student relates what happened at the party. He might
> begin by saying, 'Last night I met J. L. Aston-Martin and talked
> to him for almost an hour'. To whom does he refer at this point?
> I strongly believe the answer should be, 'to the famous philos-
> opher'. . . .
>
> The student might (also) use the name 'J. L. Aston-Martin', as
> it were, incidentally. For example: ' . . . and then Robinson tripped
> over Aston-Martin's feet and fell flat on his face'. . . . In these
> subsequent utterances to whom was the speaker referring in using
> the name 'Aston-Martin'? My inclination is to say that here it
> was to the man at the party and not to the famous philosopher.

Donnellan is talking about reference, but the same remarks seem
appropriate in response to the question, 'Who was the speaker
thinking about?' I submit that the speaker was thinking about
Aston-Martin and the man at the party in terms of (distinct) *de re*
representations, and his use of the name 'Aston-Martin' to express
both his beliefs simply reflects his supposition that the two representations represent the same individual. If he were not employing two
separate representations here, he could not subsequently come to
believe that the individuals he was thinking and talking about were
distinct. Furthermore, if we change the example and suppose the
man at the party really to have been the famous philosopher, this
would not change the fact that the student could *in principle* have
subsequently discovered that he was thinking about two different
individuals *if* there had been two individuals rather than one. Thus
even if the student really was thinking about the same individual
when he said, 'Last night I met J. L. Aston-Martin' and 'Robinson
tripped over Aston-Martin's feet', it follows that he was thinking
about that individual in two different *de re* ways. The source of the
two representations is fairly obvious. The student already had a *de
re* way of thinking of the philosopher before he went to the party.

At the party he acquired a second representation as a result of perceiving the man at the party.

The preceding observations lead to an initially startling proliferation of *de re* representations. Analogous considerations must lead us to conclude that whenever one has a number of different contacts with a single individual, it is possible for him to have a different *de re* way of thinking about that individual arising out of each contact. This is not so unreasonable as it may seem, however. The resulting proliferation of *de re* beliefs is not greater than the proliferation of *de dicto* beliefs that would be possible on traditional theories of thinking about objects, because each contact would provide different descriptions in terms of which to think about the object.

3.3 De Re *Propositions*

When one thinks of an object in a *de re* way and believes something about it, what one believes is a proposition. Such propositions might reasonably be called '*de re* propositions'. Propositions are about objects by virtue of containing propositional designators which designate those objects, so *de re* propositions must contain designators designating the objects which they are about. Those designators cannot be definite descriptions, because to believe a proposition containing only designators which are definite descriptions is to have a purely *de dicto* belief rather than a *de re* belief. Consequently, the designators involved in *de re* propositions make up a new class of erstwhile unnoticed propositional designators which we might call '*de re* designators'.[10] The existence of *de re* designators is required by the assumption that propositions are individuated by their structure and constituents.

Although there is an important connection between *de re* representations and *de re* designators, they must not be confused with one another. To say that I have a belief involving a particular *de re* representation is to say something exclusively about the phenomenological character of my cognitive state. It is analogous to reporting that I have a pain. However, unlike being in pain, my cognitive state has a propositional object whose structure determines what I believe. The *de re* representation is a mental item (like a pain or

---

[10] It should be pointed out, however, that there are similarities between my view and that of Ackerman [1979] and [1979a]. In this connection, see also Ackerman [1980].

afterimage), but the proposition believed must contain a corresponding logical item—the *de re* designator—designating the representatum of the *de re* representation. I will say that a *de re* representation *expresses* the corresponding *de re* designator.

I expect a certain amount of resistance to the positing of *de re* designators, so it is important to see how little is actually involved in such positing. The existence of *de re* designators is required by the joint assumptions that belief takes propositional objects and that propositions are individuated by their structure and constituents. Beliefs which differ only with respect to what *de re* representation is employed are beliefs in propositions with the same structure, so those propositions must contain different constituents corresponding to the different representations, i.e., they must contain different propositional designators. Those propositional designators are just what I am calling '*de re* designators'. It may still be protested that one does not understand what these designators are. This amounts to an objection to our two assumptions about propositions. But at this point the reader should recall the remarks of Chapter One about not taking propositions too seriously. As far as I am concerned, talk of propositions is just a convenient way of talking about what one believes, i.e., about types of belief states. To say that there is a proposition of a certain sort is just to say that it is possible for a person to be in a belief state of a corresponding sort. Thus to say that there are *de re* propositions and *de re* designators is to say no more than that it is possible for people to have beliefs wherein they think of objects in *de re* ways. The latter is a conclusion for which I have argued extensively, so it cannot be denied that there are *de re* designators.

The recognition of *de re* designators forces us to give up the traditional assumption that propositions are constructed exclusively out of concepts and logical operators. In *de re* designators we have a new class of propositional constituents not reducible to or constructible out of anything else. These must be regarded as primitive propositional constituents. Of course, if the arguments of Chapter One regarding first-person belief are accepted, then personal designators constitute another class of propositional designators not reducible to the classical inventory of propositional constituents.

It was argued in Chapter One that first-person propositions are logically idiosyncratic. Only I can believe a proposition containing my personal designator as a constituent. That conclusion is sufficiently surprising that it might lead us to be suspicious of the whole theory of personal designators. However, I shall now argue that personal designators are not unusual in this respect—propositions involving *de re* designators are also logically idiosyncratic, and for essentially the same reason. In order to defend this contention, let us begin by considering what is required for one and the same person to believe the same *de re* proposition on two different occasions. As maximally fine-grained objects of belief, propositions are such that if occurrently believing ϕ is phenomenologically distinguishable from occurrently believing ψ, then $\phi \neq \psi$. Thus in order to believe the same *de re* proposition twice, one's belief states must be phenomenologically the same on both occasions, and hence one must be employing the same *de re* representation on both occasions. In other words, for a single individual, different *de re* representations automatically express different *de re* designators, and hence are involved in believing different *de re* propositions. Thus a necessary condition for a single person to believe the same *de re* proposition twice is that he be employing the same *de re* representation on both occasions.

It is doubtful that the preceding criterion is even in principle applicable in attempting to determine whether two different people have the same *de re* belief. That criterion proceeds in terms of whether two different mental states are phenomenologically the same, but I doubt that interpersonal comparisons of phenomenological sameness are intelligible. Our ordinary interpersonal comparisons of mental states are in a broad sense "functional" rather than phenomenological. That is, we compare mental states in terms of the roles they play in perception or cognition, and we say that they are the same if they play the same roles. For example, I judge you to be appeared to in the same way as I am (i.e., redly) if you are appeared to in that way which, in you, stands in the same perceptual relationship to red objects as does the state of being appeared to redly in me. For this sort of judgment it is irrelevant whether our perceptual states are phenomenologically the same. Furthermore, there is no apparent way to tell whether the states of two people are phenomenologically the same. Considerations based upon the external observations of other people give us only functional information about their mental states. To make sense of interpersonal phenomenological sameness, one is reduced to saying something like, 'If God could look into the minds of two different people he could tell whether their mental states are really the same', but that makes no real sense as far as I can see. Thus I suspect that

77

the only kinds of interpersonal comparisons of mental states that do make sense are functional ones, i.e., comparisons in terms of perceptual and cognitive role.

However, even if it is insisted that interpersonal comparisons of phenomenological sameness do make sense, it can still be argued that they cannot be used in the interpersonal case to generate a criterion for when two people have the same *de re* belief. For suppose that such comparisons do make sense in a way that makes them different from functional considerations. As phenomenological sameness is something separate from functional considerations, there is no reason to suppose that phenomenologically identical states play the same functional roles in different people. For example, the "inverted spectrum" becomes a real possibility. That is, it could happen that the sensation which, in me, constitutes being appeared to redly, in you constitutes being appeared to bluely. That must be at least logically possible. Analogously, the fact that two people are employing phenomenologically identical *de re* representations gives us no reason to suppose that their representations either represent the same objects or express the same *de re* designators. The latter is a functional comparison, not a phenomenological one, and there is no reason at all to think that the phenomenological comparison gives us a basis for the functional comparison. Thus appeal to phenomenological sameness cannot help us here. If it is to be possible for two different people to have the same *de re* belief, then the relation between their *de re* representations must be a functional one rather than one of phenomenological sameness.

Consider a case in which S and S^* employ the *de re* representations τ and τ^* respectively, and for simplicity suppose that each is derived, in accordance with principle (3.2), from beliefs that there are unique objects exemplifying certain descriptions. Then it seems that the most that could conceivably be required for τ and τ^* to express the same *de re* designator is that they be derived from the same conceptual description α and that S and S^* have the same nondefective reason for believing there to be a unique thing exemplifying α. This seems to be the strongest functional condition that we could formulate. However, reflection indicates that even this very strong condition is not sufficient to guarantee that τ and τ^* express the same *de re* designator. The difficulty is that a single individual can employ two different *de re* representations which are related to one another in this way. Suppose that on some basis S comes to believe that there is a unique object exemplifying α and he comes to think of that object in a *de re* way, employing the *de re* representation τ. He may subsequently acquire many other *de re* beliefs involving τ, and eventually forget his original belief that the representatum of τ uniquely exemplifies α. Much later, he may come to believe all over again and on the same basis that there is a unique object exemplifying α, without associating that with the *de re* representation τ, and so come to think of that object in terms of a new *de re* representation ν. The representations τ and ν are derived from the same belief (that there is a unique object exemplifying α) held for the same nondefective reasons, but τ and ν are different *de re* representations and so, as we have seen, express different *de re* designators. *S**'s *de re* representation τ* cannot express the same *de re* designator as both τ and ν as they express different *de re* designators, and there is nothing to relate it more closely to one than the other, so we can only conclude that it does not express the same *de re* designator as either τ or ν. Thus the proposed functional criterion is inadequate to ensure that *de re* representations employed by two different people express the same *de re* designator. There appears to be no more stringent condition that could be required which would avoid this argument, so I think it must be concluded that there is no reasonable criterion for *de re* representations of different people to express the same *de re* designator. If the *de re* designators expressed by two *de re* representations are the same, there must be something which makes them the same. As there is nothing which can do that, it must be concluded that the *de re* representations of two different people can never express the same *de re* designator, and hence two different people can never entertain the same *de re* proposition. Consequently, *de re* propositions are logically idiosyncratic.

At the risk of belaboring the point, it is perhaps worth emphasizing once more that the content of the claim that these propositions are logically idiosyncratic is really about cognition. It is being claimed that when one thinks certain kinds of thoughts, it makes no sense to talk about someone else thinking the same thoughts. One cannot make this observation go away by denying that such cognitive states have propositional objects. Talk about *de re* propositions is really just a convenient way of saying certain things about the cognitive states themselves.

We are now in a position to repeat one of the arguments of Chapter One for the distinction between propositions and statements. It will be argued shortly that not all statements are propositions, but we are already in a position to see that the converse identification fails—not all propositions are statements. Statements must be stateable. Stating is communicating. But you cannot communicate a *de re* proposition, because as we have seen, two different people cannot entertain the same *de re* proposition. Thus *de re* propositions are not statements. This is the same argument we gave in connection with first-person propositions. It turns merely on logical idiosyncrasy. However, it may seem more compelling now because we have a much larger class of logically idiosyncratic propositions to which we can appeal.

Another interesting logical corollary of the existence of *de re* propositions and *de re* designators is that there are necessary truths which are not *a priori*. Suppose the *de re* designator δ is derived from the belief that there is a unique object exemplifying the description α. Epistemologically, δ and the definite description $\iota\alpha$ function quite differently, as we have seen, but there is a close logical tie between them. The designatum $\nabla(\delta)$ of δ is determined by α, so it seems to be a necessary truth that if δ designates anything, then it designates the same thing as $\iota\alpha$:

(3.5) $\Box[(\exists x)(x = \nabla(\delta)) \supset \nabla(\delta) = \nabla(\iota\alpha)]$.

This necessary truth is not *a priori*. A person cannot discover it simply by reflecting upon the designators δ and $\iota\alpha$. That is particularly clear in cases in which one no longer remembers from what description δ was derived. Thus the necessary proposition in (3.5) is necessary *a posteriori*.

3.4 *Propositional Designators and Concepts*

The traditional assumption was that definite descriptions built out of concepts comprise the only propositional designators. We have now seen that that is false. *De re* designators and personal designators comprise additional classes of propositional designators. Furthermore, having recognized the latter propositional designators, it is apparent that there is another kind of overlooked propositional designator. Designators of this kind are definite descriptions built not just out of concepts but also out of *de re* and personal designators. For example, given a two-place concept α and a propositional designator δ, we can construct the definite description $\iota x(\alpha : x, \delta)$. If δ is either a *de re* designator or a personal designator, then this description is not the sort countenanced by traditional theories.

The proceeding observations must lead us to reconsider our earlier definition of 'concept' as 'what can be believed of an object or sequence of objects'. The traditional view of concepts was that they were "purely qualitative" in a sense which would preclude there being such a concept as $(\alpha:x,\delta)$ where δ is a *de re* or personal designator. However, $(\alpha:x,\delta)$ is something which can be believed of an object, so it fits our definition of 'concept'. Whether we include such items as $(\alpha:x,\delta)$ as concepts is a purely verbal matter, but we should adopt some terminology which will make the distinction clear. I suggest that we define a 'purely qualitative concept' recursively to be a concept which either contains no propositional designators as constituents, or contains only propositional designators which are definite descriptions built out of other purely qualitative concepts. In talking about concepts, philosophers have generally had in mind only purely qualitative concepts.

4. Statements and Propositions

As we have seen, the traditional connotation theory proceeded from two assumptions: (a) the statement made by uttering a sentence containing a semantical occurrence of a proper name is the same as the proposition sent; (b) the only propositional designators there are are purely qualitative conceptual definite descriptions. We have seen that (b) is false. One could in principle maintain (a) and construct a liberalized version of the connotation theory on that basis. However, the way in which (b) is false leads us quickly to the conclusion that (a) is also false. The argument proceeds from logical idiosyncracy. I have argued that any proposition containing either a personal designator or a *de re* designator is logically idiosyncratic. It is in principle possible for a speaker to think of an object in terms of a purely qualitative conceptual definite description, but we are almost never in a position to do that. It is extremely rare to be able to give a purely qualitative conceptual description which uniquely characterizes some specific object. When we actually think of objects in terms of descriptions, these descriptions almost invariably proceed by relating the objects either to ourselves or to other objects. In the former case we think of ourselves in terms of our personal designators, and in the latter case we think of those other objects nondescriptively, i.e., in terms of *de re* designators. Propositions involving descriptions of either of these sorts are logically

81

idiosyncratic. It follows then that in stating by uttering a sentence containing a semantical occurrence of a proper name, the sent-proposition is almost invariably logically idiosyncratic. We have already argued that logically idiosyncratic propositions cannot be statements because statements must be communicable, so it follows that the statement one makes is not identical with the proposition one sends.

The preceding argument is quick, and I feel it is logically compelling. But it may not be totally convincing, turning as it does upon logical idiosyncracy—a notion with which I have found most philosophers to be uncomfortable. Thus it is important to observe that we would be led to precisely the same conclusions regarding the statement/proposition distinction independently of logical idiosyncracy. The argument for this turns upon the multiplicity of possible sent-propositions. In uttering the sentence $\ulcorner N$ is $F\urcorner$, it is possible to make the same statement while sending different propositions. Accordingly, the statement cannot be identified with the sent-proposition. This multiplicity of possible sent-propositions can be illustrated by returning to an example which we used against the connotation theory. Recall Professor Jones who taught his students Jacob and Rudolph all about Leibniz.[11] When Jacob and Rudolph go off and tell others

(4.1) Leibniz was an important political figure in his time.

it seems that they are making the same statement as Professor Jones. After all, they take themselves to simply be repeating what they learned from Jones. However, it also seems clear that Jacob and Rudolph are both thinking about Leibniz in ways quite different from Jones. For example, they may be thinking of Leibniz in terms of some propositional designator like 'the person Jones has been talking about all semester' (where 'all semester' includes Jones' most recent pronouncement). Jones' sent-designator will be quite different—it cannot make reference to itself. And yet they are making the same statement. Thus the speaker's sent-designator cannot be a constituent of the statement he makes in uttering a sentence containing a proper name, and accordingly that statement is distinct from his sent-proposition.

To take another example, suppose a friend rushes into the room and demands, 'Quick, give me an example of a famous physicist!',

---

[11] See page 43.

to which I, having read my Kripke, reply:

(4.2)   Richard Feynman is a famous physicist.

My friend rushes back into the next room where he informs his audience:

Richard Feynman is a famous physicist.

We have both uttered the same sentence, but with different sent-designators. My friend was, presumably, thinking of his referent as being whomever I was referring to when I uttered (4.2), and that is clearly different from the way in which I was thinking of the referent. But surely we are making the same statement.[12] My friend is simply repeating the statement that I made. Had my friend instead said:

Richard Feynman is not a famous physicist.

he would have been directly contradicting me. But that would not be possible if a difference in the sent-designator automatically guaranteed a difference in what statement is made.

The preceding examples make it reasonably clear that when we make a statement by uttering a sentence containing a proper name, that statement does not contain our sent-designator as a constituent, and hence is distinct from our sent-proposition. From this it can be concluded that the statement is not a proposition. The argument for this conclusion is that the sent-proposition is what the speaker must believe in order to "believe what he says". If the statement were a proposition, then *it* would be the proposition the speaker would have to believe in order to believe what he says. Consequently, if the statement were a proposition it would have to be the sent-proposition. As it is not, the statement is not a proposition. It is, instead, a logical abstraction characterized in terms of its diagram as described in Chapter One.

Proper names are linguistic devices for generating statements which are not propositions. When a speaker makes a statement about an object x, he will be thinking about that object in terms of

---

[12] There is something a bit odd about my friend's statement if he knows nothing about Richard Feynman except that I referred to him. When we use a proper name, we ordinarily imply that we know who or what we are talking about. However, this is only a conversational implicature, as is attested to by its cancellability in 'Richard Feynman, whoever he is, is a famous physicist'.

some propositional designator. Few such designators are purely qualitative definite descriptions. If the sent-designator is not a purely qualitative definite description, then it will be impossible for the speaker to make a statement which is about x by virtue of incorporating that designator. Furthermore, even if the speaker were to think of the referent in terms of a purely qualitative conceptual definite description (which could be incorporated into a statement), that might not be a useful statement for him to make. For example, the speaker may have reason to believe that his audience could not pick out his referent from that description because the description involves knowledge of the referent not possessed by the audience. On the other hand, the speaker may have good reason to believe that if he uses a proper name, his audience will associate it with the intended referent. This is why proper names are useful linguistic devices. We frequently have reason to believe that if we use a proper name in a certain situation, our audience will take it to refer to just what we are referring to, although our way of thinking of the object may be very different from that of our audience. This is useful because our concern is frequently to convey something about the state of some particular object, and as long as our audience seizes upon the correct object and knows what state we are attributing to it, our purpose will have been achieved. It is not part of our purpose to convey to our audience some specific way of thinking of the object, and the necessity for doing so would frequently either make our task impossible or complicate it unnecessarily. Thus proper names are devices for conveying *part* of what we believe (omitting the sent-designator).

5. The Sense of a Proper Name

My proposal will be that the sense of a proper name, as used on a particular occasion, is a statemental designator of a certain kind. Our object is to describe that designator in terms of its diagram. Let us begin by asking when two speakers using a name but sending different propositional designators are using the name with the same sense. This is equivalent to asking when they would be making the same statement by uttering a sentence of the form $\ulcorner N$ is $F \urcorner$ (supposing them to be using the predicate in the same way). We have seen that the speakers need not be sending the same propositional designator in order to be making the same statement. We have also seen that more is required than that they merely be sending designators which designate the same object. There must be some condition intermediate between these two extremes which is necessary and sufficient for them to be making the same statement. To see what it is, let us turn to a particularly simple case. Consider once more the case of my friend who simply repeats my statement by uttering 'Richard Feynman is a famous physicist'. What makes it true that he is making the same statement as I made is that his sent-designator is something like 'the person to whom Pollock was referring in using the name "Richard Feynman"'. His sent-designator is parasitic on my use of the name in a way which makes our acts of referring "convergent" in a certain sense. Insofar as either of our references are successful, they will both be successful, and they cannot but have the same referent. This is a stronger condition than sameness of referent, but a weaker condition than sameness of sent-designator. The nature of the relation between our sent-designators is such as to ensure that insofar as we are talking about anything, we are talking about the same thing. Even if there were in fact nothing to which we were referring—i.e., if Richard Feynman did not exist—it would still follow from the nature of our sent-designators that *if there were* individuals to which we were referring, we would be referring to the same individual.

On the basis of such parasitic relations, and in other ways yet to be described, different acts of referring can be convergent.[13] My proposal is that the yet to be defined notion of convergence provides the desired criterion for using a proper name with the same sense. What makes one use of a proper name express the same statemental designator as another is that they are convergent. If this is to work, convergence must be defined in such a way that it is transitive, because the notion it is intended to explicate—that of two uses of proper names expressing the same statemental designator—is clearly transitive. If we think of this in terms of chains of parasitic references, this will have the result that not only are adjacent members of the chain convergent, but so are the members at the extremities. We can achieve this result in the following way. Let us say that two sent-designators, or the corresponding acts of referring, are *directly convergent* when they stand in a direct parasitic relation to one another, or stand in any of the direct relations yet to be

[13] Under 'act of referring' we must include acts of attempting to refer, because we cannot assume that the reference is successful. Two acts of attempting to refer can be convergent even when the speakers use names in such a way that they lack referents.

described which make them convergent. Then the relation of convergence between sent-designators or acts of referring is the ancestral of the relation of direct convergence:

(5.1) Two acts of referring A and A^* are convergent iff there is a finite sequence $A_0, \ldots, A_n$ of acts of referring such that $A = A_0$ and $A^* = A_n$ and for each $i < n$, A_i is directly convergent with A_{i+1}.

The fundamental problem that remains is to define direct convergence. We will find that there are two sources of direct convergence—agreement in sent-designators and parasitic uses of names. It seems clear that if two speakers use names with the same sent-designator, then their uses are convergent. In such a case, their sent-designators are trivially such as to ensure that if their acts of referring are successful, they have the same referent—hence the convergence. But this simplest kind of convergence is also the least interesting. What is much more interesting is that two acts of referring can be convergent even when the corresponding sent-designators are distinct. I have suggested that parasitic reference is what makes this possible.

The simplest case of parasitic reference is that wherein one speaker intends to refer to whomever another speaker referred to and sends a designator to that effect. However, there are more complicated kinds of parasitic reference as well. For example, in using the name 'Aristotle' I may be sending the designator 'the well-known philosopher frequently referred to by contemporary philosophers as "Aristotle"'; and in using the name 'John Dickson Carr', I may be sending the designator 'the man well-known to mystery fans under the name "John Dickson Carr"'. In these kinds of cases it seems that my reference is parasitic on whole classes of previous references. What, precisely, is the form of my sent-designator in a case like this? In such a case, there is a class B of previous acts of referring, and it appears initially that my sent-designator is something like ⌜the thing which is frequently (often, always, etc.) the referent of the members of the class B⌝. All such designators can be regarded as having the form ⌜the thing which is the common referent of all members of the class B⌝, because B could be, for example, ⌜the largest subset of the class B^* any two members of which have the same referent⌝, where B^* is some larger class of prior acts of referring. More generally, a parasitic sent-designator may place additional constraints on its designatum, requiring it not only to be the referent of certain other acts of referring but also to have some property *F*. Thus I might send the designator 'the person who wrote *The Metaphysics* and is the most common referent of uses of "Aristotle" by contemporary philosophers'. Or more realistically, I might think of Aristotle in terms of some *de re* designator *δ* and then send the designator 'the person who is *δ* and is the most common referent of the referring uses of "Aristotle" by contemporary philosophers'. So my proposal for the general form of the sent-designator in a case of explicitly parasitic reference is:

(5.2) the thing which [is *F* and] is the common referent of the members of the class *B* of prior acts of referring.

The bracketted clause may be absent. The special case of reference parasitic on a single act of referring arises when *B* is the unit set whose only member is that single reference.

If we assume that (5.2) is a correct characterization of the sent-designator in cases of parasitic reference, it is reasonable to define:

(5.3) A propositional designator *δ* is *directly parasitic on* an act of referring *A* iff *δ* is a definite description logically equivalent to one having the form ⌜the thing which [is *F* and] is the common referent of the members of the class *B* of prior acts of referring⌝ and *A* is a member of *B* [and the referent of *A* is *F*].

A referring use of a name may be parasitic on an earlier act of referring by involving a sent-designator which is directly parasitic on that earlier act of referring. However, it seems to be the case that our sent-designators are very frequently *de re* designators. When I have more than a passing acquaintance with a person or object, the most likely way for me to think about that person or object is in terms of a *de re* designator, in which case that is apt to be my sent-designator. It appears that the use of *de re* designators can also generate cases of parasitic reference. Our initial introduction to a person or object is frequently a verbal introduction by another person. Thus Smith may tell me about his fiancée Joan, giving me a nondefective reason for believing that she exists. On that basis I may come to think of her in a *de re* way—in terms of a *de re* designator *δ*. Part of the description *α* from which my use of *δ* may be derived is the parasitic one 'the person whom Smith was telling me about'. If so, the propositional designator *ɿα* is directly parasitic on the act of referring whereby Smith originally told me about Joan. If I were to employ $\imath\alpha$ as my sent-designator, my act of referring would be convergent with Smith's. It seems to be the case that:

(5.4) $\Box[(\exists x)(x = V(\delta)) \supset V(\delta) = V(\imath\alpha)]$.

Consequently, should I employ δ as my sent-designator in my subsequent use of the name 'Joan', the relation between my act of referring and Smith's earlier act of referring is precisely the same as if I had instead sent the directly parasitic designator $\imath\alpha$. In particular, if both of our acts of referring are successful, they must be acts of referring to the same individual. Thus it seems that we should regard this as another source of convergence, ruling that if a *de re* designator is derived from a directly parasitic definite description, then the *de re* designator is also parasitic. Furthermore, this process can be repeated as the *de re* designator can become part of another definite description (e.g., $\imath x[(x \approx \delta) \wedge (\beta:x)])$,[14] which we should accordingly regard as parasitic. To capture this case, let us define:

(5.5) $\imath\alpha$ *entails* δ iff, necessarily, if $\imath\alpha$ designates an object x, δ also designates x.

Then I suggest that we define the general notion of a propositional designator being parasitic on an act of referring as follows:

(5.6)   A propositional designator δ is *parasitic on* an act of referring A iff for some $n \geq 0$ there is a sequence of propositional designators $v_0, \dots, v_n$ such that $\delta = v_0$ and v_n is directly parasitic on A and for each $i > 0$, either v_i entails v_{i+1} or v_i is a *de re* designator derived from a description α and $v_{i+1} = \imath\alpha$.

It is now my contention that, for the most part, a referring use A of a proper name is directly convergent with any use A^* of a proper name on which the sent-designator for A is parasitic. This is because the sent-designator for A is such as to ensure, given only semantical facts about prior acts of referring (specifically, about their convergence), that insofar as A has a referent it has the same referent as A^*. The exception to this is when the sent-designator for A is parasitic on two acts of referring A^* and A^{**} which are not already convergent. For example, an instance of (5.2) occurs when a speaker

---

[14] In symbolizing propositions, we use '$\approx$' for identity and '$\wedge$' for conjunction.

sends the designator

the thing which both Robinson and Smith were calling 'George'.

If the uses of 'George' by Robinson and Smith were not convergent with one another (even though they might have been references to the same individual), then the speaker's use of 'George' cannot be convergent with the uses of both Robinson and Smith.

As far as I can see, parasitic reference provides the only way in which two uses of a name can be directly convergent without having the same sent-designator. I propose that we adopt the following recursive characterization of direct convergence:

(5.7)   Two acts of referring are directly convergent iff either they involve the same sent-designator or one, A, involves a sent-designator δ parasitic on the other, A^*, without δ also being parasitic on a third act of referring A^{**} which is not already convergent with A^*.

This analysis of direct convergence constitutes the final link in our analysis of convergence. According to this proposal, the basic source of convergence will be parasitic reference, as employment of the same sent-designator is extremely rare (particulary in light of the logically idiosyncratic character of most propositional designators). It seems likely that proper names are almost always used with parasitic sent-designators. We normally (although not invariably) use proper names under one of two circumstances: (1) to refer to someone we know reasonably well (at least in the nonintimate sense in which I know Aristotle and Jimmy Carter reasonably well) and think of in a *de re* way; (2) to refer to someone about whom there is an ongoing discussion, either written or oral. In case (1), the description from which our *de re* representation is derived normally contains such information as that the person or object in question was the referent of an earlier act of referring wherein we were first introduced to or told about that person or object. In case (2), we are normally thinking of our referent in part as the object to which the other discussants were referring, in which case our sent-designator is directly parasitic. This generates a picture of convergence reminiscent of that envisaged by the historical connection theory. Ordinarily, an object acquires a name by being dubbed with that name. For example, a person is named by his parents. The next person to use the name to refer to that individual ordinarily intends to refer to the same individual as the parents were referring to. And so on. With only rare exceptions, each user of the name will use it convergently with earlier uses. Thus we generate long trees of parasitic chains with the result that almost all uses of the name to refer to that individual will be convergent with one another.[15]

6. Hereditary Designators

It has been urged that proper names are used to express statemental designators, and these statemental designators are their senses. Our account of convergence is intended to tell us when two speakers are using names to express the same statemental designator. We wish now to turn this into a description of what designator they are using it to express. For reasons that will emerge shortly, I will call these *hereditary designators*. These statemental designators can be described in terms of their diagrams. That requires us to list the dynamic parameters of the designators and describe their possible sent- and received-propositional designators for different values of the dynamic parameters. Our account in terms of convergence gives us a partial description of the sent-designators, but it is not a complete description. To describe an hereditary designator in terms of its diagram, we require an account of the sent-designators under all *possible* circumstances of using names to express that hereditary designator. The difficulty with our account in terms of convergence is that it only tells us when the sent-designators associated with *actual* uses of proper names are sent-designators for the same hereditary designator. It leaves unanswered even such simple questions as whether, if we have three referring uses of proper names R_0, R_1, and R_2, where R_1 and R_2 are both parasitic on R_0 (and hence all three are used to express the same hereditary designator), R_0 and R_1 would still express the same hereditary designator as they do now had R_2 not occurred. In other words, our account in terms of convergence tells us that the members of an actual tree of convergent parasitic uses express the same hereditary designator, but it tells us nothing about what additions or deletions could be made to that

---

[15] This does not have to be the case. For example, a person could be independently dubbed with the same name twice. In such a case we would have two separate trees of parasitic reference chains terminating on two separate dubbings, and an act of referring in one of the trees would not be convergent with an act of referring in the other tree.

tree without changing the identity of the hereditary designator expressed.

Given an act of referring A, consider the set $|A|$ of all acts of referring convergent with A. This is a *maximal convergent set* of acts of referring. The maximal convergent sets are just the equivalence classes of acts of referring under the equivalence relation of convergence. The set $|A|$ has a tree structure as is presented in Figure 1.

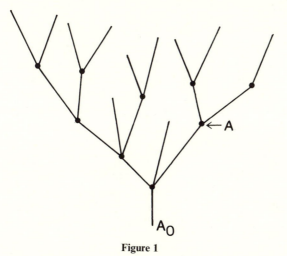

Figure 1

The terminus of the tree is a nonparasitic act of referring A_0 (or perhaps a set of nonparasitic acts all with the same sent-designator). Let us say that a member (i.e., node) of the tree is *hereditarily parasitic on* A_0 and on any node between itself and A_0. More precisely:

(6.1)   If R and R^* are acts of referring, R is *hereditarily parasitic on* R^* iff there is a finite sequence of acts of referring $R_0, \ldots, R_n$ such that $R = R_0$ and $R^* = R_n$ and for each $i < n$, R_i is parasitic on and convergent with R_{i+1}.

Thus each member of $|A|$ is hereditarily parasitic on A_0.

Let ∂ be the hereditary designator expressed by the members of $|A|$. We want to know what changes we can make to $|A|$ without changing the identity of ∂. The following principle seems obvious:

(6.2)   Only changes below A (i.e., to A_0 or between A and A_0) can affect what designator is expressed by A. Changes above A or to branches not containing A cannot affect A.

91

Now let us apply (6.2) to A_0. Principle (6.2) implies that A_0 would still express the same hereditary designator even if none of the other acts of referring in the tree had occurred. Let δ be the sent-designator for A_0. Let A^* be a second nonparasitic act of referring having the sent-designator δ, and let A^{**} be some nonparasitic act of referring having a different sent-designator. By (5.7), A^* expresses ∂ and A^{**} does not. By (6.2), if we replace A_0 in the tree by either A^* or A^{**}, we do not affect what statemental designators are expressed by A^* or A^{**}. If we replace A_0 by A^*, A^* still expresses ∂ and hence the other members of the tree, being hereditarily parasitic on A^*, also express ∂. On the other hand, if we replace A_0 by A^{**}, A^{**} still does not express ∂, and hence in that case the other members of the tree also fail to express ∂. What this shows is that it is the sent-designator for A_0 which determines the identity of ∂. An act of referring A expresses ∂ iff A is hereditarily parasitic on some nonparasitic act of referring having the sent-designator δ. Let us say that δ is the *basis designator* for ∂. We will write the hereditary designator with basis designator δ as '∂_δ'. There is a one-one correspondence between possible sent-designators δ and hereditary designators ∂_δ.

We can describe the hereditary designator ∂_δ in terms of its diagram. The dynamic parameters of ∂_δ must include those features determining which acts of referring are hereditarily parasitic on which. There are two such parameters. First, the time of the act is involved. A propositional designator γ might make reference to an act of referring R_0 in a timeless way, so that γ could be sent either before or after R_0. But only in the latter case would we get convergence, because an act of referring can only be parasitic on prior acts of referring. Thus the time of the sending is one dynamic parameter. In order to determine convergence, we must also know what prior acts of referring are convergent with one another, so we can take the second dynamic parameter to be the set of all maximal convergent sets of acts of referring occurring prior to t. Then we obtain the following characterization of the set of possible sent-designators for ∂_δ:

(6.3) γ is a possible sent-designator for ∂_δ relative to t and X for S iff $\Box(\forall R)$[if X is the set of all maximal convergent sets of acts of referring occurring prior to t & R is an act of referring occurring at t & γ is the sent-designator for R, then R is hereditarily parasitic on some nonparasitic act of referring whose sent-designator is δ] and if γ is logically idiosyncratic then it is logically idiosyncratic relative to S.

It remains to characterize the acceptable received-designators for ∂_δ. These are the designators in terms of which the members of the audience must think of the referent in order to understand what the speaker is saying. A natural suggestion is that there are no constraints on the acceptable received-designators other than that they designate the referent. However, this proposal encounters the same difficulty as the denotation theory. It is possible for a speaker to make a statement by uttering a sentence of the form $\ulcorner N$ is $F\urcorner$ despite the fact that the object to which he is attempting to refer does not exist. An historian might make a statement by saying 'Homer wrote *The Iliad*' even if Homer did not exist. If Homer did not exist, then there are no propositional designators designating Homer, and hence on this proposal there would be no acceptable received-designators for the use of 'Homer', in which case it would be impossible for anyone to understand what the historian is saying. But it *is* possible to understand what the historian is saying, so there must be acceptable received-designators. We cannot require that the acceptable received-designators designate the same thing as the sent-designator, but there must be some connection between the acceptable received-designators and the sent-designator. I suggest that the appropriate requirement is that they be convergent. This constitutes an "intensional" tie which survives reference failure. The proposal is thus:

(6.4) If ∂ is an hereditary designator, then for all values of the dynamic parameters for ∂ and for any person S, the set of acceptable received-designators for S for ∂ is the same as the set of possible sent-designators for S for ∂.

It might be wondered whether this is not too strong a requirement for understanding. Is it really required that in order for the members of the audience to come to accept what the speaker is saying, they think of the referent in a way convergent with the speaker's way of thinking of the referent? In order to answer this, we must distinguish between the proposition a member of the audience may come to occurrently believe or entertain as a result of the speaker's stating, and all the other propositions he may come to nonoccurrently believe. In order to accept what the speaker is saying, it is not required that the member of the audience come to occurrently believe an acceptable received-proposition. For example, if the speaker says 'Charles has just arrived', and Smith knows Charles well, the proposition Smith may occurrently believe as a result of hearing the speaker's utterance will most likely involve a *de re* designator.

However, if Smith believes on the basis of the stating that Charles, so conceived, has just arrived, then surely he will also have the non-occurrent belief that the person to whom the speaker is referring by using 'Charles' has just arrived. The latter involves a propositional designator parasitic upon the speaker's act of referring, and thereby ensures that Smith accepts what the speaker is saying. If the stating somehow results in Smith's believing that Charles, conceived of in a *de re* way, has just arrived, without his believing that the person the speaker is talking about has just arrived, then Smith has not merely accepted what the speaker is saying and his coming to believe the former proposition does not constitute successful communication. Similar remarks apply in general, indicating both that (6.4) constitutes only a relatively weak requirement, and that when the members of the audience do not think of the referent in terms of designators meeting this requirement, we would not agree that they have accepted or understood what the speaker is saying.

Principles (6.3) and (6.4) constitute a description of hereditary designators in terms of their diagrams. We will take them as definitive of the notion of an hereditary designator:

(6.5) ∂ is *the hereditary designator with basis* δ iff ∂ is a statemental designator and the dynamic parameters for ∂ are the time t of the sending and the set X of all maximal convergent sets of acts of referring occurring prior to the time of the sending, and a propositional designator γ is both a possible sent-designator and an acceptable received-designator for ∂ relative to t and X for a person S iff $\{\Box(\forall R)[$if X is the set of all maximal convergent sets of acts of referring occurring prior to t & R is an act of referring occurring at t & γ is the sent-designator for R, then R is hereditarily parasitic on some nonparasitic act of referring whose sent-designator is $\delta]$ & if γ is logically idiosyncratic then γ is logically idiosyncratic relative to $S\}$.

(6.6) ∂ is an *hereditary designator* iff $(\exists \delta)[\partial$ is the hereditary designator with basis $\delta]$.

We further define:

(6.7)   A proper name N is being used by a speaker S to *express* ∂ iff ∂ is an hereditary designator and S is using N to send some propositional designator δ which is a possible sent-designator for ∂ under the circumstances of the utterance.

Our claim regarding proper names is now:

(6.8)   The sense of a proper name, as used on a particular occasion, is the hereditary designator it is being used to express on that occasion.

What (6.8) requires is that when speakers use proper names in sentences by the utterance of which they make statements, the contribution of the name to the determination of what statement is made is a function solely of what hereditary designator is being expressed by the use of the name. In the case of a simple subject/predicate sentence of the form $\ulcorner N \text{ is } F \urcorner$, this seems clearly to be the case. If the speaker uses F to express a concept α and N to express an hereditary designator ∂, then the statement he makes is $(\alpha:\partial)$. In other words, the possible sent-propositions for his statement are those of the form $(\alpha:\delta)$ where δ is a possible sent-designator for ∂ and the acceptable received-propositions for his statement are those of the form $(\alpha:\nu)$ where ν is an acceptable received-designator for ∂. What (6.8) requires is that something similar be true in general. Whenever $\Theta(N)$ is a sentence containing a semantical occurrence of a proper name N, the statement made by uttering $\Theta(N)$ on a particular occasion must contain as one of its constituents the hereditary designator expressed by N, and the only role N plays in determining what statement is made by uttering $\Theta(N)$ is by supplying that designator to be a constituent of the statement. It seems reasonably clear that this is true, although a definitive argument would require a survey of a large number of English sentences, and that will not be undertaken here.

It is of interest to compare the present theory with the historical connection theory. There are obvious similarities, but there are also important differences. The historical connection theory is only a theory of reference, whereas the present theory is a theory of sense. Furthermore, the present theory implies that, as a theory of reference, the historical connection theory is either incorrect or trivial. It is incorrect if it is taken to imply that proper names can only be used to send parasitic designators. On the other hand, if the historical connection theory is merely observing that proper names *can* be used to send parasitic designators, then it is not affirming anything that anyone else would have denied. So as a theory of reference, the historical connection theory is not particularly successful. Nevertheless, there are important insights underlying the historical connection theory, and my contention is that they are basically semantical insights having to do with convergence. As such, they are incorporated into the present theory of the sense of a proper name.

7. Proper Names and Rigid Designation

Kripke [1972] introduced the notion of a rigid designator and claimed that proper names are rigid designators. That claim has been largely accepted, but my own feeling is that it is an oversimplification.

Kripke defined a *rigid designator* to be a singular term which denotes the same object in every possible world. I have some difficulty understanding this definition, although I think I understand what notion Kripke was attempting to capture by the definition. The difficulty with the definition is that it proceeds in terms of a world-relative notion of denotation. What does it mean for a term to denote an object *in a possible world*? This has a comfortable ring to it for the philosopher who is familiar with the formal semantics of modal logic, but I am not sure that it really makes sense. I understand what it is for a term to denote an object in this world. That is just for the speaker to use the term to refer to that object. But this is denotation *simpliciter*, or if you like, denotation relative to this world. How are we to understand denotation relative to other possible worlds? The most natural suggestion would be to define it counterfactually:

A term t denotes an object x in circumstances C iff a speaker in circumstances C would be using t to refer to x.

But this will not do. It is trivial that in other circumstances a speaker could use a proper name to refer to something other than what it is now being used to refer to. This should have nothing to do with the question whether proper names are rigid designators. But how else are we to define the notion of world-relative denotation? I don't see any obvious way to do it.

It seems to me to be more fruitful to pursue a different approach to the definition of 'rigid designator'. Rigid designators are to be constrasted with, for example, definite descriptions. Consider a counterfactual whose antecedent involves a definite description:

(7.1) $F(\imath x Dx) \rangle P$.

There is a familiar ambiguity here—a scope ambiguity. If we agree to use definite descriptions with narrow scope in identity sentences, then the distinction between wide- and narrow-scope in (7.1) is the distinction between

(7.2) $(\exists y)[y = \imath xDx \,\&\, (Fy \rangle P)]$

and

(7.3) $[(\exists y)(y = \imath xDx \,\&\, Fy) \rangle P]$.

In (7.2), where the description has wide scope, it is being used to select an object in this world and then we assert a counterfactual about what would be the case if *that object* were *F*. The point of rigid designators is supposed to be that they can *only* be used in this way. It seems reasonable to say that the definite description is being *used rigidly* in the wide scope case, but that definite descriptions are not rigid designators because they can also be used nonrigidly. We can capture this by defining:

(7.4)   A singular term *t* is being *used rigidly* in stating ϕ iff $(\exists \partial)(\exists A)\{t$ is being used to express ∂ and ϕ is logically equivalent either to $(\vee x)[(x \approx \partial)\,\&\,(A:x)]$ or to $(\wedge x)$ $[(x \approx \partial) \Rightarrow (A:x)]$ where *A* is an attribute not containing ∂ as a constituent}.

Definite descriptions can be used either rigidly or nonrigidly. On the other hand, it is initially plausible to suppose that proper names can only be used rigidly. For example, 'If Aristotle were alive today, contemporary philosophy would be quite different' is about Aristotle—that person who really is (or was) Aristotle. As such, the name is being used rigidly. Most sentences involving proper names seem to have this characteristic. This suggests that Kripke's notion of a rigid designator can be captured by saying that a rigid designator is a singular term that can only be used rigidly.

There are two kinds of considerations which might make a term a rigid designator. We might distinguish between them by calling them 'semantical' and 'grammatical' considerations. The semantical consideration is that the meaning of a term might be such that it can only be used to express statemental designators which are themselves rigid in the sense that they can only designate fixed objects. More precisely:

(7.5) ∂ is a *rigid statemental designator* iff ∂ is a statemental designator and there is an object *x* such that, if δ is any possible sent-designator for ∂, then, necessarily, if δ designates anything, it designates *x*.

97

Hereditary designators are not rigid in this sense, so this cannot be the explanation for the alleged rigidity of proper names.

Grammatical constraints on a term might also make it a rigid designator, and I believe that, to the extent that singular terms can only be used rigidly, it is grammatical constraints which make that the case. They do this by requiring that a sentence containing a proper name always be interpreted in such a way that the name has wide scope, i.e., such that (7.4) holds. My reason for calling this a 'grammatical constraint' is that it is not a constraint on the sense of the name, but rather on the sense of the sentence containing the name.

Nevertheless, it is an oversimplification to say that grammatical constraints make proper names rigid designators. It is true that proper names are *almost* always used rigidly, but there are exceptions. The simplest examples of this are counterfactuals with existential antecedents. Consider: 'If Jacob Horn had existed, he would have had a difficult life'. In order for 'Jacob Horn' to be used rigidly in this sentence, it would have to be equivalent to 'Jacob Horn is such that if he had existed, he would have had a difficult life', but these sentences are obviously not equivalent. The latter implies that Jacob Horn did exist. Instead, the analysis of 'If Jacob Horn had existed, he would have had a difficult life' is the straightforward one. Taking $\mathfrak{C}$ to be the concept expressed by 'exists' and ∂ to be the hereditary designator expressed by 'Jacob Horn', the statement made by uttering this sentence is $(\mathfrak{C}:\partial) \rangle (D:\partial)$.

Counterfactuals with negative existential antecedents are also counterexamples to the claim that proper names can only be used rigidly. A counterfactual of the form $\ulcorner N$ does not exist $\rangle P \urcorner$ is ambiguous. It can be understood in such a way that N is being used rigidly, but it can also be understood in such a way that N is not being used rigidly. For example, I may be unsure whether *The Horn Papers* are genuine and whether their putative author Jacob Horn existed. In such a state of mind, I might assert 'If Jacob Horn did not exist, then *The Horn Papers* would be a work of fiction'. I am clearly not asserting that Jacob Horn is such that if he did not exist then the *Horn Papers* would be a work of fiction. Instead, I am making a statement of the form $\neg (\mathfrak{C}:\partial) \rangle \phi$, and hence am not using 'Jacob Horn' rigidly.

It is also possible to use proper names nonrigidly in counterfactuals whose antecedents are neither existential nor negative existential. For example, a person who is uncertain whether Homer existed might nonetheless assert 'If Homer were the author of *The Iliad* and *The Odyssey*, he would be a literary genius'. I suggest that the proper analysis of such a statement is:

$$(\mathfrak{C} : \partial) \rangle (\vee x)[(x \approx \partial) \wedge ((W : x) \rangle (G : x))].$$

The upshot of this is that although grammatical considerations lead to proper names being used rigidly in most contexts, there are exceptions and hence it is not accurate to insist that they are rigid designators. We might say that they are "almost rigid designators".

8. The Meaning of a Proper Name

It has generally been overlooked that the traditional theories of proper names are not really theories of *meaning* at all, but theories of *sense*. The denotation and connotation theories each propose accounts of the sense of a proper name as used on a particular occasion. This is no less true of the theory of hereditary designators advanced above. All of these theories of sense are compatible with a variety of theories of meaning. At one extreme we might be tempted to identify the meaning of a proper name with its sense and say that insofar as a proper name is used with different senses on different occasions it is ambiguous. Searle [1969] adopts this course. At the opposite extreme it could be claimed that all proper names have the same meaning, that meaning being identified with the function which, when applied to any use of any proper name, determines the sense of the name on that occasion of its use.

What is the point of having a theory of meaning over and above a theory of sense? The theory of sense tells us what statements are made on various occasions. Why do we need anything more? What a theory of meaning does is systematize our theory of sense. Rather than dealing with each utterance separately, the theory of meaning provides general rules for determining senses on different occasions. These rules take the form of functions—intensions for different lexical items. However, two different accounts of meaning may agree in their assignment of senses. For example, in the case of proper names we want to identify the meaning of a name N with the function Δ_N which, to the pragmatic parameters of an utterance of N, assigns the hereditary designator expressed by N on that occasion. The theory of hereditary designators developed in Section Seven tells us what the values of Δ_N should be, but what is now at issue is what the arguments of Δ_N should be. On the one hand, we have Searle telling us that each proper name is ambiguous, so that for each name N there are a number of functions Δ_N which constitute its meanings on different occasions, each Δ_N being a constant function assigning the same sense to N on every occasion in which it is used with that meaning. On the other hand, we could group together all of the factors which go into determining the sense of any name on any occasion that it is used, including them all among the pragmatic parameters, and thus obtain a single function Δ_N which works equally for every name. What can it mean to say that one of these choices of Δ_N is objectively correct and the other objectively incorrect? Both choices would lead to exactly the same statements being made on all occasions of uttering sentences containing proper names.

Let us say that two theories of meaning are *isomorphic* if they agree in their assignment of senses. I suggest that what distinguishes between two isomorphic theories of meaning for a natural language, making one correct and the other incorrect, has to do with the way in which the users of the language process it. They design the sentences they utter by appealing to theories of lexical meaning. Although isomorphic theories of lexical meaning would lead them to utter the same sentence in order to make the same statement, they may only be thinking in terms of the rules of one of these theories of lexical meaning. The rules they are actually using are conventions of their linguistic community.

How does this help us in distinguishing between different theories of meaning for proper names? Our difficulty turns in part around the elusive distinction between indexical words and ambiguous words. Indexical words are words having fixed meanings which nevertheless enable speakers to use them with different senses on different occasions. An ambiguous word, on the other hand, can be used with different senses only because it has more than one meaning. I suggest that the difference between indexical words and ambiguous words is that in the case of an indexical word there is a single semantical rule governing all of its different uses with different senses,[16] whereas in the case of an ambiguous word, there is a different rule for each sense. When I say that *there are* such rules in our linguistic institution I mean that speakers actually

---

[16] More generally, there may be finitely many semantical rules governing a finite partition of its uses with different senses, because indexical words can be ambiguous too.

process language in terms of them—they are among the conventions underlying our conventional linguistic institution. To illustrate this, consider an ambiguous word, e.g., the predicate 'is a bank'. This predicate has at least two meanings, relating to financial institutions and river banks. What this comes to is that there are two distinct semantical rules governing its use. These rules have the form, roughly, of saying that if you use the predicate in a sentence and intend to be sending such-and-such a kind of proposition (i.e., one containing an appropriate sent-concept for a specific sense of the predicate, and being appropriate in other respects for the rest of the sentence), then you commit yourself to the appropriate statement. There are two different such rules, but speakers do not employ a single overriding rule which combines them both. With an indexical word like 'he', on the other hand, there is a single rule governing all uses of it and speakers actually think in terms of that single rule.

If we draw the distinction between indexical words and ambiguous words in the preceding manner, it immediately gives the result that no word can be infinitely ambiguous, having infinitely many different meanings. This is because speakers cannot assimilate infinitely many rules for use in processing language. They must get by with finitely many rules. Where there is infinite variation in sense, there must be a finite number of general rules governing the variation. The effect of this finite set of rules is to describe the variation in terms of finitely many intension functions, and hence it generates indexicality within at most finite ambiguity.

Now let us return to the meaning of a proper name. Consider the sentence:

(8.1)   Charles has red hair.

The meaning of (8.1) is not to be identified with its sense on any particular occasion, but with that function Δ_P which selects the sense of the sentence on different occasions of using it. So construed, does (8.1) have one meaning or many meanings? Searle believed that 'Charles' should have a different meaning for each of its bearers, but even that would not be sufficient to establish a one-one correspondence between meanings and senses. We have seen that it is not the referent but the hereditary designator which determines the sense of the name. Each proper name can be used to express infinitely many different hereditary designators designating *each* of its bearers. As we have seen, such an infinite multiplicity of

101

senses cannot be accomodated by mere ambiguity. Names must be indexical.

It seems to me that there is a single semantical rule governing a name like 'Charles', and accordingly (8.1) should be regarded as having just one meaning. The rules for making statements with (8.1) are the same on all occasions. The circumstances of utterance can change (in particular, the name can be used to send different designators), and so different statements can be made by uttering (8.1), but the rules governing what statement is made, and hence the meaning of the sentence, are in no way affected. It is fruitful to compare (8.1) with an explicitly indexical sentence:

(8.2) He has red hair.

We do not want to say that (8.2) is ambiguous just because the indexical word 'he' can be used to refer to different individuals. Rather, the rules for using such a sentence deal with how we can use 'he' to refer to different individuals and thereby make different statements. Proper names are also indexical words in that they can be used to refer to different individuals on different occasions. We have a single rule governing sentence (8.1) which, given as input how we are using the proper name, determines what statement is made in uttering (8.1), and the rule is the same regardless of how the proper name is used. It follows that the sentence, and correspondingly the proper name, has only one meaning.

Each proper name has a single meaning Δ_N which selects the hereditary designator expressed by using it on any given occasion. What designator is expressed is determined by the speaker's sent-designator taken together with the time of utterance and the set of all maximal convergent sets of acts of referring occurring prior to the time of utterance. These three parameters are pragmatic parameters of N, and hence arguments for Δ_N. There must also be a fourth pragmatic parameter. This arises from a constraint on the use of a proper name to the effect that it can only be used to refer to its bearers. Formally, this is a constraint on the domain of Δ_N. As a first approximation, we can say that Δ_N assigns an hereditary designator to a triple $\langle \delta, t, X \rangle$ only if there is a unique object x which is designated by δ and x is a bearer of the name N. We do not change the meaning of N by dubbing another object with that name. The original rules governing N (and making up its meaning) accomodate the introduction of new bearers of the name. This suggests that we should take the set of bearers of the name to be a fourth pragmatic parameter. Let us see if we can be a bit clearer about this fourth pragmatic parameter.

To begin with, the description just given of the constraint on the use of a proper name is not quite accurate, for two reasons. First, it is possible to use a proper name to refer to an object which does not bear that name. For example, if I inadvertently refer to Robert as 'Jim' and do so in such a way that my audience nevertheless knows who I am talking about, I may succeed in referring to Robert and predicating something of him despite using the wrong name. In Chapter One we distinguished between making a statement and making a statement *within* a particular language. If one misuses language, one may make a statement even though one does not conform to the rules of a particular conventional language and hence does not make a statement within any such language. In this way, by saying 'Jim did his homework', I may succeed in making a statement about Robert and thereby referring to him, but due to my misuse of the name I am not conforming to the rules of English and so am not referring to Robert within English. Thus the contraint on proper names must be that one cannot use a name to refer *within a language* to an object which is not a bearer of that name.

Our description of the constraint is inaccurate for a second reason. We can use a proper name to express an hereditary designator even when, so used, the name has no referent. For example, I can say

> I don't know whether Homer existed or not, but if he did and he wrote *The Iliad* and *The Odyssey* then he was a literary genius.

This is a proper use of the name 'Homer' even if Homer did not exist. If Homer did not exist, then different uses of 'Homer' can be "about the same individual" only by virtue of expressing the same hereditary designator. The uses of 'Homer' will form a vast tree of parasitic references, and all the references in that tree will express the same hereditary designator. The name must then be associated directly with that hereditary designator rather than with the object which is designated by it (as there is none). The mechanism by which the name becomes associated with the hereditary designator is the same as the mechanism by which, in a more normal case, it becomes associated with its bearers. In the normal case, we begin with a dubbing wherein something is "named" with the name. The dubbing simultaneously selects an object to be a bearer of the name and provides the starting point for a chain of parasitic references and hence the basis for an hereditary designator. If the dubbing is defective so that there is no object dubbed, it will still provide the basis for an hereditary designator to be expressed by the name, and then one is using the name properly if one uses it to express that hereditary designator.

It should not be supposed that an object must be dubbed with a name in order to become a bearer of that name. If a name is repeatedly used erroneously to refer to an object which is not one of its bearers or to express an attribute to which it was never dubbed, that eventually becomes a correct use of the name. Kripke [1972] gives the example of Madagascar. The Africans used 'Madagascar' to refer to a region of the mainland, but Marco Polo got it wrong and used it to refer to the island.[17] His use was picked up by other Europeans, and eventually 'Madagascar' became the name of the island.

We are now in a position to give an account of the meaning of a proper name. Let us say that a proper name N *supports* an hereditary designator ∂ iff either (1) there is a unique object x which is designated by ∂ and x is a bearer of N, or (2) N was dubbed to ∂ or has come to be associated with ∂ through being used repeatedly to express ∂. Then the meaning of the name N is given by:

(8.3) If N is a proper name, the pragmatic parameters of N are the sent-designator δ, the time t of utterance, the set X of all maximal convergent sets of acts of referring occurring prior to the time of utterance, and the set Y of all hereditary designators supported by N; and $\Delta_N(\delta,t,X,Y) = \partial$ iff $\partial \in Y$ and ∂ is the hereditary designator for which δ is a possible sent-designator at time t when X is the set of all maximal convergent sets of acts of referring occurring prior to t.

The time t and set X are both dynamic parameters for the hereditary designator expressed by N and pragmatic parameters for N. We have been forced to include them among the pragmatic parameters for N because, by contributing to the determination of the set of possible sent-designators for ∂, their specification is essential for obtaining ∂ from δ.

The general picture that emerges from all of this is that proper names constitute a special class of indexical singular terms used to

---

[17] As the island was not really named 'Madagascar', in referring to the island Marco Polo was not referring to it *within* Italian.

express hereditary designators. We will find in the next chapter that a number of other singular terms are also used to express hereditary designators, but what sets proper names apart and makes them useful is that they can only be used to refer to their bearers. Although a suitable dubbing can make anything a bearer of a name, at any given time a name will have a limited number of bearers, and this constraint facillitates communication by giving the audience a powerful clue to the identity of the speaker's referent.

IV
Singular Terms

1. Introduction

Thus far our discussion of reference has focused almost exclusively on proper names. However, we are interested in singular terms in general. Our theory of meaning for proper names can be readily generalized to other classes of singular terms. Some of the main classes of singular terms in English are: definite descriptions; the demonstratives 'this' and 'that'; the impure demonstratives $\ulcorner$this $D\urcorner$ and $\ulcorner$that $D\urcorner$ (e.g., 'this book'); the token reflexives 'I', 'here', and 'now'; and the pronouns 'he', 'she', and 'it'. There are special problems associated with the token reflexives, but the rest of these singular terms can be handled quite easily by an extension of the theory developed for proper names. We will begin with definite descriptions.

2. Definite Descriptions

A great deal has been written about definite descriptions, but it is rather remarkable that most of what has been written is inapplicable to most definite descriptions. A definite description is said to be *proper* just in case there is one and only one thing satisfying the description. Philosophers have almost invariably confined their attention to proper definite descriptions.[1] But actual speakers probably use improper definite descriptions more commonly than proper ones. There is a fairly common use of improper definite descriptions wherein they are not used to refer to specific objects. For example, I may say 'It is uncomfortable to sit in the corner' meaning 'It is

---

[1] An important exception is Donnellan [1966].

uncomfortable to sit in a corner'. In such a case, the definite description is not being used as a singular term. But even ignoring these nonreferring uses of definite descriptions, it seems that it is more common to use improper definite descriptions than it is to use proper ones. For example, I may say 'I am going to the bank'. The definite description 'the bank' is improper, because there are many banks. And yet I am referring to a specific bank. We find ourselves in the paradoxical situation that most theories of definite descriptions are inapplicable to most definite descriptions. This situation is unacceptable. An adequate theory of definite descriptions must handle all definite descriptions.

In a now classic article, Donnellan [1966] distinguished between two ways of using definite descriptions. If the description is proper, you can use it to refer to whoever or whatever uniquely satisfies the description. But you can also use it to refer to some particular individual which you (normally) believe to satisfy the description. Donnellan illustrates the distinction with the description 'Smith's murderer'. Judging from the manner of the murder, one might assert 'Smith's murderer is insane', intending to refer to whoever murdered Smith. Alternatively, as a result of witnessing Jones' behavior while he is being tried for the murder of Smith, and believing that Jones is guilty, one might assert 'Smith's murderer is insane', intending to refer to Jones. In the first case the definite description is being used *attributively*—to refer to whoever satisfies the description. In the second case the definite description is being used *referentially*—to refer to some specific individual whom the speaker takes to satisfy the description.

There are really two distinctions lurking here. On the one hand, there is a distinction between using a description to refer *within* English and using it to refer while violating the rules of English. As we have seen, one can successfully refer without conforming to the rules of the language as long as one succeeds in getting one's meaning across to one's audience. Furthermore, one can weakly statementally refer (see Principle (6.3) of Chapter One) merely by making it clear to one's audience what one's intended referent is. On the other hand, there is a distinction between two ways of using a description within English. One can use a description which is satisfied by a unique object and let that fact determine one's referent, or one can use a description which may or may not be satisfied by a unique object and use it to refer to a specific object about which one is thinking in some other way but which one takes to satisfy the

107

description. The latter of these two distinctions is the more interesting one semantically, so that is what I am calling the referential/attributive distinction, but it is arguable that Donnellan may have had the other distinction in mind.[2]

There is a connection between the attributive/referential distinction and the proper/improper distinction. Apparently only proper definite descriptions can be successfully used attributively.[3] If a speaker successfully refers using an improper definite description, he must be using it referentially. However, the two distinctions do not coincide because it appears that a proper definite description can be used either attributively or referentially.

When a speaker uses a definite description attributively, he literally says what he is talking about. The predicate itself determines what statemental designator is expressed by the definite description.. Accordingly, it seems that the attributive/referential distinction can be drawn precisely as follows:

(2.1)   A speaker is using $\ulcorner$the $F\urcorner$ *attributively* iff $(\exists A)[A$ is the attribute expressed by the predicate F under the circumstances of utterance and the speaker is using $\ulcorner$the $F\urcorner$ to express the statemental designator $\imath A]$.

(2.2)   A speaker is using $\ulcorner$the $F\urcorner$ *referentially* iff he is using it but not attributively.

Thus if a speaker makes a statement by uttering the sentence $\ulcorner$The F is $G\urcorner$ under circumstances in which F expresses an attribute A and G expresses an attribute B, and the speaker is using the definite description attributively, the statement he makes is $(B:\imath A)$.

Although (2.1) does correctly capture the notion of an attributive use of a definite description, it is not entirely adequate for the purposes of this section. The difficulty is that it proceeds in terms of what designator the speaker is using the description to express. That is a notion we have not yet defined, and when we do define it

[2] Kripke [1977] is clearly talking about the first distinction. On the other hand, Donnellan [1978] appears to be interpreting the distinction as I am.

[3] This might be resisted on the grounds that in Donnellan's preceding example I could refer to Smith's murderer by saying 'The murderer, whoever he is, is insane'. But contrary to popular opinion, the referential/attributive distinction cannot be drawn in terms of the 'whoever he is' locution. The latter locution is intimately connected with 'knows who', which is indexical in a way which precludes its being used to draw any sharp semantic distinction. The indexicality of 'knows who' is discussed in Chapter Nine.

later in the section, the definition will be in terms of whether the speaker is using the description attributively or referentially. Thus if we are to avoid circularity, we must give an alternative definition of what it is to use a definite description attributively. It seems that that can be done in terms of what propositional designator is being sent by using the definite description rather than in terms of what statemental designator is being expressed:

(2.3)   A speaker is using $\ulcorner$the $F\urcorner$ *attributively* iff $(\exists A)(\exists \alpha)[A$ is the attribute expressed by the predicate F under the circumstances of utterance & α is a possible sent-concept for A under those circumstances & the speaker is using $\ulcorner$the $F\urcorner$ to send the propositional designator $\imath\alpha].$[4]

When a speaker uses a definite description referentially, the description cannot be intended to pick out its referent simply by virtue of its own descriptive content. The descriptive part of the definite description can do nothing but place a constraint on possible referents. For example, I can use the definite description 'the bank' to refer to any bank at all. What determines to which bank I am referring in a particular case? The situation here is analogous to the use of a proper name. The name you use places a constraint on your referent—you must be referring to a bearer of the name. But which bearer of the name you are referring to is determined by how you are thinking of your referent, i.e., by your sent-designator. Analogously, when you make a statement by uttering a sentence containing a semantical occurrence of a definite description, you are sending a certain proposition and thereby using the definite description to send a certain propositional designator. What designator you are sending determines your referent. The propositional designator a speaker sends by using a definite description

---

[4] I am assuming that whenever α is a concept, there is such a propositional designator as $\imath\alpha$. One might balk at this, claiming that the propositions which purportedly contain definite descriptions do not—they are instead complex general propositions. Thus it might be claimed that the proposition we might write as $\ulcorner(\beta:\imath\alpha)\urcorner$ is really the proposition

$$(\lor x)\,[(\beta:x) \land (\land y)((\alpha:y) \Leftrightarrow (x \approx y))].$$

I am prepared to admit that these propositions are logically equivalent, but they are distinct fine-grained objects of belief. Believing $(\beta:\imath\alpha)$ is phenomenologically distinguishable from believing the above general proposition. If one were unconvinced of the Russellian analysis, one could easily believe the former without believing the latter.

referentially cannot be determined simply by the predicate in the description. What is the connection between the predicate and the sent-designator? It seems plausible to suppose that the meaning of the predicate places a constraint on the sent-designator. In using $\ulcorner$the $F\urcorner$ the speaker uses F to express some attribute A and send a concept α, and uses $\ulcorner$the $F\urcorner$ to express a statemental designator ∂ and send a propositional designator δ. The suggestion is then that α must be incorporated into δ in such a way that δ can only designate an object which exemplifies α.

However, not just any way of incorporating α into δ will suffice. The sent-concept α must be a constituent of the sent-designator δ in a particular way. We can get a grasp on this by reflecting upon what might be called the "ordinary" case of referring wherein you intend to refer to a particular object and select your singular term with that end in mind. In intending to refer to a particular object, you must be thinking of that object in a certain way—in terms of some propositional designator γ. Then what you mean by $\ulcorner$the $F\urcorner$ is, very roughly, $\ulcorner$the F I am thinking about in this way$\urcorner$. More accurately, your sent-designator has the form:

$$(2.4) \quad \imath x[\alpha:x) \wedge (x \approx \gamma)].$$

If, as I propose, the sent-designator for a definite description must always have the form of (2.4), it follows that $\ulcorner$the $F\urcorner$ can only be used to refer to an object which satisfies the predicate F. Donnellan [1966] has proposed counterexamples to this claim. For example, I might see someone drinking water from a martini glass and, believing him to be drinking a martini, refer to him by using the definite description 'the man with the martini'. It seems that I could make a statement about this many by saying 'The man with the martini is drinking it like water' despite the fact that he does not have a martini. If so, the definite description is not being used to send a designator of the form of (2.4).

Donnellan's view seems to be that $\ulcorner$the $F\urcorner$ can be used to refer to an object regardless of whether it is an F, and that the statement one makes about the object does not entail that it is an F. On this view, the definite description appears to function just like the pure demonstrative 'that'. This implies that the meaning of F makes no contribution to the meaning of $\ulcorner$the $F\urcorner$. That is at least counter-intuitive. I suggest instead that the speaker is making a statement which requires his referent to be an F, and that statement is false. But he is performing other speech acts as well. We have already remarked the general fact that a linguistic act can succeed despite the violation of linguistic rules provided it is obvious what linguistic act the speaker is attempting to perform. If he thus succeeds in performing the linguistic act, he does not perform it *within English* because he is not conforming to the rules of English, but he does perform it nevertheless. Thus I propose that, although he is making a false statement (which is about no one), the speaker in Donnellan's example is also performing a correct predication of his intended referent. If, despite his infelicitous choice of a definite description, it is obvious to his audience to whom he intends to refer, it follows from our analysis of predication (Principle (6.3) of Chapter One) that the speaker succeeds in predicating 'is drinking a martini like water' of his intended referent even though he does not succeed in making a statement wherein he ascribes that to his intended referent.

Whether Donnellan's speaker has referred to his intended referent is another matter. It is not obviously wrong simply to deny that reference has occurred, maintaining instead that as the *intended* referent was obvious, the speaker was able to predicate without referring. Alternatively, we might maintain that just as the speaker was able to predicate something of his intended referent (although not within English), he was similarly able to refer to his intended referent (but not within English). Which we say is just a convention regarding how we are going to use the term 'refer'. In Chapter One, I chose to identify referring with strong statemental referring, from which it follows that no referring takes place in Donnellan's example. But we could instead have identified referring with weak statemental referring, in which case Donnellan's speaker would have referred. It is important to realize, however, that in either case no referring occurs *within English*, and thus the example shows nothing about the meaning of definite descriptions.

The upshot of all this is that it is reasonable to insist that the sent-designator for a definite description used referentially must have the form of (2.4). Given that the speaker is sending some such propositional designator, what statemental designator is he using the definite description to express? Just as in the case of proper names, two speakers can use definite descriptions with different sent-designators and still be making the same statement (and hence using the descriptions with the same sense). This is forced upon us by all of the considerations involving logically idiosyncratic designators and privileged knowledge of the referent which led us to the analogous conclusion regarding proper names. I suggest that, as in the case of proper names, it is convergence which ties two sent-designators together as being possible sent-designators for the same statemental designator. For example, if Jones says 'The bank is on fire'. Smith can make the same statement by repeating the words 'The bank is on fire', using 'the bank' to send the propositional designator 'the bank to which Jones was referring'. In general, if two speakers use ⌜the F⌝ to send the designators

$$(2.5) \quad \imath x[(\alpha : x) \wedge (x \approx \gamma)]$$

and

$$(2.6) \quad \imath x[(\beta : x) \wedge (x \approx \xi)]$$

respectively, where they are using F to send the concepts α and β respectively (these being possible sent-concepts for the same attribute A), then they are using ⌜the F⌝ with the same sense iff the designators γ and ξ are such that if they were the sent-designators for two acts of referring under these circumstances, those acts of referring would be convergent. This implies that (2.5) and (2.6) are possible sent-designators for the same statemental designator iff α and β are possible sent-concepts for the same attribute A and γ and ξ are possible sent-designators for some hereditary designator ∂. This is equivalent to requiring that (2.5) and (2.6) be possible sent-designators for the composite statemental designator

$$(2.7) \quad \imath x[(A : x) \wedge (x \approx \partial)].$$

Consequently, we can regard this statemental designator as being the sense of the definite description. Let us define:

(2.8) ∂ is an *A-hereditary designator* iff A is an attribute and there is an hereditary designator Υ such that $\partial = \imath x[(A : x) \wedge (x \approx \Upsilon)]$.

Our claim is then that definite descriptions used referentially have A-hereditary designators as their senses.

We can now describe the meaning of ⌜the F⌝ (used referentially) as follows:

(2.9)   If F is a predicate, the pragmatic parameters of ⌜the F⌝ are the sent-designator, the time of utterance, the set of all maximal convergent sets of acts of referring occurring prior to the time of utterance, and the pragmatic parameters $v_1, \ldots, v_k$ of F; and $\Delta_{⌜\text{the } F⌝}(\delta, t, X, v_1, \ldots, v_k) = \partial$ iff $(\exists A)[\Delta_F(v_1, \ldots, v_k) = A \ \& \ \partial$ is the A-hereditary designator for which δ is a possible sent-designator at time t when X is the set of all maximal convergent sets of acts of referring occurring prior to t].

According to this account, the attributive/referential distinction in the use of definite descriptions does not pertain to the mode of reference, but to the sense of the description. When a definite description is used attributively the sense of the description is supplied by the sense of the predicate. In a straightforward sense, the speaker *says* how he is thinking of the referent. On the other hand, when a definite description is used attributively, the sense of the predicate places constraints on the sense of the description, but these constraints are not sufficient to determine the sense of the description. The sense of the description is instead an *A*-hereditary designator. This has the result that definite descriptions are genuinely ambiguous. A speaker could be thinking of his referent in the same way but using the definite description either attributively or referentially, and the difference would be reflected in a difference in the statement made.

3. Other Hereditary Singular Terms

The sense of a proper name is an hereditary designator, and the sense of a definite description used referentially is an *A*-hereditary designator. Proper names and definite descriptions comprise two classes of what may be called *hereditary singular terms*. These are singular terms whose senses are either hereditary designators or statemental designators constructed out of hereditary designators in simple ways. Having dealt with proper names and definite descriptions, it is now possible to deal with other hereditary singular terms quite cursorily. All that is required is an extension of the preceding theory.

The primary difference between different kinds of hereditary singular terms lies in differing semantical constraints. In the case of a definite description, there is a semantical constraint to the effect that the referent must satisfy the description, and this constraint arises from being built into the statemental designator expressed by the definite description. In the case of a proper name, there is a constraint to the effect that the referent must be a bearer of the name. The latter is a constraint on *whether* a statement is made rather than a constraint on *what* statement is made. It is a *presuppositional constraint*.

Kaplan [1977] has popularized the denotation theory as applied to the *pure demonstratives* 'this' and 'that', but the denotation theory of demonstratives is subject to the same difficulties as the denotation theory of proper names. First, there can be nonreferring uses of demonstratives. MacBeth would certainly have been making a statement and sending a proposition had he said 'This is a dagger I see before me', but according to the denotation theory there could be no statement or sent-proposition in that case. Second, suppose I see a boulder before me and without realizing it see the same boulder reflected in a mirror. If I say 'This is bigger than that', using 'this' to refer to the boulder before me and 'that' to refer to the boulder seen in the mirror, but my audience interprets my references in the opposite way (taking me to be saying what I would have said as 'That is bigger than this'), then my audience has misunderstood me. But according to the denotation theory, the same statement would be made by saying either 'This is bigger than that' or 'That is bigger than this', and so my audience would not have misunderstood me after all.

It must be concluded that the denotation theory of demonstratives is incorrect. I propose instead that 'this' and 'that' function much like proper names. They are used to express hereditary designators. What distinguishes them semantically from proper names is that they lack the presuppositional constraint. They can be used to refer to anything, and the hereditary designator expressed is a function merely of the sent-designator, just as in the case of proper names. As the demonstratives are used to express the same hereditary designators as proper names, the statement made by uttering a sentence containing a demonstrative is the same as the statement one could have made by uttering a sentence containing a proper name of the referent.

It has frequently been maintained that, as the name suggests, there is an intimate connection between demonstratives and "demonstrations".[5] According to this view, when one uses a demonstrative to refer to an object, he is supposed to accompany his verbal act with some sort of pointing or other overt act which demonstrates his referent. If this is correct, it is a presuppositional constraint on the use of demonstratives. It does not affect what statement is made, but it does affect whether a statement is made. However, I am inclined to doubt that the whole doctrine of demon-

[5] See for example Kaplan [1977].

114

strations makes much sense. Admittedly, if we believe that our audience may not know to what we are referring when we use a demonstrative, we may point to it and help them along, but we may do that with uses of proper names and definite descriptions too. Pointing may be more common in connection with uses of demonstratives than other singular terms, but that is only because the semantical constraints are fewer and hence the audience may need more external clues in order to ascertain the referent. Contrary to what has sometimes been claimed, the referent of a use of a demonstrative is often quite clear without any attendant demonstration, and the rules of language do not require such a demonstration. For example, if while walking down Main Street we encounter an elephant sitting atop the mayor's squashed limousine, and I am moved to remark, 'That is a big elephant', there is certainly no need for me to point to my referent in order for my act of referring to be successful.

The demonstratives 'this' and 'that' can often be used with the same senses, i.e., to express the same hereditary designators, but they do differ in meaning. The difference consists of a presuppositional constraint on their *D*-intensions. When only one demonstrative is being used, 'this' and 'that' can be used interchangeably. But when both 'this' and 'that' are being employed in the same context, 'this' is supposed to be used to refer to the "more proximate" object (if there is one). The kind of proximity involved may concern physical location, temporal location, time at which the objects were last mentioned or will next be mentioned, proximity in thought (i.e., 'this' refers to the object you are thinking about now, or perhaps you have a mental image involving perspective and 'this' refers to the object closer in your mental image), etc. This "proximity requirement" is only a presuppositional constraint. It does not affect what statement is being made. A speaker using 'this' and 'that' implies that the referent of 'this' is more proximate than the referent of 'that', but this is only a conversational implicature. Just as one can violate the presuppositional constraint on proper names and use a name to refer to an object which does not bear it (provided the speaker's intent is obvious to his audience), so a speaker can violate the presuppositional constraint on 'this' and 'that' and use them to refer to objects not satisfying the constraint (provided, again, his intent is obvious to his audience), and if he does so the statement he makes is not automatically false by virtue of his misuse of 'this' and 'that'. This indicates that the statement does not logically entail that the referent of 'this' is more proximate than the referent of 'that', and hence the constraint is only presuppositional and does not result from the content of the statement made.

The *impure demonstratives* ⌜this F⌝ and ⌜that F⌝ are a cross between the pure demonstratives and definite descriptions used referentially. The sense of either is the same as the sense of the definite description ⌜the F⌝ used referentially—an A-hereditary designator. In referring to something as ⌜this F⌝ or ⌜that F⌝, one's statement entails that the referent is an F. But the impure demonstratives differ from definite descriptions in that impure demonstratives are subject to the same presuppositional constraint regarding relative proximity as are the pure demonstratives.

The personal pronouns 'he' and 'she' are subject to obvious semantical constraints regarding the sex of the referent.

The pronoun 'it' seems to have a semantical constraint, roughly, to the effect that the referent have a certain degree of nonsentience. The pronoun 'it' can be used without restriction to refer to inanimate objects, but cannot ordinarily be used to refer to human beings, and seems inappropriate for highly intelligent animals. The word can, however, be used to refer to idiots and sufficiently young children.

The general picture which emerges is that most singular terms are hereditary singular terms, and that they differ only with respect to their semantical constraints. Some have presuppositional constraints which do not affect what statement is made but do affect whether a statement is made. Others have semantical constraints which do affect what statement is made. The latter accomplish this by making the sense of the singular term an A-hereditary designator rather than a hereditary designator. The purpose of the varying constraints is to provide clues to the audience regarding the identity of the referent. The speaker's choice of a singular term will give the audience important information regarding the intended referent and this facilitates communication.

4. Token Reflexives

What Reichenbach [1947] called 'the token reflexive pronouns' are the words 'I', 'here', and 'now'. For reasons that will shortly become apparent, I will call them merely *token reflexives*. It is generally felt that the token reflexives are importantly different from the other singular terms we have considered, and importantly like one another. Accounts will now be proposed of the meanings of the token reflexives. There are a number of other words which are intimately related to the token reflexives, e.g., 'we', 'yesterday', and 'tomorrow', but they will not be discussed explicitly. Given the accounts of the token reflexives, it will be fairly obvious how to deal with related words.

It is generally felt that 'I', 'here', and 'now' are importantly alike. I will conclude that there are strong similarities between 'I' and 'now', but that 'here' has little in common with the others.

4.1 'I'

In Chapter One, it was alleged on epistemological grounds that we have a privileged way of thinking of ourselves, and that the propositions entertained while thinking of ourselves in that way involve a special propositional designator—our *personal* designator. There would seem to be an intimate connection between 'I' and the speaker's personal designator. In fact, it would seem natural to propose that if ι_S is S's personal designator and F is a predicate expressing a concept α, then the statement S makes by saying $\ulcorner$I am $F\urcorner$ is $(\alpha:\iota_S)$. This cannot be right, however, because the latter proposition is logically idiosyncratic and hence not a statement. It was urged in Chapter One that rather than being the statement which S makes, $(\alpha:\iota_S)$ is his sent-proposition. In using 'I' to refer to himself, S expresses a statemental designator $I(S)$ and his sent-designator is ι_S. Let us call $I(S)$ S's *personal statemental designator*.

The sense of 'I' as used by a speaker S is $I(S)$. We will describe this statemental designator in terms of its diagram. One possible sent-designator for $I(S)$ is ι_S. In Chapter One it was alleged that ι_S is the only possible sent-designator for $I(S)$. However, Kaplan [1977] asserts that 'I' is *purely referential* in the sense that if S makes a statement by saying $\ulcorner$I am $F\urcorner$, another speaker can make the same statement by saying $\ulcorner$You are $F\urcorner$ (using 'you' to refer to S). This suggests that perhaps *any* designator designating S is a possible sent-designator for $I(S)$.

There are actually two separable claims here. First, there is the claim that in the case of S himself, any designator which designates S is a possible sent-designator for $I(S)$ for S. Second, there is the claim that for another person S^*, any designator which designates S is a possible sent-designator for $I(S)$ for S^*. Let us address the first claim first. Suppose δ designates S, but S is unaware of this fact. For example, S might see his own reflection in a hall of mirrors, but not realize that it is his own reflection. S could not reasonably say 'I look tired' using 'I' with the intention to refer to the person he sees in the mirror (and believes to be someone other than himself). One can only use 'I' to knowingly refer to oneself. But S could properly say 'You look tired', using 'you' with the intention to refer to the person he sees in the mirror. Would he still be expressing $\mathbf{I}(S)$ and hence making the same statement he would have made had he, knowingly seeing his own reflection, said 'I look tired'? My intuition is that he would not be. Even if he were unwittingly talking about himself, he would be making a different statement by saying 'I look tired'. It seems to me that in saying 'You look tired', S would still be making the same statement even if he were seeing someone else in the mirror (just as long as his way of thinking of whomever he is seeing remains unchanged). But in that case it is perfectly clear that he is making a different statement than in saying 'I look tired', because it might even have a different truth value. If this is right, it must be concluded that ι_S is the only possible sent-designator for $\mathbf{I}(S)$ for S.

What about another person S^*? If S^* says 'You look tired' using 'you' to refer to S, can he express $\mathbf{I}(S)$ and make the same statement as S could make by saying 'I look tired'? If S^* uses 'you' to send a propositional designator which is not logically idiosyncratic, then S could use 'you' to send the same propositional designator and thereby make the same statement as S^*. But we have just seen that the statement S makes by saying 'You look tired' is different from the statement he would make by saying 'I look tired', so it follows that the statement S^* makes by saying 'You look tired' is different from the statement S would make by saying 'I look tired'. S^* cannot make the same statement as S. Apparently, if $S^* \neq S$, there are no possible sent-designators for $\mathbf{I}(S)$ for S^*.

Turning to the acceptable received-designators, we must again distinguish between the acceptable received-designators for $\mathbf{I}(S)$ for S and those for another person S^*. If $S^* \neq S$, it appears that any propositional designator δ which designates S is an acceptable received designator for $\mathbf{I}(S)$ for S^*.[6] The case in which $S^* = S$ is different. In unusual cases it is possible for a person to be a member of his own audience. For example, one might write

---

[6] The analogous claim was rejected for proper names on the grounds that speakers can make statements and be understood while using the proper names in such a way that they fail to refer. But reference failure is impossible for a use of 'I'.

oneself notes in order to jog a fallible memory. In this case, it appears that one is making a statement to oneself. When one reads such a note, it does not appear that one has understood what the speaker (i.e., oneself) has said unless one knows that the speaker is oneself and so receives one's first-person designator in connection with any uses of 'I' in the note. Thus it appears that ι_S is the only acceptable received-designator for $\mathbf{I}(S)$ for S himself.

We can now describe the diagram of $\mathbf{I}(S)$ as follows:

(4.1)   The sole dynamic parameter of $\mathbf{I}(S)$ is the set X of all propositional designators designating S; and if ζ is the diagram of $\mathbf{I}(S)$ and $\zeta(X) = \langle \Sigma, \Omega \rangle$, then for each S^*:

$$\Sigma(S^*) = \begin{cases} \{\iota_S\} \text{ if } S^* = S; \\ \varnothing \text{ otherwise;} \end{cases}$$

$$\Omega(S^*) = \begin{cases} \{\iota_S\} \text{ if } S^* = S; \\ \{\delta \mid \delta \in X \ \& \text{ if } \delta \text{ is logically idiosyncratic, then} \\ \quad \text{it is logically idiosyncratic relative to } S^*\} \\ \text{otherwise.} \end{cases}$$

It follows from (4.1) that the statements we make using 'I' are themselves idiosyncratic in the sense that no one else can make them. However, they are not idiosyncratic in the strong sense exemplified by logically idiosyncratic propositions. These statements are still public objects of use in communication.

We have described the statemental designators $\mathbf{I}(S)$ which are expressed by 'I'. The statemental designator $\mathbf{I}(S)$ is the sense of 'I' as it is used on a particular occasion by a speaker S. The identity of the speaker is the only pragmatic parameter. So identifying the meaning of 'I' with its D-intension, the meaning is that function $\Delta_{\mathbf{T}}$ which, to a speaker S, assigns the designator $\mathbf{I}(S)$.[7]

The preceding account is based more upon intuition than argument. My only reason for rejecting the direct reference account of 'I' is that it conflicts with certain intuitions. The direct reference account is perfectly coherent, and there is no reason why 'I' couldn't function in that way, regardless of whether it really does. Which way it actually functions is an empirical question about English,

---

[7] It may be protested that this account of the meaning of 'I' is inadequate because it does not enable us to deal with Castañeda's "quasi-indicator" uses of 'I', as in 'I believe that Jones believes that I am wealthy'. I deny this charge, but its discussion will be postponed until Chapter Nine.

and although I have given reasons for preferring my account to the direct reference account, I must acknowledge that they are not conclusive. I know of no very strong arguments in favor of either account, so in the end it is perhaps best just to lay out both accounts and let the reader decide which is more plausible.

4.2 'Now' and Temporal Reference

The second token reflexive is 'now'. It has frequently been suggested that 'now' is a pronoun synonymous with 'the present time'. In point of fact, 'now' generally functions as an adverb rather than as a pronoun. In its adverbial use it can be roughly paraphrased as 'at the present time'. For example, we can say 'He is coming now' meaning 'He is coming at the present time'. We cannot treat 'now' in this context as a pronoun paraphrased as 'the present time' and obtain the sentence 'He is coming the present time'. The latter is ungrammatical.

Unfortunately for linguistic neatness, the behavior of 'now' is heterogeneous. It does not always function adverbially. It might reasonably be considered a pronoun in any of the following sentences:

I did not believe it until now.
I will behave from now on.
Now is the time for all good men to come to the aid of their country.

In any of these sentences we can paraphrase 'now' as meaning approximately 'the present time'.[8]

The adverbial use of 'now' is much more common than the pronominal use. Perhaps for this reason, recent investigations of temporal logic have tended to concentrate on the sentence operator 'it is now the case that'.[9] However, there is reason to believe that despite its comparative rarity, the pronominal use is logically more fundamental. If we allow ourselves some reasonably contorted constructions, it is plausible to suppose that the adverbial use of 'now' can always be replaced by pronominal uses. For example, 'He is

---

[8] I am indebted to Rolf Eberle for these examples and for dissuading me of my earlier opinion that 'now' functions only adverbially.

[9] See for example Prior [1968], Kamp [1971], and Kaplan [1977].

coming now' could be paraphrased as:

(4.7) There is a time which is now and which is such that he is coming at that time.

Or, importing a bit of logical notation:

$(\exists t)[t = \text{now} \,\&\, \text{he is coming at } t]$.

Conversely, it does not seem possible to paraphrase pronominal uses of 'now' in terms of the adverbial use. For example, what would you do with 'I did not believe it until now'?

My concern in this section will be with the pronominal use of 'now', and derivatively with the adverbial use. It will be assumed that the adverbial use can be defined in terms of the pronominal use.

The word 'now' is used (pronominally) to refer to a time (the present time). It is so used in the context of making statements, and presumably the statement made by uttering a sentence containing 'now' is a function in part of the statemental designator expressed by 'now'. This designator is the sense of 'now' on that occasion of its use. Thus, in order to explain the meaning of 'now', we must ascertain what statemental designator it expresses on different occasions. This statemental designator will be characterized in terms of its diagram, and the latter will be constructed out of the propositional designators in terms of which we think of times. These propositional designators are constituents of propositions which are *temporal* in the sense of being about what is the case at specific times. Most of the propositions which we believe are temporal in this sense. For example, when I believe that there is a book on the table, the proposition I believe is about that particular time and if, at a later time, I again believe that there is a book on the table, I am believing a different proposition which is about that later time.

In order to describe the statemental designator expressed by 'now', we must first understand how temporal propositions can be about specific times. What may seem initially puzzling about temporal propositions is that there need be no introspectible difference between believing the same thing of two different times. For example, suppose I believed yesterday that there was a book on the table, and I believe today that there is a book on the table. My belief states may be phenomenologically indistinguishable, but we want to insist that I believe two different propositions (at least, construing propositions as maximally fine-grained objects of belief). Sameness

or difference of belief here is determined not just by the phenomenological character of your belief state, but also by the time when you
are in that state. Equivalently, what temporal proposition you
believe is determined *jointly* by your psychological state and the
time when you are believing it.

If we are to differentiate between propositions in terms of structural descriptions of them, we must endow temporal propositions
with a constituent which reflects the time. For example, we might
describe the proposition you believe when you believe that there
is a book on the table as having the form:

$$(\vee x)(\vee y)[(B:x,\dagger) \wedge (T:y,\dagger) \wedge (O:x,y,\dagger)]$$

where $\dagger$ designates a particular time. Different times will be represented by different designators $\dagger$. As each time of belief generates a
different temporal proposition, we must say that for each time t,
there is a propositional designator $\dagger_t$ which designates t and only t.
If at time t I believe that there is a book on the table, then the proposition I believe is:

$$(\vee x)(\vee y)[(B:x,\dagger_t) \wedge (T:y,\dagger_t) \wedge (O:x,y,\dagger_t)].$$

Differences in $\dagger_t$ are not reflected by differences in our psychological
state. (We cannot tell time by introspection.)

I expect that some philosophers will balk at the designators $\dagger_t$,
insisting that there is no reason to believe that there are such propositional constituents and insisting that temporal propositions are
instead directly referential. But we really have no substantive disagreement here. Nothing I have said precludes taking the designators
$\dagger_t$ to be the times themselves, in which case temporal propositions
are directly referential. On the other hand, I doubt that it actually
makes any sense to argue over whether the designator in a temporal
proposition is the time itself or a surrogate of the time. The only
objective fact is that different times generate different temporal
propositions, and if we are going to differentiate between propositions in terms of their structure and constituents, then we must
regard temporal propositions as containing designators designating
times.

When you believe a proposition containing $\dagger_t$, the particular
designator $\dagger_t$ that is contained in the proposition you believe is
determined by the time of the belief. In other words, $\dagger_t$ must always
be the designator for the present instant. It is possible to believe

temporal propositions which are about times other than the present, but these propositions generally contain temporal designators constructed out of the designators $\dagger_t$. For example, if I believe that there was a book on the table twenty four hours ago, I believe the proposition

$$(\vee x)(\vee y)[(B\!:\!x, (\dagger_t - 24)) \wedge (T\!:\!y, (\dagger_t - 24)) \wedge (O\!:\!x,y, (\dagger_t - 24))]$$

where $\ulcorner(\dagger_t - 24)\urcorner$ is short for some definite description involving $\dagger_t$ and designating the time twenty-four hours prior to t.

Let η be the statemental designator expressed by the speaker's use of 'now' at t. We will call such designators *temporal designators*. Our objective is to describe them in terms of their diagrams. Suppose a speaker makes a statement by saying $\ulcorner N$ is now $F\urcorner$ using N to express ∂ and F to express A. His statement has the form $(A\!:\!\partial,\eta)$. If, on a later occasion, a speaker makes a statement by uttering the same sentence, and in doing so again uses N to express ∂ and F to express A, his statement once again has the form $(A\!:\!\partial,\eta)$. Thus the two speakers make the same statement on these two occasions iff the temporal designator expressed by 'now' is the same on both occasions. However, if the speakers make their statements at different times, then they are making different statements. They are reporting two different states of affairs, with the result that their statements need not even have the same truth values. Thus 'now' must express two different temporal designators on the two different occasions. Let η_t be the temporal designator expressed by 'now' at t. If $t \neq t^*$, then $\eta_t \neq \eta_{t^*}$.

Let ϕ_t be $(A\!:\!\partial,\eta_t)$. If $t^* \neq t$, you cannot state ϕ_t by saying $\ulcorner N$ is now $F\urcorner$ at time t^*. Is there any other way you can state ϕ_t at time t^*? It does not seem that there is. To do so one would have to utter a sentence of the form $\ulcorner N$ is F at time $T\urcorner$ where T is some term like a definite description used to refer to t. But different choices of the term T will normally result in different statements being made. If the statements are different from one another, they cannot all be the same as ϕ_t. Thus at most a few sentences of the form $\ulcorner N$ is F at time $T\urcorner$ could be used to state ϕ_t. But I can see no reason for regarding some such sentences as more intimately connected with ϕ_t than are other such sentences. Thus it seems likely that none of them can be used to state ϕ_t, and hence that ϕ_t cannot be stated at any time other than t.

The preceding indicates that the time t^* of utterance must be regarded as one of the dynamic parameters of η_t. If $t^* \neq t$, then there are no possible sent-designators for η_t relative to t^*. On the other hand, if $t^* = t$, then it seems clear that $\dagger_t$ is a possible sent-designator for η_t relative to t^*. Are there any other possible sent-designators for η_t relative to t? My intuition is that there are not, but I have no strong argument for this position. It just seems to me intuitively that no other way of thinking of t is an appropriate way of thinking of the present time in connection with a use of 'now'. I might think of (what is in fact) the present time as 'the time of the fifth eruption of Mt. St. Helens in this century', but I could not express my thought appropriately using 'now'. If this is correct, then $\dagger_t$ and only $\dagger_t$ is a possible sent-designator for η_t at time t.

Turning to the received-designators, we might think initially that $\dagger_t$ is also the only acceptable received-designator for η_t. But this overlooks the fact that there is invariably some time lag between the speaker's making the statement and the audience's receiving it. Consequently, the received-designator does not designate the time when the audience receives the communication, but designates an earlier time. As such, I can see no basis for any restrictions on acceptable received-designators. It would seem that any designator of the time t is an acceptable received-designator for η_t.

Having described the diagrams of the temporal designators η_t, we can describe the meaning of the pronominal use of 'now' as follows:

> (4.8) The sole pragmatic parameter of 'now' is the time of utterance, and $\Delta_{\cdot\text{now}}$ is that function which, to a time t, assigns the temporal designator η_t as the sense of 'now' at t.

Note that our semantical account of 'now' is exactly parallel to our semantical account of 'I'.

4.3 'Here'

The remaining token reflective is 'here'. It has typically been claimed that 'here' is a pronoun used to refer rigidly to the physical location of the speaker.[10] Let us call this 'the received view on "here"'. I am inclined to think that the received view is wrong in almost all respects.

Like 'now', 'here' is generally used as an adverb rather than a pronoun. As an adverb, 'here' can be roughly paraphrased as 'in this place'. 'He is here' means roughly 'He is in this place', not 'He is

---

[10] For example, see Kaplan [1977].

this place'. Unlike 'now', however, I do not believe that 'here' is ever used as a pronoun. At this point I part company with most linguistic sources, who regard 'here' as functioning pronominally in prepositional constructions like 'in here' or 'under here'. Let me postpone discussion of these prepositional constructions until later in this section.

If it is agreed that 'here' is an adverb rather than a pronoun, we might accomodate this by weakening the received view and saying that 'here' is an adverb exclusively to talk about the physical location of the speaker. However, this would still be false. First, as the *Oxford English Dictionary* observes, 'here' is not used exclusively to talk about physical locations. It can also be used to talk about times: 'Consider the seventeenth century. Here we find . . . '; about stages of development: 'First the butterfly crawls out of the cocoon. Here he is apt to . . . '; about points or periods in speech or thought: 'Here we see that . . . '; about matters before us or in question: 'Here more than anywhere it is important to . . . '; etc.

Perhaps it will be claimed that 'here' has more than one meaning and that in its *basic* meaning it is used to talk about physical locations. That seems plausible, but even if it is true and it is accordingly claimed that philosophical theories about 'here' only relate to this basic meaning, there is still little resemblance between the received view of 'here' and the facts. Even using 'here' to talk about physical locations, it need not be used to refer to the location of the speaker. For example, if I spot a lost earring under a nearby table, I may report, 'It is under here'. I am referring to a location which is under the table, but that is not my location. Or, standing at the mouth of the cave in which he has cornered the fugitive, the sheriff might announce, 'He is in here'. The sheriff is talking about the spatial region within the cave, but he is not in that spatial region. Or if I am describing a civil war battlefield, I might say, 'Here you would find many interesting things', although the battlefield may be hundreds of miles away.

It is false that in using 'here' to talk about physical locations, it can only be used to talk about the location of the speaker. What seems to have led philosophers to that mistaken view is a proximity requirement closely related to the one we discussed in connection with ⌜this F⌝. When a speaker uses ⌜this F⌝ and ⌜that F⌝ to talk about two different F's, he implies that the referent of ⌜this F⌝ is "more proximate" than the referent of ⌜that F⌝. The kinds of proximity that can be involved include physical proximity, temporal

125

proximity, mental proximity, logical proximity, etc.[11] Analogously, when a speaker uses 'here' to talk about one place and 'there' to talk about another, he implies that the former is closer to him than the latter. The proximity requirements regarding 'here' and 'there' appear to be just what we would get automatically from the paraphrases 'this place' and 'that place'. For example, I can refer to the region under the table by saying 'It is under here' because I am close by that region, and the sheriff can refer to the interior of the cave by saying 'He is in here' because the sheriff is close by the cave. I can refer to the civil war battlefield by saying 'Here you would find many interesting things' just as I could refer to it by saying 'In this place you would find many interesting things'. In this context the proximity requirement requires temporal proximity to the time at which the place was last referred to. In this case, physical proximity is not required by the use of either 'here' or 'this place'.

All of this suggests that 'here' should be analyzed as meaning 'in this place'. This would make 'here' much simpler than philosophers have generally supposed. There is nothing special about 'this place' to make it behave differently than other impure demonstratives. I believe that this proposal is right in most respects, but it overlooks some linguistic complexities.

The first of the linguistic complexities has to do with the behavior of 'here' when combined with prepositions, e.g., 'in here' or 'under here'. It looks initially as if in such contexts 'here' is functioning as a pronoun meaning 'this place' rather than as an adverb. However, the appearance is misleading. Suppose, having found the earring under the table, I say 'It is under here'. This does not mean 'It is under this place'. The word 'here' is not being used to talk about the place which the earring is under; rather, it is being used to refer to the place occupied by the earring. 'It is under here' means 'It is here under that', where 'that' refers to the table, and hence it can be paraphrased as 'It is in this place under that'.

Similarly, when the sheriff reports the presence of the fugitive in the cave by saying, 'He is in here', this is not the same thing as saying 'He is in this place'. The location 'in here' can only be used in talking about enclosures—caves, holes, rooms, houses, auditoriums, etc. I cannot say 'He is in here' referring to a football field or meadow.[12] The 'in' of 'in here' is in the 'in' of 'within'. 'He is in here'

---

[11] See pages 115–116.

[12] Instead we might say 'He is out there' meaning 'He is outside in this place'.

means 'He is here within', i.e., 'He is in the enclosure here', which can be paraphrased as 'He is in this place within the enclosure'.

These examples illustrate that although occurrences of 'here' in combination with prepositions can be paraphrased in terms of 'in this place', the paraphrases are occasionally complicated and vary depending upon the preposition and the context. Nevertheless, these examples suggest that there is an interchangeability between 'here' and 'in this place' provided we make the required transformations.

Although 'here' is not a singular term, it is nevertheless used in referring to places, in the same sense that the adverbial phrase 'in this place' is used in referring to places. The grammatical peculiarities of 'here' are not of philosophical significance. Does 'here' exhibit any other peculiarities which *are* of philosophical interest and would serve to set it apart from other terms used in referring? Kaplan [1977] asserts that 'here' is a rigid designator. In claiming this, he is taking 'here' to be a pronoun rather than an adverb, but we can reformulate the question and inquire whether, in an extended sense, 'here' is a rigid designator. That 'here' is not a rigid designator is illustrated by the following example:

If we were in China, people here would be speaking Chinese.

As far as I can see, there is nothing about 'here' which sets it apart philosophically from other terms used in referring.

V
The Traditional Theory of Predicates

1. Introduction

Predicates have not been supposed to create nearly so many difficulties for the traditional theory of language as have singular terms. In fact, it has often seemed that the source of the difficulties for singular terms lay primarily in the fact that traditional theories of language were tailor-made for predicates and the attempt to fit proper names and other singular terms into those theories occurred mainly as an afterthought. Having dealt with singular terms, the reader may feel that there is little that needs to be said about predicates because they are adequately treated by the traditional theories. It will be my contention, however, that the traditional theories do not handle predicates any better than they do singular terms.

Predicates are those linguistic items which are used to predicate, i.e., to ascribe attributes to things. Attributes can be one-place or many-place, so this definition includes relations as many-place predicates, or as we will say, relational predicates. In English, linguists distinguish between common nouns, noun phrases, predicates, verbs, and adjectives, but we will lump these together and call them all 'predicates'. The justification for doing this is that they can all be regarded as expressing attributes. This should not be taken as implying that I think there are no important differences between these different kinds of linguistic items. Rather, most of those differences are unimportant for our present purposes, which are really rather crude.

We say that an object (or sequence of objects) *satifies* a predicate (as used on a particular occasion) when the object (or sequence of objects) exemplifies the attribute which the predicate expresses. An object or sequence of objects satisfying a predicate will be called an *exemplar* of the predicate. The set of all exemplars of a predicate (as used on a particular occasion) is the *extension* of the predicate (as used on that occasion).

The traditional theory regarding predicates is just the original propositional theory according to which a predicate expresses a concept which constitutes its meaning and an object satisfies the predicate just in case it emplifies that concept. This concept is the *intension* of the predicate. The sense in which a predicate is supposed to "express" its intension is that the intension is supposed to be a constituent of statements made by assertively uttering sentences containing semantical occurrences of the predicate.

In order to handle predicates like 'is here' which contain indexical elements it is best to generalize this account a bit. It is alleged that such predicates are still used to express concepts, but they may be used to express different concepts on different occasions. The concept expressed by the predicate on a given occasion is its sense on that occasion, and the meaning of the predicate is constituted by that function which determines its sense on each occasion. This is the "indexical version" of the traditional theory of predicates.

The move to the indexical theory may seem less important for predicates than it did for sentences. Sentences are virtually never used to make the same statements from one occasion to another because they almost invariably contain indexical elements (at least an implicit 'now'). Similarly, syntactically complex predicates frequently contain indexical elements, but if we look at one-word predicates, it is apt to appear initially that most of them are non-indexical. We will discover, eventually, that this appearance is misleading, but it is true that the indexicality of syntactically simple predicates is generally of a lower order than that of sentences and singular terms. Proper names are *strongly indexical* in the sense that, even in a fixed social setting, a speaker can use a name to express different senses by merely sending different propositional designators. On the other hand, we will find that there is a central class of predicates which are only *weakly indexical* in the sense that they are indexical but when one of these predicates is used with its conventional meaning (or if it is ambiguous, with any one of its conventional meanings) in a fixed social setting, it can only be used to express a fixed sense. Let us say that a predicate is *elementary* iff it is either nonindexical or weakly indexical, i.e., iff, when used with any one of its conventional meanings in a fixed social setting it always expresses the same sense. Syntactically simple predicates

129

prove to be almost uniformly elementary. Syntactically complex predicates may be elementary or not, depending upon whether they contain indexical elements.

In Chapter One we formulated an alternative theory of meaning for predicates which was claimed to be virtually a truism. That theory proposed that the meaning of a predicate is constituted by its A-intension, the latter being that function from pragmatic parameters to attributes which determines what attribute the predicate expresses on any given occasion of its use. The attribute expressed is the sense of the predicate. The defense of this proposal was as follows. Attributes are, by definition, what predicates express, and which attribute a predicate expresses on a particular occasion is presumably determined by the meaning of the predicate. Conversely, if we know what attribute a predicate expresses on any given occasion of its use, there would seem to be nothing further we would have to know in order to know the meaning of the predicate. Thus the meaning is constituted by its A-intension. However, this account of meaning is not particularly informative without a fuller account of the attributes expressed, and should best be regarded as the framework for a theory of meaning rather than a theory all by itself. To generate a full-fledged theory we must flesh the framework out by saying what the attributes are like which predicates express. We can generate the traditional theory by identifying these attributes with concepts. In this connection, however, it should be pointed out that we have already found some predicates which express attributes that are not concepts. These are predicates containing semantical occurrences of proper names (e.g., 'brother of John') or other singular terms. But it may reasonably be felt that these attributes are atypical, and that most attributes, and in particular those expressed by elementary predicates, are concepts. One of the major contentions of this book will be that this traditional supposition is incorrect.

2. Analytic and Synthetic Predicates

We will begin our investigation of predicates by concentrating exclusively on elementary predicates, which express fixed attributes in a fixed social setting. The traditional theory alleges that these attributes are concepts. The traditional theory has generally been embellished with a theory about the nature of concepts according to which a concept is to be analyzed in terms of its *a priori* logical relationships to other concepts. Our discovery in Chapter Three of concepts which are not purely qualitative must force us to reject this traditional view. However, the only nonqualitative concepts we have encountered are logically idiosyncratic, and as such are not reasonable candidates for the senses of predicates anyway. If we consider only purely qualitative concepts, it still seems reasonable to suppose that concepts can be analyzed in terms of their *a priori* logical relationships to one another. However, this view of concepts creates unexpected problems when combined with the traditional theory of predicates. According to the latter theory, elementary predicates are used to express concepts. It should follow that the sense of an elementary predicate on a given occasion can be characterized by its *a priori* logical relationships to the senses of other predicates.[1] Sometimes this appears to work. For example, as 'bachelor' expresses the concept of being a bachelor and the latter concept is equivalent to the concept of being an unmarried man (so we are told), it follows that the sense of the predicate 'bachelor' is logically equivalent to the sense of the predicate 'unmarried man', or equivalently that one states a necessary truth by saying 'A person is a bachelor iff he is an unmarried man'. All uses of elementary predicates should be analyzable in analogous ways. On any particular occasion, the sense of an elementary predicate must stand in sufficiently many *a priori* logical relations to the senses of other predicates for the set of these logical relationships to determine completely the sense of the initial predicate.

The difficulty for all this lies in the paucity of logical connections. When we begin to look for the logical connections required by this theory, we find that they do not generally exist. For example, how would you set about defining 'horse'? *Webster's New World Dictionary* gives the following definition:

> A large four-legged, solid-hoofed animal with flowing mane and tail, domesticated for drawing loads, carrying riders, etc.

Whatever this definition is, it is not a report of *a priori* logical features of the sense of the predicate 'horse'. Having four legs is obviously not an *a priori* necessary condition for being a horse. If a horse loses a leg in an accident or is deformed at birth, it is still a horse. And none of the other conditions listed fares any better. This definition does not provide *a priori* necessary and sufficient conditions for being a horse. Nor does it seem possible to construct

---

[1] Provided our language contains predicates expressing the appropriate concepts.

an alternative definition which is any more satisfactory in this respect. The only conditions which could with any plausibility at all be claimed as *a priori* necessary conditions for being a horse are conditions like 'occupies space', 'has weight', 'is alive', etc. I am not convinced that these conditions *are a priori* necessary for being a horse, but even if they are they are clearly not sufficient to completely characterize the sense of 'horse'. The predicate 'horse' just does not have the logical features required by the traditional theory.

To take another example, consider 'electron'. Here we encounter a problem which appears initially to be just the opposite of that for 'horse'. There are too many conditions which seem to be *a priori* necessary and sufficient for being an electron. A physicist could enumerate quite a list of such "definitions" of 'electron'. But now the difficulty is in choosing between them. They cannot all be *a priori* necessary, but none of them seems particularly more privileged than any other, and upon reflection it seems that any of them could be rejected by subsequent physical discovery. For example, if we define an electron to be a negatively charged particle of such-and-such a mass, it is certainly possible for subsequent experiments to lead us to revise our value for the mass of an electron. Consequently, having that mass is not *a priori* necessary for being an electron. Similarly, if we define an electron to be a negatively charged particle having the smallest rest mass of any elementary particle, this would not prevent us from subsequently discovering a new class of particles having one third the mass and charge of an electron.[2] It is not even an *a priori* truth that electrons are negatively charged. We can easily imagine discovering that in certain high energy interactions electrons temporarily lose their charge. It seems that nothing about electrons is sacrosanct, and hence the predicate 'electron' also lacks the logical features required by the traditional theory.

The traditional theory of predicates does not seem at all plausible when we attempt to apply it to predicates like 'horse' or 'electron'. However, the traditional theory is based upon what seems to be a strong argument, which goes as follows. When we employ a predicate to make a statement about its exemplars, we must be thinking of those exemplars in some particular way. The only way to think collectively about the members of a class of objects, supposedly, is in terms of some description of them, or what comes to the same

---

[2] This shows that what are called 'definitions' in this context are not definitions in the philosopher's sense of providing logically necessary and sufficient conditions.

thing, under some concept. Thus when a speaker uses a predicate, he is using it to express a certain concept, that concept being the one in terms of which he is thinking of the exemplars of the predicate.

This is a persuasive defense of the traditional theory. However, it will not withstand close scrutiny. For example, let us consider a strictly regimented society on a tropical island whose economy is based on the production of lemon juice. The society has a caste structure. The lowest caste consists of the lemon pickers. The lemon pickers know nothing about what becomes of the lemons after they pick them. The next higher caste consists of the people who transport the lemons to the juicing factory. The next caste consists of the people who extract juice from the lemons, and a higher caste yet consists of those persons who transport the lemon juice to the docks where it is shipped to market. The highest caste consists of the priests who organize all of this and collect the proceeds. The priests do not want the members of the lower castes to learn for themselves how to make and market lemon juice, so it is strictly forbidden, on pain of death, for the members of two different castes to communicate with one another in any way about lemons. But let us suppose that two foolhardy individuals, one from the pickers' caste and one from the juice transporters' caste, meet and fall in love. To demonstrate their trust in one another, they begin to talk about lemons. The odd thing is that they have almost no knowledge in common about lemons. The pickers do not know anything about what becomes of the lemons after they are picked, and in particular they have no idea that lemons contain juice. The juice transporters, on the other hand, know nothing about the origin of the juice they transport. They know it to be the juice of lemons, but they have no idea what a lemon is. Thus when they share their knowledge with one another, each is amazed. Now we come to the moral of the story. Although they are both using the predicate 'lemon', and have no difficulty in communicating with one another, there can be no common concept which they both have in mind. They share no common knowledge about lemons, so there can be no common concept which they both express when they use the predicate. One might suppose that they must be using the predicate with two different senses, but that is hard to defend. It seems that if they are using the predicate with two different senses, then they should be unable to communicate about lemons, but in fact they would have no difficulty at all in communicating. The juice-transporter certainly understands his friend when she tells him that lemons are little yellow fruits that grow on trees, and she in turn would have no difficulty in understanding him when he tells her that lemons are important for their juice. Furthermore, each is clearly able to communicate with members of the priestly caste (with whom each does share knowledge about lemons), so it seems that each is using the word 'lemon' with the same sense as the priests, and hence each is using the word with the same sense as the other.

When one uses a predicate like 'lemon', one must be thinking about its exemplars in some way, but one can be using the predicate in the same sense while thinking of its exemplars in different ways. Thus the sense of the predicate is not identical with the concept in terms of which one thinks of its exemplars.

Apparently the senses of many predicates do not have the logical features required by the traditional theory of predicates. On the other hand, there are some predicates whose senses do seem to have the *a priori* features required by the traditional theory. Well-known examples include 'bachelor', 'sibling', 'invisible' (defined as 'not visible'), and perhaps most of the predicates of mathematics. The traditional theory was constructed by looking at these few examples, but what is true of them does not seem to be true in general. We must distinguish between two kinds of elementary predicates: *analytic* predicates, which fit the tranditional theory at least in that their senses are characterized by *a priori* features; and *synthetic* predicates whose senses lack the *a priori* features required by the traditional theory. This distinction is founded upon a distinction between two kinds of attributes which serve as the senses for the two kinds of predicates. We might call these *analytic* and *synthetic attributes* respectively.[3] To make the distinction more precise, we might try defining:

(2.1)   An attribute *A* is analytic iff there are other attributes whose *a priori* relationships to *A* are jointly sufficient to uniquely characterize *A*.

This definition is subject to a perplexing difficulty. We would like to say that the attribute of *being invisible* is analytic, because there

---

[3] This indicates that it is slightly misleading to talk about a distinction between two kinds of predicates. At least in principle, a predicate might express analytic attributes under some values of its pragmatic parameters and synthetic attributes under others. However, I know of no such predicates.

are *a priori* relationships between *being invisible* and the attribute of *being visible* which constitute a definition of *being invisible*. However, these *a priori* relationships would equally enable us to define *being visible* in terms of *being invisible*, and we do not thereby want to count *being visible* as an analytic attribute. An analogous move would make all attributes analytic. We want to distinguish between *being invisible* and *being visible* on the grounds that the *a priori* relationships between them are in some sense "constitutive" of the former but not of the latter. At this point it is impossible to make it clear just what this notion of a *constitutive logical relationship* involves. We will obtain a precise explication of it in Chapter Seven, but for now we must be content with a rough intuitive grasp of it. Utilizing this notion, we can define:

(2.2) An attribute *A* is *analytic* iff there are other attributes whose *a priori* relationships to *A* are jointly sufficient to uniquely characterize *A* and are constitutive of *A*. A predicate is *analytic* iff it is elementary and its senses are analytic.

(2.3) An attribute is *synthetic* iff it is not analytic. A predicate is *synthetic* iff it is elementary and its senses are synthetic.

Obviously, these definitions leave much to be desired, and we are not yet in a position to repair their shortcomings. However, the present definitions should be sufficient to give a grasp of the distinction we are trying to illuminate, and they will prove sufficient for our present purposes.

On the assumption that purely qualitative concepts are characterized by their *a priori* relationships to other purely qualitative concepts, it follows that synthetic predicates do not express concepts. On this assumption, purely qualitative concepts will be analytic attributes and so will not be expressed by synthetic predicates. Nonqualitative concepts are logically idiosyncratic, so they cannot be expressed by any predicates. Thus synthetic predicates do not expresses concepts.

The failure of the traditional theory for the case of synthetic predicates could be indicative either of a failure of our theory of concepts or of an incorrect theory of the relationship between predicates and concepts. Donnellan [1962], Kripke [1972], and Putnam [1975] have taken it as indicative of the former, but I shall argue that it is actually indicative of the latter.

3. The Historico-Scientific Theory

Saul Kripke [1972] and Hilary Putnam ([1973] and [1975]) have proposed a theory which is intended to meet the difficulties that have been raised regarding synthetic predicates. The theory has been called 'the historico-scientific theory'.[4] This is a theory about the meaning of "substance words" like 'water', "natural kinds" like 'lemon', 'tiger', 'electron', physical magnitude terms like 'temperature', etc. Perhaps it is a theory about the meaning of synthetic predicates in general.

According to the historico-scientific theory,[5] the extension of a predicate like 'water' is determined by two factors. The predicate is introduced stipulatively, by dubbing some quantities of liquid as water. Then another quantity of liquid is water iff it has the "same nature" as the initially dubbed quantities. What it is to "have the same nature" is something to be discovered by scientists, but Putnam tells us that according to contemporary science, this amounts to having the same molecular structure. Thus science provides us with a relation $same_L$, the dubbing provides us with an initial quantity of water W, and a new quantity of liquid is water iff it stands in the relation $same_L$ to W.

Putnam cites two reasons for holding this theory. On the one hand, he has argued, much as I did above, that the extension of a synthetic predicate, as used on a particular occasion, is not determined by a concept in the minds of the speakers, so he is looking for an alternative way in which that extension could be determined. The historico-scientific theory is his proposal. On the other hand, he is looking for a theory which makes it possible for one and the same predicate to occur, with the same meaning, in two different scientific theories. For example, classical electrodynamics and quantum electrodynamics both employ the predicate 'electron', and common sense tells us that they are theories about the same things—electrons. However, if we embrace the traditional theory of predicates and insist that the meaning of 'electron' must be given by some definition, and then we observe that these two electrodynamic theories contain different definitions for 'electron', we are forced to conclude that the predicate does not have the same meaning in the

----

[4] This name was proposed by Zemach [1976].

[5] What follows is Putnam's formulation, which is much clearer than Kripke's. Perhaps the theory thus formulated should only be attributed to Kripke with reservations.

two theories. Putnam is looking for a theory of predicates which enables them to be meaning-invariant under scientific advancement with its attendant changes in scientific theories, and he believes that the historico-scientific theory satisfies this desideratum.

Although the historico-scientific theory seems initially clear, there are some examples which make its precise formulation somewhat problematic. Both Kripke and Putnam cite the example of jade. As Putnam [1973] observes: "Although the Chinese do not recognize a difference, the term 'jade' applies to two minerals: jadeite and nephrite. Chemically, there is a marked difference. Jadeite is a combination of sodium and aluminum. Nephrite is made of calcium, magnesium, and iron. These two quite different micro-structures produce the same unique textural qualities!" This creates a difficulty regarding what is to be included in the initial dubbing of a predicate like 'jade'. Perhaps the initial samples of jade were all instances of jadeite rather than nephrite. Does this mean that contemporary mineralogists are mistaken in calling nephrite 'jade'? Presumably not. The dubbing must be taken to include some instances of nephrite. But this makes it difficult to see just how to draw the line between the initial dubbing and the subsequent use of the predicate to classify new substances as jade.

The preceding considerations suggest a serious difficulty for the historico-scientific theory. It has been observed by both Lycan [1975] and Zemach [1976] that the historico-scientific theory is in danger of making it impossible for us to know whether a present-day substance is water, or jade, or of any other natural kind introduced into our language at some time in the distant past. The difficulty is that for a predicate like 'water' or 'jade', we really have no idea what the initial instances were in terms of which the predicate was introduced. Nor can we simply trust the judgments of past speakers to the effect that the different things which have been called 'water' or 'jade' down through the ages were really of the same nature as the things that were previously called 'water' or 'jade', and hence ultimately of the same nature as the initial instances of water or jade. This is because what is regarded as constituting *being of the same nature* is determined by science, and science has changed its mind on this question many times. When 'water' and 'jade' were introduced into the language, no one knew anything about molecular structure, but according to Putnam, that is what is now regarded as constituting sameness of nature. Thus past speakers, who were mistaken about what constituted *being of the same nature*, may have been frequently or even predominantly wrong about what things were water or jade. Hence we cannot simply take their word for it in determining what things are water or jade. Consequently, the historico-scientific theory seems to lead us to a kind of absurd skepticism in which no one knows what substances are really water or jade.

This difficulty can be overcome if we change the theory a bit and suppose that the dubbing goes on continually. At any given time, to be water is to be of the same nature as the stuff that is *now* considered water. According to this version of the theory, each time a new quantity of stuff is reasonably judged to be water (or jade, etc.) it becomes included in the class of paradigms against which new candidates are judged, and as the older paradigms cease to exist or are forgotten they drop out of the class of paradigms. Thus dubbing becomes an ongoing process. This version of the theory is suggested by some of the remarks in Putnam [1975]. We might call this the *evolving version* of the historico-scientific theory.

The evolving version of the theory avoids the danger of skepticism, but does so only at the expense of ceasing to satisfy Putnam's second desideratum, according to which a predicate like 'water' should be meaning-invariant in the face of scientific change. Through mistaken assimilations, the present-day paradigms of water may be of an entirely different nature than the original paradigms in terms of which the predicate was introduced. Thus what was originally of the same nature as the paradigms is quite different from what is now of the same nature as the paradigms. In other words, the extension of the predicate 'water' has changed. But if the extension has changed, then the meaning must have changed. Furthermore, changing our scientific theories about water will almost automatically lead to some change in what concrete substances we class as water, and hence will change our paradigms, and correspondingly the extension and the meaning of the predicate. Thus it will rarely be the case that the meaning of the predicate 'water' will remain invariant in the face of a change in our theories about water.

By reflecting once more upon 'jade', we can see that there is an even more crucial difficulty for the evolving version of the historico-scientific theory. As we formulated it, the theory would require that for something to be jade it must be of the same nature as the present paradigms of jade. But this formulation presupposes that all of the present paradigms are of the same nature, which is false of jade. Nor can we require that a piece of jade be of the same nature as *most* of the present paradigms. As jadeite is much less common than nephrite, it would follow that jadeite is not jade. Is it enough, instead, to require that a piece of jade be of the same nature as *some* of the present paradigms? This will only be sufficient if we can be confident that all of the present paradigms of jade really are jade. This forces us to be more careful in deciding what we mean by 'paradigm'. If by 'paradigm' we just mean those things which are confidently and reasonably *considered* to be jade, then it is possible that we have made a mistake and included some "fool's jade" among our paradigms. If a new hunk of stuff is of the same nature as some of this fool's jade, this does not make it jade. The only obvious way to avoid this difficulty is to define 'paradigm' in such a way that the present-day paradigms of jade are those things which we currently *know* to be jade. But this makes the theory circular. In order to decide whether we know a putative paradigm to be jade we must already know what it is to be jade, and that is precisely what is at issue. We might attempt to avoid circularity by making the account recursive, defining what it is to be a paradigm at a given time in terms in part of being of the same nature as the previous paradigms. But this would have the effect that, throughout history, the nature of the paradigms cannot change, and so would reduce to the original (nonevolving) version of the historico-scientific theory, and hence once more to skepticism. I do not see any simple way out of this difficulty. But without some solution, the historico-scientific theory must be forsaken.

VI
Synthetic Predicates

1. Synthetic Predicates and Social Knowledge

We seek a theory of meaning for predicates. It is convenient to begin by looking exclusively at synthetic predicates. Furthermore, it will be helpful to initiate the investigation by asking a somewhat easier question, viz., what determines the extension of a synthetic predicate? The answer to this question will lead us, eventually, to an account of meaning for synthetic predicates.

Let us simplify our discussion as much as possible by considering a synthetic predicate which is not ambiguous. Such a predicate has just one extension. This extension consists of the class of all objects satisfying the predicate. How do we determine whether an object satisfies such a predicate? The traditional theory was that a predicate expresses a concept and we determine whether an object satisfies the predicate by seeing whether it exemplifies that concept. But synthetic predicates do not work in this way. A synthetic predicate expresses no such concept. When a speaker employs a synthetic predicate on some specific occasion, there must be some way that he is thinking about the things which satisfy the predicate. But what makes a synthetic predicate peculiar is that different speakers can be using the predicate conventionally, with the same sense, and yet be thinking about its extension in different ways. Recall the use of the predicate 'lemon' in the island community whose economy was based on the production of lemon juice. The different members of the society were each thinking about lemons in particular ways, under particular descriptions, but there was no single "analytic" description they had to be employing in order to be using the predicate in accordance with its conventional meaning. Similarly, physicists could produce any number of descriptions of electrons, and one speaker (who is a specialist in one area) may employ one such description while another (who is a specialist in a different area) employs a different description, but both may be using the predicate 'electron' conventionally. The situation seems to be that there is a great deal of socially shared knowledge about lemons and electrons. Any description which can be put together from that social knowledge is as good as any other, and each is subject to potential correction in terms of the rest of our social knowledge. This social knowledge is shared, not in the sense that everyone possesses it all, but in the sense that different members of society possess different parts of it and can in principle obtain the other parts from the other members of society.

In ascertaining whether an object satisfies a synthetic predicate like 'electron' or 'lemon', one has at his potential disposal everything that is known in the society about electrons or lemons, and all of this socially entrenched knowledge operates more or less on a par in determining the extensions of the predicates. Different speakers may be thinking about the exemplars of a synthetic predicate in different ways, using different "definitions", but as long as all of their definitions are drawn from our social knowledge involving the predicate, the different speakers are all using the predicate with the same sense—that determined by its conventional meaning. Contrary to the traditional theory of predicates, there is no single "analytic" definition. Rather than being determined by a single such analytic definition, it seems that the extension of a synthetic predicate must be determined jointly by all of our social knowledge involving it.[1] How can our social knowledge involving a synthetic predicate determine its extension?

My answer to this question will proceed in terms of the notion of a set of objects satisfying the statements comprising our social knowledge. For reasons that will become apparent later, I do not want to assume that those statements are extensional. Thus we must define 'satisfies' in a more complicated way than is customary. Let us say that a *concept* satisfies a statement relative to a particular attribute occurring in the statement iff replacement of the attribute by the concept throughout the statement yields a truth. Then a *set* satisfies the statement iff it is the extension of some concept satisfying the statement. We will say that the set satisfies the statement relative

---

[1] That social knowledge is a set of statements. For precision, let us say that a statement ϕ *involves* a predicate F iff it is possible for ϕ to be expressed by some sentence containing a semantical occurrence of F wherein F is used with its current sense.

to a predicate F iff the set satisfies the statement relative to the attribute expressed by F.

It is now quite simple to explain how our social knowledge could determine the extension of a synthetic predicate. The principles in our socially shared knowledge about, say, electrons, must be true—otherwise they would not be knowledge. In order for them to be true they must be satisfied by the extension of the predicate. Thus the extension of a synthetic predicate must automatically satisfy our social knowledge involving that predicate. If the social knowledge is going to *determine* that extension, then the extension of the predicate must be the *unique* set satisfying that social knowledge.

Unfortunately, the relation between our social knowledge and the extension of a synthetic predicate cannot be quite as simple as the preceding proposal would have us believe. The difficulty is that we may have very little actual social knowledge. Scientific theories almost invariably turn out to be false in the end, in which case they are not included in our actual social knowledge. They are only putative social knowledge. Putative social knowledge is that which purports to be social knowledge, and is accepted as such by the members of our society, but may not be because it may turn out to be false. A great deal of our putative social knowledge will consist of "near misses" rather than actual social knowledge. But then it seems quite likely that we do not have enough actual social knowledge about, say, electrons, for that to determine the extension of the predicate. A more plausible account would be that all of our putative social knowledge enters into the determination of the extension, and the extension is the set which comes closest to satisfying all of that putative social knowledge.

A set of statements is *satisfied* just in case there is some set which satisfies it. If our putative social knowledge involving a synthetic predicate F is all true, then it is satisfied by the set of all F's. Thus if we ascertain that our putative social knowledge is not satisfied, we can conclude that some of it is false. How do we decide which part of it to reject? We have no independent standard by which to judge which bits of our putative social knowledge are true of F's, because what it is to be an F is determined by what part of our putative social knowledge survives as actually true. The only way we can test a bit of putative social knowledge is by comparing it with the rest of our putative social knowledge. The test is one of "coherence" in something like the traditional sense of coherence theories of truth or knowledge. For example, if we ascertain that there is a class of objects satisfying all of our putative social knowledge about electrons except for that regarding the rest mass, then we will rationally conclude that we were wrong about the rest mass and use the remainder of our putative social knowledge to help us ascertain a new value for the rest mass. In general, when we discover that our putative social knowledge about F's is unsatisfied, we seek to make it satisfied by minimally weakening it. The simplest way to weaken it is to delete some principle or principles from it. However, not every minimal deletion will constitute a minimal weakening. There may be more than one way to make our putative social knowledge satisfied through deletion, and one of those deletions may constitute a greater weakening than another. For example, suppose some situation required us to either give up the principle that electrons are negatively charged or reject some specific value for the rest mass of the electron. If we had to choose between these two options, there is no question but that we would choose the latter as constituting a much less significant change to our putative social knowledge. Thus in deciding which of two deletions is smaller, we do not simply count the number of principles being deleted. Some principles are more important than others and receive correspondingly greater weights. It is unclear precisely what the basis for this weighting is, but it is clear that some such weighting is involved in the notion of a minimal weakening. Presumably, the weight a principle receives has to do with systematic considerations concerning the organization of our putative social knowledge.

To further complicate matters, a weakening of our putative social knowledge does not always consist of an outright deletion. We sometimes weaken specific principles rather than simply rejecting them. For example, by appealing to the rest of our putative social knowledge about electrons, we might conclude on the basis of some experiment that in certain high energy interactions electrons temporarily lose their charge. In such a case, the weakening of our putative social knowledge about electrons may consist of qualifying the principle that electrons are always negatively charged rather than completely rejecting it. This can be important because it might happen that if we simply rejected the principle that all electrons are negatively charged, without simultaneously replacing it with this weakened principle, the resulting set of putative social knowledge would no longer be strong enough to uniquely determine an extension for the predicate 'electron', whereas the putative social knowledge resulting from merely qualifying the principle would be sufficient to uniquely determine an extension. It is apparent that it is difficult to give a precise characterization of this notion of minimally weakening our putative social knowledge in order to make it satisfied. For now we must be content with the very rough characterization just given.

If we can make our putative social knowledge about F's satisfied through minimal weakening, we have thereby determined which part of it is true, viz., that part which remains. The truths among our putative social knowledge constitute our actual social knowledge. However, our putative social knowledge about F's may contain no actual social knowledge, because it may be that every principle contained in that putative social knowledge has to be weakened or qualified in some way. The truths that result from this weakening were implied by the principles in our putative social knowledge, but were not themselves among those principles. In such a case, our putative social knowledge may lead us to truths sufficient to determine the extension of the predicate F, but those truths need not be contained in our actual social knowledge about F's. Everything we believe about F's may be "a little wrong". This seems to be a congenial picture of what is often the actual state of science.

In realistic circumstances it generally seems to be the case that there is a unique weakening which will make our putative social knowledge about F's uniquely satisfied. But two less fortunate situations are at least possible. It could happen that there are two distinct ways of making our putative social knowledge uniquely satisfied through minimal weakening, or it could happen that there is no way to do this. The former case is illustrated by the predicate 'mass' as it occurred in Newtonian physics and relativistic physics.[2] For the sake of the example, let us pretend that the special theory of relativity is literally true. In the latter, there are two predicates for mass: 'rest mass' and 'inertial mass'. In Newtonian physics there is the single predicate 'mass'. The change in putative social knowledge involved in the transition from Newtonian physics to relativistic physics contained the recognition that the Newtonian putative social knowledge involving 'mass' was unsatisfied. There are two different ways of making it satisfied, one of which yields 'rest mass' and the other 'inertial mass'. Neither change is significantly smaller than the other, so there is no rational basis for preferring one of the changes to the other. Accordingly, we conclude

[2] This is a relational predicate relating objects and real numbers.

that there is no such thing as Newtonian mass rather than concluding either that it is really relativistic rest mass or that it is really relativistic inertial mass.

It can also happen that there is no way to render our putative social knowledge about F's uniquely satisfied through weakening. We can always weaken it enough to render it satisfiable, but it is harder to ensure that it be uniquely satisfiable. If every way of weakening it enough to make it satisfiable has the effect of making it so weak that it no longer characterizes any unique class, then again there is no straightforward way of seizing upon any particular class as the actual set of all F's, so once again we should conclude that there are no F's. Thus science has concluded that neither the electromagnetic ether nor phlogiston exists.

Summarizing our conclusions so far, it seems that we should be able to characterize the extension of a synthetic predicate as follows:

(1.1)   If F is a synthetic predicate and Γ is the set of statements comprising our putative social knowledge about F's, then a set X is the extension of F iff either: (1) there is a unique set Λ which is a minimal weakening of Γ sufficient to render it uniquely satisfied, and X is the unique set satisfying Λ with respect to F; or (2) there is no unique set Λ which is a minimal weakening of Γ sufficient to render it uniquely satisfied, and $X = \varnothing$.

However, (1.1) oversimplifies. The first difficulty is that we cannot assign extensions to individual predicates piecemeal. Rather, we must assign extensions to all synthetic predicates simultaneously. This is because statements in our putative social knowledge involving F will typically involve other synthetic predicates as well. We cannot delete a statement from the putative social knowledge involving F and retain it in the putative social knowledge involving G. What we must seek is a minimal weakening of our entire set of putative social knowledge sufficient to render it uniquely satisfied with respect to all synthetic predicates simultaneously. Then we should have the following:

(1.2)   If there is a unique set Λ which is a minimal weakening of our putative social knowledge sufficient to render it uniquely satisfied simultaneously with respect to all the synthetic predicates involved in it, and there is an assignment of extensions to the synthetic predicates involved in

145

> our putative social knowledge which satisfies Λ relative
> to those synthetic predicates and which assigns X to F,
> then X is the extension of F.

It may seem that is is impossible for any reasonably strong set of statements to be uniquely satisfied. This is rather like having a large set of uninterpreted axioms and then looking for the unique assignment of extensions to the predicates in the axioms which will make them all true. We know from logic that there rarely is a unique assignment of extensions which will satisfy a set of axioms. As a general rule, if a set of axioms is satisfiable, it will be satisfied by infinitely many different assignments of extensions. In the present context, this would have the unfortunate result that the extensions of our synthetic predicates would not be uniquely determined. However, this is to misconstrue the problem of assigning extensions to synthetic predicates. Describing our procedure in the above manner overlooks the fact that our putative social knowledge involves analytic predicates as well as synthetic ones. Our putative social knowledge includes such things as the characteristic taste and feel of water, the look of a tiger, the shape of a lemon, the smell of hydrogen sulphide, etc. The presence of such analytic predicates in our putative social knowledge has the effect that it cannot after all be regarded as a set of uninterpreted axioms. Some of the predicates have their extensions antecedently fixed by the concepts they express. This anchors the whole structure so that an assignment of extensions to synthetic predicates must fit in with the predetermined extensions of the analytic predicates, thus making it possible for the assignment to be unique.

Principle (1.2) only deals with the case in which there is a unique minimal weakening of our putative social knowledge sufficient to render it uniquely satisified. Let us define:

(1.3) A set of statements is *reducible* iff there is a unique minimal weakening of it sufficient to render it uniquely satisfied with respect to all of the synthetic predicates involved in it.

Thus (1.2) deals with the case in which our putative social knowledge is reducible. How do we assign extensions when our putative social knowledge is irreducible? Irreducibility is a failing of the *set* of statements comprising our putative social knowledge, but we want to lay the blame for it on just a few of our synthetic predicates and not let it interfere with assigning extensions to the others. How do we locate the troublesome predicates which are responsible for the irreducibility, and how do we assign extensions to the others? Ordinarily, there will be just one or a small set A of related predicates which cause the irreducibility, and if we simply delete statements involving them from our putative social knowledge Γ, what is left will be reducible. Let 'Γ/A' denote the latter set. Let us say that a *deletable* set of predicates is a minimal set which is such that the deletion of all statements involving predicates in that set from our putative social knowledge will render our putative social knowledge reducible. It seems that if our putative social knowledge Γ is irreducible, there will normally be a unique deletable set A. Then we should take the predicates in A to have empty extensions, delete statements involving members of A from our putative social knowledge, and assign extensions to other synthetic predicates by applying (1.2) to the reducible set Γ/A of statements that are left.

It is, however, at least logically possible that there is more than one deletable set of synthetic predicates. If A and B are both deletable sets of predicates, then our putative social knowledge Γ can be rendered reducible by paring it down to either Γ/A or Γ/B. Which deletion should we adopt? It is important to realize that this sort of case does not arise from there being two unrelated sources of irreducibility in our putative social knowledge, e.g., 'phlogiston' and 'electromagnetic ether'. If the irreducibility resulting from A and the irreducibility resulting from B were unrelated, it would be necessary to delete all of $A \cup B$ in order to achieve reducibility. Deleting just A or just B would not be sufficient to guarantee reducibility. The case in which there are two deletable sets A and B arises instead when the predicates in A and those in B all work together to generate the irreducibility, but the forced irreducibility can be eliminated by deleting just some of the conspiring predicates without deleting them all. It is doubtful that a real case of this sort has ever occurred in the history of science, so we cannot appeal to actual examples to guide us in deciding what should be done in this sort of case. It seems at least plausible, however, to rule that all of the conspirators should be deleted as they are all involved equally in the irreducibility of our putative social knowledge and there is nothing to favor some over others. This suggests that in case there is more than one deletable set of synthetic predicates, we should assign empty extensions to all deletable predicates and then take the extensions of nondeletable predicates to be determined by applying (1.2) to the remaining putative social knowledge. That putative social knowledge comprises the set:

(1.4) $\Gamma_1 = \Gamma/\bigcup\{A \mid A$ is deletable relative to $\Gamma\}$.

However, there appears to be no logical guarantee that Γ_1 will be reducible. If it is not, this means in effect that there are additional conspirators among our synthetic predicates besides those captured in deletable sets. In this case, we should continue the process of deletion by deleting predicates which are deletable with respect to Γ_1, and so on. In general, we can define:

(1.5) $\Gamma_0 = \Gamma$;

$\Gamma_{n+1} = \Gamma_n/\bigcup\{A \mid A$ is deletable relative to $\Gamma_n\}$.

If, at some point n, we arrive at a reducible set Γ_n, then for any $m > n$, $\Gamma_m = \Gamma_n$. Thus we can characterize that reducible set as the intersection of all the Γ_n's:

(1.6) $\Gamma_\omega = \bigcap\{\Gamma_n \mid n \in \omega\}$.

On this basis we can define a nonrelational sense of deletability:

(1.7) A synthetic predicate F is *deletable* iff, if Γ_0 is our putative social knowledge, then F is deletable relative to some Γ_n.

Finally, it seems that we can characterize the extensions of our synthetic predicates as follows:

(1.8) If F is a synthetic predicate involved in our putative social knowledge Γ, the extension of F is X iff either: (a) F is deletable and $X = \varnothing$; or (b) F is not deletable and if Λ is a unique minimal weakening of Γ_ω sufficient to render it simultaneously uniquely satisfied with respect to all synthetic predicates involved in it, then there is an assignment of extensions to the synthetic predicates involved in Λ which satisfies Λ relative to the set of those synthetic predicates and assigns X to F.

One final modification to this principle will be suggested in the next section.

2. Change of Sense

It has been argued that the extension of a synthetic predicate is determined by the putative social knowledge involving that predicate. It follows that a change in putative social knowledge can, on occasion, lead to a change in the extension of a synthetic predicate. For example, the extension of 'chemical compound' changed with the assimilation of Dalton's atomic theory into our putative social knowledge. Prior to Dalton's work, solutions were regarded as chemical compounds, but after Dalton's work they were not. A change in the extension of a predicate automatically results in a change in the truth values of certain statements made by uttering sentences containing the predicate. But this change in truth values comes about without any change in the way the world is (all that has happened is that we have acquired more putative social knowledge). Thus the statements made by uttering sentences containing the predicate cannot themselves be changing truth value—instead, what is changing must be the identity of the statement made by uttering a sentence containing the predicate. As a different statement is being made, the sentence and hence the predicate must have changed sense. Thus, at least on occasion, a change in putative social knowledge can result in a change of sense for a synthetic predicate.

Under what circumstances does a change in putative social knowledge result in a change in sense? It must at least do so whenever it results in a change in extension. It might be supposed that is the only time a change in sense results. Let us call this hypothesis *the conservative sense change theory*. At the opposite extreme, it might be supposed that any change at all in the putative social knowledge involving a synthetic predicate results in a change in its sense. Let us call this *the radical sense change theory*. We will eventually formulate and endorse a theory intermediate between the conservative and radical sense change theories, although at this point it is not obvious how to do that.

2.1 *The Radical Sense Change Theory*

According to the radical sense change theory, any change in the putative social knowledge involving a synthetic predicate results in a change in sense for the predicate. This is reminiscent of the views of Feyerabend [1962] and Kuhn [1962], and similar views have been endorsed by other philosophers of science. In assessing this theory, it should be observed that the extent of the sense change wrought by scientific advancement would be even broader and more far reaching than we might initially suppose. This arises from the fact that the statements comprising the putative social knowledge involving one synthetic predicate will characteristically involve other

149

synthetic predicates as well. A change in our putative social knowledge involving a particular predicate consists of the addition or
deletion of some statement involving that predicate. According to
the radical sense change theory, once this occurs, the predicate
changes sense. This in turn alters what statement is expressed by
any sentence containing a semantical occurrence of that predicate.
There will characteristically be other synthetic predicates which are
such that the putative social knowledge involving them contains
some statements involving the first predicate. Our putative social
knowledge is normally enshrined in sentences. Thus a change in
the sense of the first predicate results in a change in the identity of
some of the statements comprising the putative social knowledge
involving these other predicates. We thereby get a *dispersion effect*
wherein a change in the putative social knowledge involving one
predicate results in a change in its sense, which results in a change
in the putative social knowledge involving other predicates and a
consequent change in their senses, and so on. Our overall putative
social knowledge forms a network which ties all of our synthetic
predicates together. Thus, according to the radical sense change
theory, a change anywhere in our putative social knowledge is apt
to result in sense changes for *all* of our synthetic predicates simultaneously.

The dispersion effect is a most implausible consequence of the
radical sense change theory. Given the dispersion effect and the
rapidity of current scientific advancement, senses may not hold still
long enough for us to get sentences out of our mouths. We may
begin making one statement and end up making another as senses
change in mid utterance. Furthermore, once a change in putative
social knowledge has occurred, it will be impossible to repeat or
deny any statement involving a synthetic predicate which was made
prior to the change. For example, suppose that the accepted value
for the charge on an electron is 4.8025×10^{-10} e.s.u., but that
subsequent measurements lead us to accept the revised value of
4.8024×10^{-10} e.s.u. This is a change in putative social knowledge,
so according to the radical sense change theory, the sense of 'electron'
has changed. Thus it becomes impossible for us to say truly, 'We
were wrong before in thinking that the charge on an electron was
4.8025×10^{-10} e.s.u.', because that is not what we believed. Nor
can someone who questions the reliability of the measurements
leading to the revised value insist, 'We should continue to hold that
the charge on an electron is 4.8025×10^{-10} e.s.u.'. We cannot

continue to hold that because, due to the change in sense of 'electron', that is not anything that we ever did hold. These conclusions seem preposterous. The observation that the radical sense change theory is committed to them at least creates a strong presumption against that theory. Accordingly, unless there are compelling reasons for endorsing the radical sense change theory, alternative theories would seem to be more plausible.

Are there any good arguments in favor of the radical sense change theory which would be sufficient to overcome the presumption against it? In this connection it is natural to look to Feyerabend [1962] as its most ardent defender.[3] However, if we look to Feyerabend for arguments we are going to be disappointed. Feyerabend merely observes that different theories make different claims about, e.g., electrons, and then moves directly from that observation to the conclusion that 'electron' must mean something different in the different theories. But this is just to assume that any difference in the claims made involving a predicate automatically results in a change in sense, which is the very question at issue. Thus Feyerabend supplies us with no argument.[4]

I know of no other arguments in the literature which are any better, nor do I know how to propound one. In light of the implausible consequences of the radical sense change theory, the only reasonable course is to explore its alternatives. Let us turn then to consideration of the conservative sense change theory.

2.2 The Conservative Sense Change Theory

According to the conservative sense change theory, changes in putative social knowledge only result in a change of sense for a synthetic predicate insofar as they result in a change of extension. This theory avoids the undesirable consequences of the radical sense change theory, but it has a surprising consequence of its own. Let F and G be any two coextensive synthetic predicates. If we interchange the putative social knowledge involving F and the putative social knowledge involving G, we have not thereby altered

---

[3] Feyerabend and Kuhn are often discussed together, but Kuhn's position is much less radical. Kuhn maintains only that meaning change occurs with more frequency than we might suppose—not that it occurs with every little change in putative social knowledge.

[4] See Putnam [1965] for a similar assessment of Feyerabend's defense of his views on meaning change.

the extension of F, and hence according to the conservative sense change theory, we have not altered the sense of F. Presumably, if the putative social knowledge involving two synthetic predicates is the same (e.g., 'water' in English and 'Wasser' in German), then the predicates are synonymous (i.e., have the same sense). Thus F after the change has the same sense as G before the change. But as the sense of F has not changed, it follows that F was also synonymous with G before the change in putative social knowledge. Consequently, the conservative sense change theory implies that any two coextensive synthetic predicates are synonymous.

Every freshman philosophy student is taught that coextensive predicates need not be synonymous. However, the standard examples which are supposed to illustrate this concern predicates like 'creature with a heart' and 'creature with a kidney'. It is noteworthy that these are analytic predicates rather than synthetic predicates. It is more difficult to get convincing examples of nonsynonymous coextensive synthetic predicates, although such examples can be found. The simplest examples involve synthetic predicates having empty extensions, like 'unicorn' and 'dragon'. Such predicates are coextensive, but not synonymous. One is not making the same statement if he says 'There used to be unicorns in England' as he is if he says 'There used to be dragons in England'.

A more illuminating example of a pair of coextensive synthetic predicates which are not synonymous can be constructed as follows. Suppose there are two kinds of stars—A-stars and B-stars—where 'A-star' and 'B-star' are synthetic predicates, and suppose that all A-stars are B-stars and all B-stars are A-stars. Suppose further, however, that according to current astrophysical theory (which we can suppose to be correct in this respect), this is just a physical accident. Whether there are A-stars which are not B-stars or B-stars which are not A-stars is a function of the total mass of the universe. Had the universe been somewhat less massive than it is, there would have been A-stars which were not B-stars; and had the universe been somewhat more massive than it is, there would have been B-stars which were not A-stars. Furthermore, we can suppose that the universe could have been either more massive or less massive—that is not dictated by physical laws. Thus we can make a true statement by saying:

(2.1)   There could have been A-stars which were not B-stars.

But we could not make a true statement by saying:

(2.2)   There could have been *A*-stars which were not *A*-stars.

And yet these two sentences would be synonymous if the coextensive predicates '*A*-star' and '*B*-star' were synonymous. Thus, once again, coextensive synthetic predicates need not be synonymous, and hence the conservative sense change theory must be rejected.

2.3 *Nomic Equivalence*

Apparently, the radical sense change theory countenances too much change of sense, and the conservative sense change theory countenances too little. Some intermediate theory must be correct. The key to understanding change of sense lies in considering how a change in the putative social knowledge involving '*A*-star' and '*B*-star' could be erroneous if it leaves their extensions unchanged. This can only happen if the putative social knowledge involving these predicates contains statements in which the predicates function nonextensionally. A little reflection indicates that our putative social knowledge does indeed contain such nonextensional statements. Statements of physical law are nonextensional. The logical form of a physical law is that of what I called a *subjunctive generalization* in Pollock [1976]. Subjunctive generalizations can be expressed in English by sentences of the form $\ulcorner$Any F would be a $G\urcorner$, and can be symbolized as $\ulcorner Fx \Rightarrow Gx \urcorner$.[5] Because physical laws are thus subjunctive, they are not extensional. For example, 'Any *A*-star would be a *B*-star' is false, but 'Any *A*-star would be an *A*-star' is true. Our putative social knowledge involving a synthetic predicate will normally contain at least one putative physical law. This is because it will normally contain at least one "definition" of the predicate. Definitions in this sense have the form of subjunctive generalizations. Let us define *nomic equivalence* as follows:

(2.3) $Fx \Leftrightarrow Gx$ iff $[(Fx \Rightarrow Gx) \ \& \ (Gx \Rightarrow Fx)]$.

Then a scientific definition of a synthetic predicate F which we might write somewhat sloppily as

(2.4)   *F*'s are things which are *G*

---

[5] In this symbolization, '$\Rightarrow$' is a variable-binding operator, binding the free variables in the antecedent and consequent.

really has the form $\ulcorner Fx \Leftrightarrow Gx \urcorner$. For example, the definition of 'electron' as 'the smallest negatively charged particle' amounts to affirming the two subjunctive generalizations:

> Any electron would be a negatively charged particle which was such that no other negatively charged particle had a smaller rest mass.

> Any negatively charged particle such that no other negatively charged particle had a smaller rest mass would be an electron.

Frequently, our putative social knowledge will contain several such definitions for a synthetic predicate, and perhaps a number of other putative physical laws as well.

We can now understand how a rational change in putative social knowledge can leave the extension of a predicate unchanged but be incorrect nonetheless. It follows from the definition of 'satisfaction' that a set of objects satisfies a subjunctive generalization $\ulcorner Fx \Rightarrow Gx \urcorner$ with respect to F (or with respect to G) iff it satisfies the corresponding material generalization $\ulcorner (\forall x)(Fx \supset Gx) \urcorner$. The extensions of F and G satisfy the material generalization $\ulcorner (\forall x)(Fx \supset Gx) \urcorner$ iff the material generalization is true. But the truth of the material generalization does not entail the truth of the subjunctive generalization. Thus the subjunctive generalization may be satisfied by the extensions of its predicates without being true. Consequently, if a change in the putative social knowledge involving a particular predicate amounts to the addition of a subjunctive generalization involving that predicate, that subjunctive generalization may be satisfied by the original extension of the predicate (i.e., the corresponding material generalization may be true of that extension) without that subjunctive generalization being true.

The observation that subjunctive generalizations are nonextensional amounts to the observation that they are not just about *sets* of objects—they are about *kinds* of objects. For example, A-stars and B-stars comprise two different kinds of objects despite the fact that the same objects happen to be objects of those kinds. It seems that our putative social knowledge does more than determine the extension of a synthetic predicate F—it determines what kind of things F's are. For want of better terminology, let us say that a synthetic predicate *connotes* a kind. We will consider shortly how this notion of connotation is to be defined, but in the meantime we can rely upon our intuitive understanding of the notion. Kinds can be regarded as satisfying subjunctive generalizations (and also

154

extensional statements) in a straightforward sense:

> (2.5) A kind *K satisfies* a statement relative to a certain predicate iff, if that predicate is taken to connote that kind, then the statement will be true.

Then the way in which our putative social knowledge determines what kind of things *F*'s are is that the kind connoted by a synthetic predicate is that kind which maximally satisfies the putative social knowledge involving that predicate. The extension of a synthetic predicate is determined only indirectly as the set of all objects of the kind connoted by the predicate.

In the preceding paragraph, we have made free use of the notion of a *kind of object*, but that is a problematic notion which requires considerable clarification. What are these kinds which are connoted by synthetic predicates? One kind of kind is a concept. We might call concepts *logical kinds* because, on the one hand, they pick out classes of objects (thus making it reasonable to call them 'kinds'), and on the other hand, they are individuated by their logical relationships to one another. You cannot have two nonequivalent definitions of the same logical kind. However, logical kinds do not behave in the manner required of the kinds connoted by synthetic predicates. The difficulty is that there will not normally be a *unique* logical kind which maximally satisfies the putative social knowledge involving a synthetic predicate. Whenever there are two nonequivalent definitions of a synthetic predicate, those definitions will yield distinct logical kinds which are nomically equivalent and hence both of which satisfy the putative social knowledge involving that predicate to precisely the same degree. We want a notion of 'kind' according to which two such definitions characterize the same kind. Let us call these *nomic kinds*. We want two definitions to connote the same nomic kind just in case the kinds defined by those definitions satisfy the same subjunctive generalizations. But that is equivalent to saying that the definitions are nomically equivalent. Thus we can say that two different concepts characterize the same nomic kind iff the concepts are nomically equivalent. It is tempting to simply *define* a nomic kind to be a set of nomically equivalent concepts, but let us hold that in abeyance temporarily. In the meantime, we at least have:

> (2.6) Two synthetic predicates (or the same synthetic predicate at two different times) connote the same nomic kind iff they are nomically equivalent.

VI. Synthetic Predicates

Now let us return to the question at hand, viz., when does a change in putative social knowledge result in a change in the sense of a synthetic predicate? A sufficient condition for meaning change is that the predicate comes to connote a different nomic kind, because then there will be subjunctive generalizations which change in truth value. This is illustrated by the example of the predicates '*A*-star' and '*B*-star'. Such a change can occur without a change in extension. I propose that this is also a necessary condition for change of sense. To suppose that it is not a necessary condition is to suppose that two synthetic predicates can connote the same nomic kind but still have different senses. That would be to suppose that the sense of a synthetic predicate is determined by some more narrowly individuated sort of kind. The only obvious candiate for that is logical kinds, i.e., concepts. But we have already seen that synthetic predicates do not express concepts. Thus the following is at least quite plausible:

(2.7)   Two synthetic predicates are synonymous iff they connote the same nomic kind.

Equivalently:

(2.8)   If *F* and *G* are synthetic predicates, *F* and *G* are synonymous iff they express nomically equivalent attributes.

2.4 *Nomic Kinds*

Having concluded that the meaning of a synthetic predicate is a function of the nomic kind which it connotes, it becomes imperative to understand nomic kinds. We have concluded that two descriptions describe the same nomic kind iff they are nomically equivalent. This implies that nomic kinds are individuated by the sets of nomically equivalent concepts describing them. Let us call the latter the *characteristic concepts* of the kind. The set of all characteristic concepts of a kind is its *characteristic set*. The characteristic set of a nomic kind contains information about what laws the kind satisfies, because subjunctive generalizations can always be translated into nomic equivalences: $\ulcorner Fx \Rightarrow Gx \urcorner$ is equivalent to $\ulcorner Fx \Leftrightarrow (Fx \mathbin{\&} Gx) \urcorner$, and $\ulcorner Gx \Rightarrow Fx \urcorner$ is equivalent to $\ulcorner Fx \Leftrightarrow (Fx \vee Gx) \urcorner$.[6]

It is tempting simply to identify nomic kinds with sets of nomically equivalent concepts. There is, however, reason for defining the

---

[6] For a discussion of the logical properties of '$\Rightarrow$', see Pollock [1976], 54–62.

notion a bit more broadly. I will take nomic kinds to be sets of concepts, but will not require that the concepts all be nomically equivalent. Let us say that a set of concepts is *actualized* iff all of its members are nomically equivalent to one another. The reason for countenancing nonactualized nomic kinds concerns deletable synthetic predicates, i.e., those which are such that the putative social knowledge involving them is irreducible. An example is 'Newtonian mass'. Relativistic rest mass and relativistic inertial mass satisfy the prerelativistic putative social knowledge for Newtonian mass equally, and hence that putative social knowledge does not select a unique extension for the predicate or a unique actualized nomic kind to be connoted by it. Nevertheless, it seems reasonable to say that *Newtonian mass* is a nomic kind,[7] and that there are true laws regarding it, e.g., 'The Newtonian mass of an object would be unaffected by its velocity'. The latter is a true counterlegal, as objects do not actually have Newtonian masses. That it is more than a convention to say that deletable synthetic predicates connote nomic kinds is evidenced by the fact that we need an account of when two deletable synthetic predicates are synonymous, and it appears that we want to reaffirm (2.7) in this connection, taking the predicates to be synonymous iff they connote the same nomic kind.

Our prerelativistic putative social knowledge regarding Newtonian mass contains or implies a number of logically nonequivalent definitions, but those definitions are not nomically equivalent either. If they were nomically equivalent, then that putative social knowledge would be satisfied. Nor is there any way to isolate a subset of these definitions which *are* nomically equivalent and regard them as characterizing the kind, because that would be to suppose that the putative social knowledge selects a unique actualized kind after all and hence is reducible. Consequently, we cannot regard the nomic kind *Newtonian mass* as consisting of a set of nomically equivalent concepts. We can still take it to be a set of concepts, but we cannot require those concepts to be nomically equivalent.

What concepts should we include in the characteristic set of the nomic kind connoted by a deletable synthetic predicate like 'Newtonian mass'? It seems that we should at least include all of

---

[7] *Newtonian mass* is a binary kind, relating objects and real numbers, the latter being the measure of the mass.

the definitions contained in or implied by the putative social knowledge involving that predicate. It might be supposed that those are the only definitions which should be included in the characteristic set. That supposition, however, would have the consequence that any change in our putative social knowledge which led to the adoption of a new definition would result in the predicate connoting a different nomic kind, and hence would result in a change of sense for the predicate. That consequence is almost as objectionable as the radical sense change theory. The putative social knowledge involving a deletable synthetic predicate characteristically undergoes considerable change over a period of time before the predicate is discovered to be deletable. We do not want to be forced to say that the predicate changes sense each time that happens. Given some of the definitions we have already got for an unactualized kind, we can be led rationally to others. A proposed new definition for the unactualized kind would be correct iff, were the kind actualized, that definition would be nomically equivalent to the other definitions we already have for the kind. Equivalently, the nomic kind connoted by a deletable synthetic predicate must satisfy the conditions:

$$(2.9) \quad (\forall \alpha)[(K \text{ is actualized} \rangle K \cup \{\alpha\} \text{ is actualized}) \supset \alpha \in K].$$

I suggest, then, that the nomic kind connoted by a deletable synthetic predicate F is the smallest nomic kind containing all of the definitions implied by the putative social knowledge involving F and closed under (2.9), viz.:

$$\bigcap \{X \mid X \text{ contains all of the definitions for } F \text{ implied by our putative social knowledge } \& \ (\forall \alpha)[(X \text{ is actualized} \rangle X \cup \{\alpha\} \text{ is actualized}) \supset \alpha \in X]\}.$$

For an actualized kind, (2.9) is equivalent to requiring that any concept equivalent to a member of the kind is itself a member of the kind. I suggest then that we take (2.9) to be the defining characteristic of nomic kinds:

(2.10) K is a *nomic kind* iff K is a set of concepts such that $(\forall \alpha)[(K \text{ is actualized} \rangle K \cup \{\alpha\} \text{ is actualized}) \supset \alpha \in K].$

The members of a kind are its *characteristic concepts*. They characterize what it is for an object to be of that kind:

158

(2.11) *x is of kind K* iff *K* is actualized and *x* exemplifies some (equivalently, all) concepts in *K*.

(2.12) The *extension* of a nomic kind is the set of all objects of that kind.

We can now give a precise definition for the relation of connoting. The idea behind the proposed definition is that our putative social knowledge determines the extension of a synthetic predicate only indirectly by first selecting the nomic kind connoted by it, and the nomic kind connoted by a particular synthetic predicate is the one which maximally satisfies the putative social knowledge involving that predicate. In order to make this precise, recall that an assignment of concepts to predicates satisfies a set Γ of statements iff the result of replacing the senses of the predicates by the corresponding concepts throughout Γ yields a set of truths. Let us say that an assignment of nomic kinds to predicates satisfies Γ iff every assignment of concepts which assigns characteristic concepts of those kinds to the corresponding predicates satisfies Γ. Let us revise our understanding of what it is to say that Γ is uniquely satisfied with respect to its synthetic predicates. Previously, we took this to mean that there was a unique assignment of extensions satisfying Γ, but now let us understand this to mean that there is a unique assignment of actualized nomic kinds satisfying Γ. With this revised understanding, we can leave definitions (1.3)–(1.7) unchanged, and replace (1.8) with:

(2.13) If *F* is a synthetic predicate involved in our putative social knowledge Γ, *F connotes* a nomic kind *K* iff either (a) *F* is deletable and *K* is the smallest nomic kind containing all of the definitions for *F* implied by Γ; or (b) *F* is not deletable and if Λ is the unique minimal weakening of Γ_ω sufficient to render it uniquely satisfied with respect to all synthetic predicates involved in it, then there is an assignment of actualized nomic kinds to the synthetic predicates involved in Λ which satisfies Λ relative to the set of those synthetic predicates and assigns *K* to *F*.

The extension of a synthetic predicate is then the extension of the nomic kind it connotes. This differs slightly in theory (but probably not in practice) from (1.8). If there were two coextensive actualized

159

nomic kinds which satisfied our putative social knowledge regarding F equally and to a greater extent than any other kind, principle (1.8) would result in their extension being the extension of F, but by our revised understanding of unique satisfaction, our putative social knowledge involving F would not be uniquely satisfied and hence our new account will make the extension of F empty.

The appeal to nomic kinds is supposed to illuminate meaning with regard to synthetic predicates. Principle (2.7) alleges that two synthetic predicates are synonymous iff they connote the same nomic kind. It may be questioned, however, whether all synthetic predicates do connote nomic kinds. Schwartz [1978] has recently raised doubts about Putnam's theory as it applies to artifacts, and his objections suggest similar objections to the present theory. The basic difficulty is that if we consider a synthetic predicate like 'pencil' or 'chair' whose exemplars are artifacts, there do not appear to be any true natural laws regarding them. How can such a predicate connote a nomic kind? However, there is no real difficulty here. Even for such predicates our putative social knowledge supplies us with at least one concept whose extension is the same as that of the predicate. This is a perceptual concept characterizing the exemplars in terms of their appearance.[8] Let α be such a concept. It may well be that α is not nomically equivalent to any other concept. But in that case, the unit set $\{\alpha\}$ is a nomic kind and it is connoted by the predicate.

3. Synthetic Attributes

Thus far we have argued that two synthetic predicates are synonymous iff they connote the same nomic kind. This tells us when two synthetic predicates have the same sense, but it does not tell us what that sense is. The sense of a synthetic predicate is a synthetic attribute. Attributes are characterized by their diagrams, the latter being constructed out of possible sent-concepts and acceptable received-concepts. Synthetic predicates connote nomic kinds, the

---

[8] This is not to say that, for example, it is necessary and sufficient for being a chair that an object have a certain appearance. Rather, appearance provides us with a *prima facie* reason for judging that something is or is not a chair, and the defeaters for these *prima facie* reasons are inductive. Concepts of this general sort were discussed at length in Pollock [1974]. There I took them to be expressed by the corresponding predicates, but if the predicates are synthetic, then they are only related to the perceptual concepts in the present more indirect way.

latter being sets of concepts, so it is natural to suggest that the possible sent-concepts and acceptable received-concepts for the synthetic attribute expressed by a synthetic predicate are just the characteristic concepts contained in the nomic kind. Regardless of whether the characteristic concepts are among the possible sent-concepts and acceptable received-concepts, it is clear that they cannot exhaust the set of possible sent- and acceptable received-concepts. The possible sent-concepts for *electron* are the concepts in terms of which the speaker can be thinking of electrons. It could happen that no one knows any of the characteristic concepts of *electron*. As we have seen, all of our putative social knowledge involving a synthetic predicate might be "a little wrong". It would still be possible for us to use the predicate correctly, so that cannot require us to be thinking of electrons in terms of the characteristic concepts.

To enable us to employ a synthetic predicate despite our not knowing any of the characteristic concepts of the kind connoted by the predicate, we might include among the possible sent-concepts and acceptable received-concepts any concept which our putative social knowledge alleges to characterize the nomic kind, whether it actually characterizes that kind or not. Let us call these *putative characteristic concepts*. However, putative characteristic concepts need not have the same extension as the predicate. If they don't and we attempt to use these putative characteristic concepts to construct the possible sent-propositions for statements involving synthetic predicates, the purported sent-propositions may not even have the same truth values as the statements for which they are supposed to be sent-propositions, and that is impossible. Thus we cannot include merely putative characteristic concepts among the possible sent-concepts and acceptable received-concepts.

Suppose F is a synthetic predicate, K the nomic kind connoted by F, and ξ the synthetic attribute expressed by F. The diagram of ξ must include more than just the characteristic concepts of K, but it can only include concepts which, in some sense, accurately depict K. What might these additional concepts be? One reasonable candidate might be the concept expressed by $\ulcorner$ is of the kind connoted by $F \urcorner$. This is precisely the way in which nonexperts often think of the exemplars of a synthetic predicate. For example, Putnam [1975] observes that he cannot distinguish between aluminum and molybdenum but that this does not prevent him from using the predicate 'aluminum' in saying things like 'The kettles in my kitchen are made of aluminum'. It seems that those of us who are not metallurgists generally think of aluminum as something like 'the stuff called "aluminum"'.

Putnam suggests that most of us can get away with thinking of aluminum as 'the stuff called "aluminum"' only because some of us are experts who can think of aluminum in terms of its actual characteristic concepts.[9] It is worth pointing out that that is wrong. The predicate 'aluminum' would work perfectly well if all of us thought of aluminum only as 'the stuff called "aluminum"'. This is because the kind connoted by the predicate is determined by our putative social knowledge. The existence of that putative social knowledge requires there to be experts who have views about aluminum, those views being incorporated into our putative social knowledge. But it does not require that those views be correct. And in holding those views, there is nothing to prevent the experts from thinking of aluminum as 'the stuff called "aluminum"' just as the rest of us do. The logical mechanism whereby the kind connoted by the predicate is determined by our putative social knowledge functions perfectly well without anyone thinking of aluminum in any way other than as 'the stuff called "aluminum"'.

The preceding observation might suggest that in using a synthetic predicate F, we are constrained to think of its exemplars metalinguistically as ⌜things of the kind connoted by F⌝. These would be the only possible sent- and received-concepts. However, imagine an undergraduate physics student who habitually confuses the predicates 'proton' and 'positron' with one another. On some occasion of his saying 'Positrons are much more massive than electrons', one of his friends might explain, 'He means "protons"'. In such a case, the student is presumably sending a concept appropriate for 'proton' rather than 'positron', but does not realize this. Clearly, that concept is not a metalinguistic one involving the predicate 'proton'. He is, instead, thinking of protons in terms of their putative characteristics but calling them 'positrons'. It may be that none of the putative characteristics he ascribes to protons are totally accurate, but this does not prevent his thinking about protons. I suggest that he is thinking of them as 'things of the kind reputed to have these characteristics'. This in turn suggests that *any* concept of the form ⌜is of the kind which is κ⌝, where κ uniquely describes K, will also be among the possible sent- and acceptable received-concepts. Let Υ be the binary concept of x *being of the*

---

[9] Of course, Putnam does not put it in quite this way.

kind y. My proposal is that if κ is any propositional designator designating K, then $(\Upsilon:x,\kappa)$ is a possible sent-concept and acceptable received-concept for ξ (the attribute expressed by F).

Next let us reconsider whether the characteristic concepts of K are among the possible sent- and received-concepts for ξ. That they are not can be seen by considering the attributes expressed by predicates connoting unactualized nomic kinds. The characteristic concepts for such a kind will not normally have the same extension as the kind (whose extension is empty), and hence cannot be possible sent-concepts for the attribute expressed by the predicate connoting that kind. It seems instead that speakers exploit the characteristic concepts to enable them to think of the kind under such descriptions as ⌜the familiar kind having the characteristic concept α⌝. As any of our synthetic predicates *could* turn out to express unactualized kinds, it seems that this must be the way characteristic concepts enter into possible sent-concepts in general. In other words, possible sent-concepts and acceptable received-concepts for ξ are those of the form $(\Upsilon:x,\kappa)$. κ can be any propositional designator designating K. Thus κ can make appeal to the characteristic concepts of K, or to the predicate conventionally used to connote K, or to anything else which is sufficient to pick out K. κ will frequently be a *de re* designator.

Given a nomic kind K, any two synthetic predicates connoting K are synonymous and hence express the same synthetic attribute. Thus there is a one-to-one correspondence between synthetic attributes and nomic kinds. Let us say that a synthetic attribute *connotes* the corresponding nomic kind. If K is nomic kind, let

(3.1) $\mathscr{D}_K = \{\kappa | \kappa$ is a propositional designator designating $K\}$.

If ξ_K is the synthetic attribute connoting K, we can take $\mathscr{D}_K$ to be the sole dynamic parameter for ξ_K, and can define ξ_K in terms of its diagram as follows:

(3.2) ξ_K is *the synthetic attribute connoting the nomic kind K* iff ξ_K is that attribute whose sole dynamic parameter is the set $\mathscr{D}_K$ and which is such that for each person S, the sets $\Sigma(S)$ and $\Omega(S)$ of possible sent-concepts and acceptable received-concepts for ξ_K for S given $\mathscr{D}_K$ are: $\Sigma(S) = \Omega(S) = \{(\Upsilon:x,\kappa) | \kappa \in \mathscr{D}_K$ & S can entertain $\kappa\}$.

The sense of a synthetic predicate is then that synthetic attribute connoting the nomic kind which the predicate connotes.

4. Meaning

We finally have all of the elements required for an account of the meaning of a synthetic predicate. The meaning of a synthetic predicate F is constituted by its A-intension, which is a function Δ_F from values of the pragmatic parameters of F to its sense. The simplest account that might be proposed for Δ_F would take the pragmatic parameters of F to be (1) the sent-concept, and (2) the set $\mathscr{D}_K$ where K is the nomic kind connoted by F, and would then define Δ_F as follows:

(4.1) $\Delta_F(\alpha, X) = \xi$ iff $(\exists K)[F$ connotes K & $X = \mathscr{D}_K$ & ξ is the synthetic attribute connoting K & $(\exists \kappa)(\kappa \in \mathscr{D}_K$ & $\alpha = (\Upsilon : x, \kappa))]$.

Principle (4.1) would make synthetic predicates nonindexical. A change in sense would require a change in meaning. But notice that there is an alternative account available according to which synthetic predicates are weakly indexical. This alternative account takes the pragmatic parameters of F to be: (1) the sent-concept; (2) the function $\{\langle K, \mathscr{D}_K \rangle \,|\, K$ is a nomic kind$\}$; and (3) the nomic kind connoted by F. Then Δ_F is defined as follows:

(4.2) $\Delta_F(\alpha, \mathscr{D}, K) = \xi$ iff $[F$ connotes K & ξ is the synthetic attribute connoting K & $(\exists \kappa)(\kappa \in \mathscr{D}(K)$ & $\alpha = (\Upsilon : x, \kappa))]$.

According to (4.2), although changes in the nomic kind connoted by F require a change in sense, they do not require a change in meaning. Rather, synthetic predicates are indexical, one of the pragmatic parameters being the kind connoted by the predicate.

In order to decide between (4.1) and (4.2), we must recall our discussion of indexicality in section eight of Chapter Three. The proposal there was that indexicality has to do with what the rules are in terms of which language users actually process the language. The correctness of (4.1) would require that language users process the use of a synthetic predicate in terms of a different rule whenever it comes to connote a different nomic kind. Principle (4.2), on the other hand, would require there to be a single rule in terms of which language users process the use of a synthetic predicate regardless of what nomic kind it connotes. Put in this way, it seems clear that (4.2) is the correct alternative. The nomic kind connoted by a synthetic predicate normally changes only because we are making mistakes in developing our putative social knowledge. As such, we are unaware that the change is occurring. It can hardly be required that, when the change occurs, we start processing the use of the predicate in terms of a different rule. Rather, we have a single rule which accommodates the possibility that the kind connoted may change.

Synthetic predicates are indexical, but their degree of indexicality is much less than that of a proper name. A speaker can use a proper name to refer to any of its bearers simply by varying his sent-designator. Analogously, the sent-concept is a pragmatic parameter for a synthetic predicate, but it plays a less significant role. In order to use a synthetic predicate to express its sense, a speaker must be sending an appropriate concept, but unlike proper names, he cannot vary the sense he expresses merely by varying the sent-concept. Synthetic predicates are only weakly indexical, whereas proper names are strongly indexical.

The endorsement of (4.2) has the consequence that the A-intensions of two different synthetic predicates F and G are precisely parallel. The only difference between them is that the definition of Δ_F mentions F where the definition of Δ_G mentions G. We might regard this difference as sufficient to make the meaning of F different from the meaning of G, but if we do then it will equally imply that no two synthetic predicates in different languages ever have the same meaning either. It would not be unreasonable to say that all synthetic predicates have the same meaning, although whether we say this or not appears to be a matter of how we are going to talk and not a substantive issue. Even if we say that all synthetic predicates have the same meaning, they will have different senses, and it is the senses that are of primary importance. Notice that we could equally say that all proper names have the same meaning.

VII
Nonsynthetic Predicates

1. Conceptual and Definitional Predicates

Having dealt with synthetic predicates, it may seem that it is now trivial to give an account of analytic predicates. The reason it was difficult to deal with synthetic predicates was that synthetic predicates do not express concepts. According to the traditional theory of predicates, all predicates should express concepts, but synthetic predicates do not accord with that theory. However, it may seem that analytic predicates are precisely the predicates that do fit the traditional theory, and hence little needs to be said about them.

In fact, the situation regarding analytic predicates is more complex than one might initially suspect. First, recall the definition of 'analytic predicate'. An analytic predicate is an elementary predicate expressing an analytic attribute, where that is an attribute which stands in sufficiently many logical relations to other attributes to characterize it completely, the latter relationships being in some sense constitutive of the analytic attribute. It has been argued that synthetic attributes do not express concepts, but it does not follow from this that analytic predicates *do* express concepts. The traditional theory of predicates was formulated by looking at a rather short list of paradigms like 'bachelor', 'sibling', 'red', etc. These are all analytic predicates. But in light of our discussion of synthetic predicates, it now takes little reflection to realize that the traditional theory does not work even for most analytic predicates. Consider everybody's favorite example—'bachelor'. It is generally agreed that the attribute of being a bachelor is logically equivalent to the attribute of being an unmarried man, and this equivalence would seem to be, in the appropriate sense, constitutive of the attribute of being a bachelor. Supposing that this is so, it follows that 'bachelor' is an analytic predicate. But does 'bachelor' express a concept? It is rather obvious that it does not. Both 'man' and 'married' are synthetic predicates, and as they do not express concepts, then presumably neither does the compound predicate 'unmarried man'. But then 'bachelor' does not express a concept. Similar remarks apply to 'sibling', and most of the other traditional examples of analytic predicates.

Apparently we must distinguish between two kinds of analytic predicates—those which express concepts, and those which do not. What are the latter like? They appear to be predicates like 'bachelor' or 'sibling' expressing attributes that are involved in logical relationships which actually constitute definitions of those attributes. If one or more of the attributes in the definiens is synthetic, then the defined attribute will not be conceptual. More generally, if the definition of an attribute $\mathscr{A}$ proceeds in part in terms of any statemental constitutent which is not also a propositional constituent (e.g., an hereditary designator, or a personal statemental designator), then $\mathscr{A}$ will not be a concept. Let us define:

(1.1)   An attribute $\mathscr{A}$ is *definitional* iff there are logical relationships involving $\mathscr{A}$ and constitutive of $\mathscr{A}$ which jointly comprise a definition of $\mathscr{A}$ (a specification of necessary and sufficient conditions for something to exemplify $\mathscr{A}$) in terms, in part, of at least one statemental constituent which is not a propositional constituent.

(1.2)   A predicate is *conceptual* (in one of its senses) iff it expresses a concept.

(1.3)   A predicate is *definitional* (in one of its senses) iff it expresses a definitional attribute.

My conjecture is that all nonsynthetic predicates are either conceptual or definitional. If this conjecture is correct, it is relatively easy to give an account of nonsynthetic predicates, although we must handle conceptual predicates and definitional predicates separately.

Nonsynthetic predicates need not be analytic. Analytic predicates are, by definition, elementary, i.e., they are not strongly indexical. However, the restriction to elementary predicates now seems arbitrary. Elementary and nonelementary definitional predicates appear to work in essentially the same way, the difference lying only in what elements enter into the definition; and conceptual predicates appear to be uniformly elementary. Thus rather than confining our attention to elementary predicates in this chapter, we will consider nonsynthetic predicates in general.

2. Definitional Predicates

Definitional predicates are predicates expressing definitional attributes. Definitional attributes are attributes definable in terms, in part, of statemental constituents which are not propositional constituents. The definition of a definitional attribute is supposed to be, in some as yet unexplained sense, constitutive of it. We can now make this precise. Consider the attribute $\mathscr{IV}$ of *being invisible*. This is a definitional attribute, because it is definable as the negation of the synthetic attribute $\mathscr{V}$ of *being visible*. The sense in which $\mathscr{IV}$ is so definable, and the sense in which that definition is constitutive of $\mathscr{IV}$ but the converse definition of $\mathscr{V}$ (as the negation of $\mathscr{IV}$) is not constitutive of $\mathscr{V}$, can be made clear by considering the diagrams of these attributes. Since $\mathscr{V}$ is a synthetic attribute, its diagram is as described in Chapter Six. Logical relationships between attributes are to be explained in terms of logical relationships between their possible sent- and acceptable-received concepts. The force of saying that $\mathscr{IV}$ is the negation of $\mathscr{V}$ is that the possible sent-concepts for $\mathscr{IV}$ are the negations of the possible sent-concepts for $\mathscr{V}$ and the acceptable received-concepts for $\mathscr{IV}$ are the negations of the acceptable received-concepts for $\mathscr{V}$. The converse is not true. The possible sent-concepts and acceptable received-concepts for $\mathscr{V}$ are not negations at all—they are all of the form $(\Upsilon:x,\kappa)$. The latter are, of course, *equivalent* to negations of possible sent- and acceptable received-concepts for $\mathscr{IV}$, but that is a different matter altogether.

The preceding account can be generalized to deal with all definitional attributes. For example, the attribute $\mathscr{B}$ of *being a bachelor* is the conjunction of the attribute $\mathscr{M}$ of *being a man* and the negation of the attribute $\mathscr{R}$ of *being married*, i.e., $(\mathscr{B}:x) = [\neg(\mathscr{R}:x) \wedge (\mathscr{M}:x)]$. This means that β is a possible sent-concept (or acceptable received-concept) for $\mathscr{B}$ iff there are possible sent-concepts (or acceptable received-concepts) ρ and μ for $\mathscr{R}$ and $\mathscr{M}$ respectively such that $(\beta:x) = [\neg(\rho:x) \wedge (\mu:x)]$. Similarly, the attribute $\mathscr{S}_{\mathscr{R}}$ of *being a sister of Robert* is definable in terms of the two-place attribute $\mathscr{S}$ of *being a sister of* and the hereditary designator ∂ expressed by 'Robert': $(\mathscr{S}_{\mathscr{R}}:x) = (\mathscr{S}:x,\partial)$. The expressions '$[\neg(-:x) \wedge (-:x)]$' and '$(-:x,-)$' can be regarded as expressing *definition schemes*. When we replace the dashes by appropriate propositional constituents, these give us definitions of concepts, and when we replace the dashes by appropriate statemental constituents, they give us definitions of attributes. Definitional attributes are now those which are definable in the preceding manner. That is:

(2.1) $\mathscr{A}$ is a *definitional attribute* iff there are statemental constituents $\mathscr{B}_1, \ldots, \mathscr{B}_n$ at least one of which is not a propositional constituent and there is a definitional scheme $\mathscr{D}$ such that (1) the dynamic parameters of $\mathscr{A}$ consist of all the dynamic parameters of $\mathscr{B}_1, \ldots, \mathscr{B}_n$ taken together, and (2) for each possible set of values of those parameters, the possible sent-concepts and acceptable received-concepts for $\mathscr{A}$ result from applying $\mathscr{D}$ to the possible sent-objects and acceptable received-objects for $\mathscr{B}_1, \ldots, \mathscr{B}_n$.

Principle (2.1) makes precise the sense in which the definition of a definitional attribute is constitutive of it. It is constitutive of it by virtue of providing a description of its diagram. I propose that we adopt (2.1) as our official definition of 'definitional attribute', taking our earlier (1.1) as merely a heuristic explanation of the concept of a definitional attribute. I propose that we also replace our earlier vague definition of 'analytic attribute' by the following precise definition:

(2.2)   An attribute is *analytic* iff it is either a concept or a definitional attribute.

Having drawn a precise distinction between conceptual predicates, synthetic predicates, and definitional predicates, we might now set about sorting predicates into these three categories. In many cases, that proves surprisingly difficult to do. The most obvious examples of definitional predicates tend to be syntactically complex (including among the latter both multi-word predicates and predicates constructed with the help of prefixes and suffixes). Complex predicates are typically (but not invariably) definitional. They carry their definitions with them, so there is no difficulty in supposing that when people use them they send and receive concepts constructed in accordance with those definitions.

It is much more difficult to find convincing examples of syntactically simple definitional predicates, and difficulties arise even in connection with the most plausible of these examples. One frequent difficulty is that we are often unable to distinguish between several related but distinct definitions of a seemingly definitional predicate and say which is the correct definition. For example, philosophers are fond of defining 'sibling' as 'brother or sister', but my dictionary gives the definition 'offspring of the same parents'. Which definition gives the meaning of 'sibling'? One might wonder why we should have to choose between these two definitions. After all, they are equivalent aren't they? Surprisingly, they are not equivalent. From the fact that x is an offspring of the same parents as y we cannot conclude that x is a brother or sister of y without first knowing that all offspring are either male or female. The latter, although presumably true, is not necessarily true. Furthermore, even if these definitions were equivalent, they are still distinct definitions which would yield distinct attributes having distinct diagrams. The mere logical equivalence of two definitions does not guarantee that they provide the same sense for a definitional predicate.

It is hard to know what to do with this difficulty, but I suspect that its solution is that the predicates involved are simply ambiguous. If the connection between two definitions is sufficiently intimate, then there is little reason to choose between them, and accordingly there will be little to lead our linguistic conventions to develop in such a way as to select one of these definitions rather than the other as providing the meaning of the predicate. It is probable that mere convention will never select an absolutely unique linguistic institution as the linguistic institution of a particular linguistic community. Convention will always leave some features of a linguistic institution underdetermined. Those will be the features for which there is no strong motivation for the conventions to develop one way rather than a slightly different way. This seems to be what is happening in connection with the two definitions of 'sibling'.

Notice that there are two different ways in which words can be ambiguous. A word like 'bank' can be said to be *sharply ambiguous* because it is well determined that we are operating within a linguistic institution which contains two different conflicting meaning rules for this word. The word 'sibling', on the other hand, is *fuzzily ambiguous* in the sense that the meaning rules governing it are simply not well determined and could be made more precise in either of two ways.

A difficulty which is closely related to the previous one is that there are groups of predicates which are to a certain extent interdefinable. Given such a group, we can choose different members as primitive (taking them to be synthetic) and define the others in terms of them. Consider, for example, predicates ascribing quantities of force and mass. We could regard 'mass' as a synthetic predicate and define 'force' as 'mass times acceleration'; or we could regard 'force' as a synthetic predicate and define 'mass' as 'force divided by acceleration'. Similarly, we could define 'centimeter' in terms of 'meter', or we could define 'meter' in terms of 'centimeter'. Which way should the definitions go? These examples are particularly problematic because they appear to undermine the analytic-predicate/synthetic-predicate distinction itself. For each of these pairs of predicates, there seems to be no way to determine which member is analytic and which is synthetic.

A possible response to this difficulty would be to claim once more than the predicates involved are fuzzily ambiguous, being analytic on one meaning and synthetic on the other. This is probably correct for a few pairs, like 'meter' and 'centimeter' (whose connection is enshrined in the syntax). My suspicion, however, is that most of these pairs of predicates, and in fact most putatively definitional predicates, are not really definitional at all. The relations between predicates like 'force' and 'mass' which appear at first to be analytic are probably just very well-established generalizations. If this is correct, we should be able to describe reasonable scenarios in which we would rationally reject these generalizations. It seems that this can generally be done. For example, the relations between comparable units of measure are customarily supposed to be analytic. Consider angstroms and meters. One angstrom is 10^{-10} meters. Angstroms are used in measuring atomic distances. Suppose that a natural catastrophe resulted in the death of everyone who knew the precise conversion between angstroms and meters and resulted in the destruction of all records in which that conversion was contained. Nevertheless, if certain standard atomic distances were known in angstroms, scientists could continue to use 'angstrom' by comparing other distances with these known distances, and could rediscover the conversion between angstroms and meters by measuring these standard distances in meters. Due to inaccuracies in the measuring process, however, they might end up with a slightly different conversion, e.g., 9.978×10^{-11} meters. (They might suspect from this that an angstrom was originally defined to be 10^{-10} meters, but they could not be sure; it might instead have been defined in terms of some standard atomic distance coincidentally close to 10^{-10} meter.) Thus if they knew enough else, scientists could use 'angstrom' without knowing the conversion between angstroms and meters, and they could empirically confirm a generalization incompatible with the "standard" conversion. Clearly, their sent- and received-concepts for 'angstrom' are not constructed out of the standard definition of 'angstrom' in terms of 'meter'. It seems likely that 'angstrom' and 'meter' are just two synthetic predicates which are such that our putative social knowledge contains empirical definitions of each in terms of the other.

With a bit of imagination, similar scenarios can be constructed for most putatively definitional predicates, the conclusion being that they are actually synthetic. But there are a few cases in which such scenarios do not seem at all plausible. The predicate 'bachelor' is one such case, and 'sibling' is another. In the construction of a similar scenario for these predicates, I find myself repeatedly protesting that the development of the scenario involves an illicit change of meaning. It seems to me that the reason I react differently to a scenario for 'bachelor' than I did to a scenario for 'angstrom' is that my sent-concept for 'bachelor' really is constructed out of the definition 'unmarried man', but my sent-concept for 'angstrom' is not similarly constructed out of a definition of angstroms in terms of meters. The predicate 'angstrom' is like 'aluminum' in that one can use it with perfect propriety without being able to define it. Scientific neophytes use it all the time, and I doubt that many of them could characterize angstroms beyond saying that an angstrom is a unit of atomic distance. It seems, on the other hand, that one is not using 'bachelor' correctly if one is not thinking of bachelors in terms of the definition 'unmarried man'. I think it must be concluded that 'bachelor' is definitional, but 'angstrom' and almost any other "interesting" putatively definitional predicate is really synthetic. There are very few syntactically simple definitional predicates.

The reason there are so few syntactically simple definitional predicates seems to be roughly that given by Putnam [1962a]. It is likely that many predicates start life as definitional predicates, but after a while they come naturally to be treated as synthetic predicates (which is to say that they *become* synthetic predicates). In the beginning, a predicate is introduced by a definition, and at that point our sent-concept must be constructed in accordance with the definition. However, if a great deal is known involving the predicate, keeping track of the definition involves a certain amount of mental effort. For most purposes, a speaker need not know the definition—

all he must know is that certain statements involving the predicate are true. Whether they are analytic or not is unimportant. Thus speakers can be forgiven for losing track of definitions. But once they have done so, they are using the predicate as a synthetic predicate; and once enough speakers do this, that becomes the conventional way of using the predicate. It is only when people know very little of importance involving the predicate that it is easy to keep track of the definition. Consequently, that is the only time speakers are apt to use it consistently as a definitional predicate. This is the current situation with regard to 'bachelor'. Thus 'bachelor' and a few other syntactically simple predicates are definitional, but they constitute an extreme minority. Once a nonconceptual predicate becomes involved in interesting beliefs, it becomes synthetic. If there are to be any interesting analytic predicates, they must be conceptual.

3. Conceptual Predicates

Little needs to be said about conceptual predicates. These are predicates whose senses are concepts. About the only interesting question to ask about conceptual predicates is whether there are any and if so which predicates they are. As far as I can see, there is no reason why there would have to be any conceptual predicates. We cannot do without concepts, because they are what nonconceptual attributes are constructed out of, but language could function all right without there being any predicates which express concepts. Among the syntactically simple predicates, very few are conceptual, the only ones tending to be basic ones like 'red' which play an important epistemological or logical role in our thought. Of course, given a few syntactically simple conceptual predicates, we can generate infinitely many syntactically complex conceptual predicates by combining the simple ones in various ways.

It is noteworthy that even predicates like 'red' do not seem to be unequivocally conceptual. Rather, they tend to be fuzzily ambiguous, being conceptual on one of their meanings and synthetic on the other. It is the synthetic use of 'red' which makes it possible for a blind person to use this predicate correctly. Presumably a blind person cannot grasp the concept of being red, and so cannot use the predicate with its conceptual meaning. But there is no more obstacle to his using the predicate with its synthetic meaning than there is to most of us using the predicate 'aluminum' without being able to give a scientifically satisfactory characterization of aluminum. This sort of fuzzy ambiguity is presumably also responsible for the possibility of the growing divergence between the "phenomenal" use of a predicate like 'hot' and the "scientific" use. Such a divergence eventually results in a sharp ambiguity wherein the predicate has two well-determined meanings, one conceptual and the other synthetic.

VIII
The Alethic Modalities

1. Propositional Modalities

The traditional *de dicto* alethic modalities include *necessary truth*, *a priori truth*, and *analyticity*. The first two have generally been regarded as propositional modalities and the third as a sentence modality. We now have a third kind of entity intermediate between sentences and propositions—statements. We can also define alethic modalities for statements. The purpose of this chapter will be to explore various features of these alethic modalities in the light of our preceding theory of language and thought.

We can reasonably take the propositional modalities to be the fundamental ones, with the statemental and sentential modalities being defined in terms of them. Where ψ is a proposition, let us abbreviate $\ulcorner \psi$ is necessarily true$\urcorner$ as $\ulcorner Nec(\psi) \urcorner$, and $\ulcorner \psi$ is *a priori* true$\urcorner$ as $\ulcorner A(\psi) \urcorner$. We can define possibility and implication and equivalence relations in terms of these modalities:

(1.1) $Poss(\psi)$ iff $\sim Nec(\neg \psi)$;

(1.2) $\psi \rightarrow \chi$ (ψ *entails* χ) iff $Nec(\psi \Rightarrow \chi)$;

(1.3) $\psi \leftrightarrow \chi$ (ψ is *logically equivalent* to χ) iff $Nec(\psi \Leftrightarrow \chi)$;

(1.4) ψ *A-implies* χ iff $A(\psi \Rightarrow \chi)$;

(1.5) ψ is *A-equivalent* to χ iff $A(\psi \Leftrightarrow \chi)$.

Necessity and possibility are *properties* of propositions. But it is also customary to talk about necessity and possibility as modal operators. There are *modal propositions* which contain these modal operators as part of their structure, e.g., the proposition that it is necessary that $2 + 2 = 4$. It is intriguing to ask what the relationship is between modal operators and modal properties. I suggest that their relationship turns upon there being a special way of thinking about propositions. For example, consider the proposition that $2 + 2 = 4$. We can *employ* the proposition in believing it. We can also think *about* the proposition, believing that it is true. The latter consists of believing a proposition containing a propositional designator designating that proposition. One way of thinking about a proposition is in terms of some contingent description like 'John's favorite proposition', but that is clearly not the way we normally think of propositions in judging them to be true. It is possible to think of a proposition in a direct fashion which does not involve thinking of it under a description which designates it only contingently. A proposition proposes that something is the case, and we can think of it directly in terms of what it proposes. This is to think of it in terms of its content. Thinking of it in this way, we can go on to affirm it, deny it, judge it to be necessary, etc. If we could not think of propositions in terms of their content, it would be a mystery how we could ever make judgments *about* them. How could we ever judge that a proposition is true or necessary if we could not think of it in terms of its content?

It must be admitted that there is a sense in which we can think of a proposition "directly" in terms of its content. In order to construct a suitable propositional object for the beliefs we have when we think of propositions in this way, we must countenance the existence of a class of special propositional designators $\langle \psi \rangle$ which are necessarily such that they designate specific propositions ψ. To think of ψ in terms of $\langle \psi \rangle$ is to think of ψ in terms of its content. That, in turn, is to think of ψ in terms of its structure. For example, we think of a conjunction *as* a conjunction, a disjunction *as* a disjunction, etc. In employing $\langle \psi \rangle$ we think of ψ in terms of a description which involves its being constructed in a certain way out of concepts, logical operators, propositional designators, etc. We must also be thinking of these logical items directly in terms of their content rather than in terms of contingent descriptions of them. This requires that for each propositional constituent α, there is a propositional designator $\langle \alpha \rangle$ which designates α necessarily, and there is a privileged way of thinking of α which involves employing $\langle \alpha \rangle$. Let us call the propositional designators $\langle \psi \rangle$ and $\langle \alpha \rangle$ *logical designators*.

The recognition of logical designators suggests a way of introducing modal operators in terms of modal properties. Let $\mathscr{N}$ be the concept of *being necessarily true*. The modal operator can then be defined as follows:

(1.6) $\Box\psi = (\mathcal{N}:\langle\psi\rangle)$.

(1.7) $\Diamond\psi = \neg\Box\neg\psi$.

According to (1.6), $\Box\psi$ is a proposition which is about ψ, because it contains a propositional designator designating ψ, but it is about ψ in a very special way. To think of ψ in terms of the designator $\langle\psi\rangle$ is to think of ψ in terms of its content. Thus there is a reasonable sense in which $\Box\psi$ is also about whatever ψ is about. It is important to recognize that $\Box$ is an operator, not a concept, because $\Box$ is appended to the proposition ψ itself to form the proposition $\Box\psi$. $\Box$ is not appended to a designator designating ψ. It is only possible to construct such an operator, however, because there are the privileged designators $\langle\psi\rangle$.

2. *De Re* Necessity

The necessary truth of a proposition is called '*de dicto* necessity'. To be distinguished from this is *de re necessity* which is a relation between an object and either a concept or an attribute. For example, it may be asserted that two is necessarily the square root of four, that Michael is necessarily not a number, that this table is necessarily not made of ice, or that Queen Elizabeth necessarily has the parents she does.[1] Where α is a concept, let us abbreviate $\ulcorner x$ is necessarily such that it exemplifies $\alpha\urcorner$ as $\ulcorner\text{Nec}[x,\alpha]\urcorner$. We can define:

(2.1) $\text{Poss}[x,\alpha]$ iff $\sim\text{Nec}[x,\neg\alpha]$.

Until recently, most philosophers viewed *de dicto* necessity as philosophically respectable, but viewed *de re* necessity with considerable suspicion. That has changed in the last fifteen years. Although I know of no compelling arguments that have been given in its defense, the prevailing view is now that *de re* necessity is legitimate although philosophically puzzling.

We can define concepts and operators for *de re* necessity in a manner analogous to our treatment of *de dicto* necessity. Let $\mathcal{N}_{dr}$

---

[1] The latter two examples are from Kripke [1972].

be the concept expressed by $\ulcorner Nec[x,y] \urcorner$. Then we can define $\square \alpha$ to be the concept:

(2.2) $\quad \square \alpha = (\mathcal{N}_{dr} : x, \langle \alpha \rangle)$;

(2.3) $\quad \diamondsuit \alpha = \neg \square \neg \alpha$.

(2.2) has the result that x exemplifies $\square \alpha$ iff $Nec[x,\alpha]$.

3. Statemental Modalities

The recent literature contains several kinds of objections to the traditional theory of necessary truth, but most of them involve confusing propositions and statements. One sort of objection concerns the difficulty in finding *a priori* truths involving synthetic predicates.[2] We have seen that that pertains to statements rather than propositions, and we discussed it fully in Chapter Six. Another sort of difficulty has been urged by Kripke [1972] and Putnam [1975]. They maintain in connection with "natural kinds" that many truths which would traditionally have been regarded as only physically necessary are actually necessary "in the strictest possible sense".[3] Although they do not quite commit themselves to this, they at least suggest that no distinction can be drawn between physical necessity and logical necessity with regard to natural kinds. However, natural kind terms are synthetic predicates and so statements involving them are not propositions. Thus, once again, this does not pertain directly to the propositional modalities. In order to resolve it we must ask in what sense statements can be necessary.

Given our propositional modalities of necessity and *a prioricity*, we can define analogous statemental modalities in an obvious manner in terms of the possible sent-propositions for a statement:

(3.1) If ϕ is a statement, $NI(\phi)$ (ϕ is *internally necessary*) iff ϕ is necessarily such that for all possible values of the dynamic parameters, all possible sent-propositions for ϕ are necessarily true.[4]

---

[2] In this connection, see Donnellan [1962] and Putnam [1962] and [1962a].

[3] Kripke [1972], pg. 320.

[4] It should be observed that there is nothing suspicious or potentially circular about our use of $\ulcorner x$ is necessarily such that it is $F \urcorner$ in this definition or in similar definitions in this section and the next. We only use it in cases in which F expresses a concept, in which case $\ulcorner x$ is necessarily such that it is $F \urcorner$ is just a more idiomatic way of saying $\ulcorner Nec[x,\alpha] \urcorner$ where α is the concept expressed by F.

(3.2)   If ϕ is a statement, $A(\phi)$ (ϕ is *a priori true*) iff ϕ is necessarily such that for all possible values of the dynamic parameters, all possible sent-propositions for ϕ are true *a priori*.

We can define corresponding implication and equivalence relations as we did for the propositional modalities.

There is another way of defining a notion of necessity for statements, viz., *de re* necessary truth:

(3.3)   If ϕ is a statement, $Nec(\phi)$ (ϕ is *externally necessary*) iff ϕ is necessarily such that it is true.

One might reasonably expect that our two notions of statemental necessity coincide. It is extremely interesting, then, that they do not. This is related to the suggestion of Kripke and Putnam that physical necessity and logical necessity coincide for natural kinds. To make precise what is actually true in this connection, we need the notion of a law statement. Recall from Chapter Six that '$\Rightarrow$' is the logical connective involved in law statements (i.e., strong subjunctive generalizations). Let us use the same symbol for the logical operator which is a constituent of propositions. Thus $(\alpha \Rightarrow \beta)$ is the proposition that any α would be a β. Given attributes A and B, we can define the subjunctive generalization statement $(A \Rightarrow B)$ to be the statement whose sent- and received-propositions have the form $(\alpha \Rightarrow \beta)$ where α and β are sent- and received-concepts for A and B. The following theorem is then a consequence of our account of synthetic attributes in Chapter Six:

(3.4)   If A and B are distinct synthetic attributes and $(A \Rightarrow B)$ is true, then $(\wedge x)[(A:x) \Rightarrow (B:x)]$ is externally necessary but not internally necessary.

This theorem is established as follows. As A and B are synthetic attributes, they express some nomic kinds K and K^* respectively. Let us define:

(3.5) $K \Rightarrow K^*$ iff $(\forall \alpha)(\forall \beta)[(\alpha \in K \mathbin{\&} \beta \in K^*) \supset ((\alpha:x) \wedge (\beta:x)) \in K]$.

It then follows from the definition of 'nomic kind' that

(3.6) $(A \Rightarrow B)$ is true iff $K \Rightarrow K^*$.

The set of characteristic concepts of a nomic kind is an essential feature of that kind, so

(3.7) $K \Rightarrow K^* \supset \square(K \Rightarrow K^*)$.

Trivially:

(3.8) $\Box[K \Rightarrow K^* \supset (\forall x)(x \text{ is of kind } K \supset x \text{ is of kind } K^*)]$.

If we abbreviate $\ulcorner x$ exemplifies $A\urcorner$ as $\ulcorner A^{\ulcorner}x\urcorner$, our account of the extension of a synthetic attribute gives us:

(3.9) $\Box(\forall x)(A^{\ulcorner}x \equiv x \text{ is of kind } K)\&\Box(\forall x)(B^{\ulcorner}x \equiv x \text{ is of kind } K^*)$.

From (3.6)–(3.9) we get:

(3.10)   If $(A \Rightarrow B)$ is true, then $\Box(\forall x)(A^{\ulcorner}x \supset B^{\ulcorner}x)$.

But the consequent of (3.10) is equivalent to saying that

$$(\wedge x)[(A:x) \Rightarrow (B:x)]$$

is necessarily such that it is true. Thus the material generalization corresponding to a true subjunctive generalization involving synthetic attributes is externally necessary. That material generalization is not internally necessary, however. The possible sent-propositions for $(\wedge x)[(A:x) \Rightarrow (B:x)]$ have the form

(3.11) $(\wedge x)[(\Upsilon:x,\kappa) \Rightarrow (\Upsilon:x,\kappa^*)]$

where κ and κ^* are propositional designators designating K and K^* respectively. κ and κ^* may designate K and K^* only contingently. For example, κ might be a definite description of the form $\ulcorner$the nomic kind generally considered to be such that ...$\urcorner$. It is a contingent fact what nomic kind satisfies such a description. Accordingly (3.11) will normally be a contingent proposition.

Principle (3.4) partially vindicates the intuitions of Kripke and Putnam. If $(A \Rightarrow B)$ is true, then $(\wedge x)[(A:x) \Rightarrow (B:x)]$ is necessarily such that it is true, and this is (*de re*) necessity "in the strictest possible sense". It is not, however, the strictest possible statemental modality. Internal necessity is stricter than external necessity, in the sense that an internally necessary statement must also be externally necessary, but not vice versa. Nevertheless, for many purposes external necessity is the more interesting of the two modalities.

A second source of external necessities that are not internally necessary lies in certain kinds of identity statements. There is a distinction between the statements $(x \approx y:\partial,\partial)$ and $(x \approx x:\partial)$. $(\delta_1 \approx \delta_2)$ is a possible sent-proposition for $(x \approx y:\partial,\partial)$ whenever δ_1 and δ_2 are distinct possible sent-designators for ∂, but $(\delta_1 \approx \delta_2)$ is a possible sent-proposition for $(x \approx x:\partial)$ only when δ_1 and δ_2 are the *same* possible sent-designator for ∂. It follows from this that if ∂ is either a hereditary designator or an A-hereditary designator and $\mathfrak{E}$ is the concept of *existing*, $[(\mathfrak{E}:\partial) \Rightarrow (x \approx x:\partial)]$ is internally necessary, but $[(\mathfrak{E}:\partial) \Rightarrow (x \approx y:\partial,\partial)]$ is not. However, the latter statement is externally necessary, i.e., it is necessarily such that it is true. This can be illustrated by the case of a person who knows of Aristotle both as a philosopher and as a biologist, but thinks they were different individuals. Let us suppose that although he does not know it, his use of 'Aristotle' in both cases is hereditarily parasitic on the use of the name by a single person, and hence he is using the name with the same sense in referring either to the biologist or the philosopher. Thinking exclusively of the philosopher (i.e., sending a single designator) he may say 'If Aristotle existed, then Aristotle was Aristotle', expressing the internally necessary and *a priori* statement $[(\mathfrak{E}:\partial) \Rightarrow (x \approx x:\partial)]$. Using the name 'Aristotle' to send two different designators, one for the putative biologist and one for the putative philosopher, he may say 'If Aristotle existed, then Aristotle was Aristotle' and express the statement $[(\mathfrak{E}:\partial) \Rightarrow (x \approx y:\partial,\partial)]$, which is not *a priori* and which he takes to be false but which is in fact externally necessary.

Having distinguished between *de dicto* internal and external necessity for statements, we can make a similar distinction for *de re* necessity involving attributes. Taking *de re* necessity involving concepts as basic, we can define *de re* internal and external necessity as follows:

(3.12) $\mathrm{Nec}_I[x,A]$ iff x and A are necessarily such that if α is any possible sent-concept for A then $\mathrm{Nec}[x,\alpha]$.

(3.13) $\mathrm{Nec}_E[x,A]$ iff x and A are necessarily such that x exemplifies A.

The same considerations that led to the existence of externally necessary statements that are not internally necessary lead to there being attributes A such that some objects are externally necessarily such that they are A without being internally necessarily such that they are A. For example, suppose B and C are synthetic attributes such that $(\wedge x)[(B:x) \Rightarrow (C:x)]$ is externally necessary without being internally necessary. Then for any object y, $\mathrm{Nec}_E[\, y, ((B:x) \Rightarrow (C:x))]$ but $\sim \mathrm{Nec}_I[\, y, ((B:x) \Rightarrow (C:x))]$.

In discussing the propositional modalities, we introduced *de dicto* necessity both as a property of propositions and as a modal operator transforming propositions into modal propositions. Thus far we have discussed *de dicto* necessity for statements only as a property of statements, but we can define a modal operator for statements too by utilizing our propositional modal operator. If the sense of a sentence P is the statement ϕ, then $\Box\phi$ is the statement one would make by saying ⌜It is necessary that P⌝. It seems clear that, in saying the latter, one's sent-proposition is of the form $\Box\psi$ where ψ is some possible sent-proposition for ϕ. This indicates that $\Box\phi$ can be described in terms of its diagram as follows:

(3.14) If ϕ is a statement, then $\Box\phi$ is that statement which has the same dynamic parameters as ϕ and whose possible sent- and acceptable received-propositions are just those of the form $\Box\psi$ where ψ is a possible sent- or acceptable received-proposition for ϕ.

A necessary constraint on the diagram of a statement is that, under any given circumstances (which include a specification of the values of the dynamic parameters), all of the possible sent- and acceptable received-propositions for that statement have the same truth value. It follows from (3.14) that if there is to be such a statement as $\Box\phi$, under any given circumstances either all of the possible sent- and acceptable received-propositions for ϕ are necessary or they are all contingent. Otherwise, not all of the possible sent-propositions and acceptable received-propositions for $\Box\phi$ will have the same truth value. We have already had occasion to remark (in Chapter One) that this seems like a plausible restriction on statements. It would be extremely peculiar if one person could accept a statement by believing a contingent proposition while another person accepted the same statement by believing a necessary proposition. My hypothesis is that this provides a necessary constraint on the diagrams of statements:

(3.15) Necessarily, if ϕ is a statement and ψ and θ are possible sent- or acceptable received-propositions for ϕ relative to some specific values of the dynamic parameters, then $(\mathrm{Nec}(\psi) \equiv \mathrm{Nec}(\theta))$.

Perhaps the best argument for this is that it is required in order for there to be modal statements, and hence, as we will see in the next section, it is required in order for modal sentences to make sense. Modal sentences clearly do make sense, so (3.15) must be correct.

There is an intimate connection between the *de dicto* statemental modal operator $\square$ and internal necessity:

(3.16)   If ϕ is a statement, $\square\phi$ is true iff $NI(\phi)$.

It is interesting that there is no obvious way to introduce a statemental modal operator bearing a similar relationship to external necessity. In order for there to be an operator $\boxplus$ with the characteristic that $\boxplus\phi$ is true iff $\text{Nec}(\phi)$, it would have to be possible to construct $\boxplus\phi$ in terms of its diagram, but there is no apparent way to construct an appropriate diagram for such a putative statement. The fact that modal operators must express internal necessity rather than external necessity is perhaps the main reason internal necessity is of interest. Furthermore, modal sentences express modal statements, so internal necessity is intimately connected with our ordinary use of the adverb 'necessarily'. This connection will be discussed in the next section.

Turning to *de re* necessity, a sentence like 'Michael is necessarily not a number' expresses a modal statement of the form $(\square A:\partial)$ in which $\square$ occurs as a *de re* modal operator transforming attributes into modal attributes. In light of (3.14), the description of $\square A$ in terms of its diagram seems obvious:

(3.17)   If A is an attribute, then $\square A$ is that attribute which has the same dynamic parameters as A and whose possible sent- and acceptable received-concepts are just those of the form $\square\alpha$ where α is a possible sent- or acceptable received-concept for A.

A necessary constraint on the diagram of an attribute is that under any given circumstances, all of the possible sent- and acceptable received-concepts for that attribute have the same extension. Thus a necessary condition for there always to be such an attribute as $\square A$ is:

(3.18)   Necessarily, if A is an attribute and α and β are possible sent- or acceptable received-concepts for A relative to some specific values of the dynamic parameters, then $(\forall x)(\square\alpha^\ulcorner x \equiv \square\beta^\ulcorner x)$.

Principle (3.18) is probably less obvious than (3.15), although it must be true for similar reasons. First, if (3.18) failed, then one person could believe an object x to exemplify A by believing x to exemplify a concept α such that x necessarily exemplifies α, while a second person might believe x to exemplify A by believing x to exemplify a concept β such that x only contingently exemplifies β. That is at least peculiar. Second, and perhaps more compelling, (3.18) is required for the existence of *de re* modal operators for statements, and hence for the existence of *de re* modal operators for sentences. Such operators do make sense, so (3.18) must be true.

In analogy to (3.16) we have:

(3.19)   If A is an attribute, $\Box A^{\mathsf{r}} x$ iff $\mathrm{Nec}_I[x,A]$.

4. Sentential Modalities

Given our three alethic statemental modalities, we can define four interesting alethic sentential modalities:

(4.1)   If P is a declarative sentence and Δ is (one of) its S-intensions, then P is $\begin{cases} analytic \\ internally\ necessary \\ externally\ necessary \\ weakly\ analytic \end{cases}$ (relative to Δ) iff Δ is

necessarily such that $(\forall \pi)[$if π is the sequence of values of the

pragmatic parameters then $\Delta(\pi)$ is $\begin{cases} a\ priori \\ internally\ necessary \\ externally\ necessary \\ true \end{cases}]$.

On the assumption that *a priori* propositions are also necessary, it follows that analytic sentences are internally necessary, internally necessary sentences are externally necessary, and externally necessary sentences are weakly analytic. But the converses all fail. For example, 'I exist' is weakly analytic but not externally necessary; a sentence employing synthetic predicates to connote nomic kinds and thereby express a true subjunctive generalization about them will be externally necessary but not internally necessary; and if a proposition can be necessary but not *a priori*, then a sentence expressing it will be internally necessary but not analytic. Weak analyticity is a relatively unfamiliar modality, but it has recently attracted a bit of interest.[5]

[5] See van Fraassen [1977], and Kaplan [1978].

One of the more interesting topics concerning sentential modalities is that of sentential modal operators. The words 'necessary' and 'possible' usually occur in English only within the phrases 'it is necessary that' and 'it is possible that', the latter phrases being equivalent to the adverbs 'necessarily' and 'possibly' used in their *de dicto* senses. Syntactically, these are operators rather than predicates. They take sentences as complements rather than terms. Philosophers abbreviate them as '$\Box$' and '$\Diamond$', respectively. The use of these operators is commonplace in philosophy, and we have used them repeatedly throughout the book. It is obvious, in light of our discussion of modal operators for propositions and statements, that these modal operators are to be analyzed as follows:

(4.2)   If P is a declarative sentence, then for any values of its pragmatic parameters, the sense of $\ulcorner \Box P \urcorner$ is $\Box \phi$ where ϕ is the sense of P.

(4.3)   If P is a declarative sentence, the sense of $\ulcorner \Diamond P \urcorner$ is the same as that of $\ulcorner \sim \Box \sim P \urcorner$.

Philosophers have often found modal operators puzzling and tried to replace them with predicates.[6] There is a trivial connection between '$\Box$' and the *statemental* predicate 'internally necessary':

(4.4)   Given any fixed set of values for the pragmatic parameters, $\ulcorner \Box P \urcorner$ expresses a true statement iff P expresses an internally necessary statement.

However, there appears to be no simple connection between the modal operator and the *sentential* predicate 'internally necessary'. In particular, we do not have:

(4.5)   Given any fixed set of values for the pragmatic parameters, $\ulcorner \Box P \urcorner$ expresses a true statement iff P is internally necessary.

Principle (4.5) holds in the special case in which P is nonindexical (so that its sense is the same for any values of the pragmatic parameters), but it does not hold in general. If P is indexical, it may express an internally necessary statement on certain values of the pragmatic parameters even if it is not internally necessary. A simple example of such a sentence is 'That is so'.

---

[6] In this connection, see particularly Montague [1963] and Skyrms [1978].

If we consider the very special case of a language which is devoid of indexicality, (4.5) will hold.[7] But even in that special case, (4.5) cannot be taken as *defining* the modal operator '$\square$'. That would require the sense of $\ulcorner \square P \urcorner$ to be a statement about the sentence *P*. Instead, $\ulcorner \square P \urcorner$ is about whatever *P* is about. The attempt to define modal operators in terms of modal predicates reflects the feeling that somehow modal predicates must be basic and modal operators constructed in terms of them. That feeling is correct, but that construction cannot take place at the level of sentences, or even at the level of statements. It must take place at the level of propositions where by virtue of having the logical designators $\langle \psi \rangle$ we can construct propositions which, although about propositions, are also about whatever those propositions are about. We do not have anything similar for either sentences are statements. Accordingly, modal operators for sentences are constructed in terms of modal operators for statements, the latter being constructed in terms of modal operators for propositions, and only these last modal operators can be constructed directly on the basis of modal predicates.

For a nonindexical language (which philosophers frequently pretend to be dealing with) our construction of the *de dicto* sentential modal operator gives us an operator directly connected with internal necessity (i.e., (4.5) holds). There is no obvious way to construct additional modal operators which bear the analogous relation to any of our other sentential alethic modalities. In particular, we cannot simply postulate, as philosophers are wont to do, that

(4.6) $\ulcorner \boxplus P \urcorner$ is true (i.e., expresses a true statement) iff $\mathfrak{H}(P)$

where $\mathfrak{H}$ is some modal predicate (e.g., weak analyticity). Principle (4.6) purports to give us the truth conditions for some statement, but as we have noted, there is no guarantee that there is a statement having those truth conditions. There is such a statement only if we can construct an appropriate diagram for it, and there is no obvious way to do that if $\mathfrak{H}$ is any modal predicate other than 'internally necessary'.

As we have defined it, '$\square$' is a *de dicto* modal operator, but the adverb 'necessarily' is also used as a *de re* modal operator in English.

---

[7] Such a language would be very restricted in the subject matter about which it could talk. For example, it could not be used to make statements reporting contingent events, because that requires sentences to be indexical with respect to time.

We can say such things as '2 is necessarily the square root of 4'. This *de re* modal operator transforms predicates into modal predicates. If F is a predicate, we can characterize the modal predicate $\ulcorner \Box F \urcorner$ in terms of its A-intension as follows:

(4.7)   If F is a predicate, then for any values of its pragmatic parameters, the sense of $\ulcorner \Box F \urcorner$ is $\Box A$ where A is the sense of F.

This has the result, for example, that if the sense of F is A and the sense of N is ∂, then the sense of $\ulcorner N$ is $\Box F \urcorner$ is $(\Box A : \partial)$.

IX
Doxastic and Epistemic Sentences

1. Introduction

Doxastic and epistemic sentences are notorious for creating difficulties for theories of meaning. The objective of this chapter is to
present a theory of meaning for such sentences which is compatible
with our account of the meanings of singular terms and predicates.

There is a traditional analysis of doxastic and epistemic sentences
which must be rejected. It goes as follows. The objects of knowledge
and belief are propositions. Given a sentence P and an occasion on
which it is used to express a proposition, let $\P P$ be the proposition
it expresses ("the proposition that P"). Let $\mathfrak{B}$ be the concept of
believing something, i.e., the concept expressed by 'x believes y'.
Analogously, let $\mathfrak{K}$ be the concept expressed by 'x knows y'. Then
the natural and traditional analysis of $\ulcorner S$ believes that $P \urcorner$ and $\ulcorner S$
knows that $P \urcorner$ proposes that if S is used to express the statemental
designator ∂, then the sentences are used to make the statements
$(\mathfrak{B}:\partial,\P P)$ and $(\mathfrak{K}:\partial,\P P)$ respectively. The main difficulty with this
analysis is that we have now concluded that most sentences do not
express propositions. They are used to express statements instead,
and most statements are not propositions. If P is used to make a
nonpropositional statement, then there is no such proposition as
$\P P$, and hence the traditional analysis makes no sense. As sentences
containing most singular terms and most predicates can only be
used to express nonpropositional statements, the analysis of $\ulcorner S$
believes that $P \urcorner$ or $\ulcorner S$ knows that $P \urcorner$ when P is such a sentence must
be more complicated than has traditionally been supposed.

2. Propositional Doxastic Sentences

Let us begin our investigation of doxastic and epistemic sentences
by examining the simplest case—sentences of the form $\ulcorner S$ believes

188

that $P^\urcorner$ and $^\ulcorner S$ knows that $P^\urcorner$ where P does express a proposition. When S is used to express the statemental designator ∂ and P to express the proposition ψ, let us symbolize those statements which are the senses of these sentences as $^\ulcorner B_\P[\partial,\psi]^\urcorner$ and $^\ulcorner K_\P[\partial,\psi]^\urcorner$ respectively. The truth conditions of these statements are simple enough. Using $^\ulcorner\mathfrak{K}_S\psi^\urcorner$ and $^\ulcorner\mathfrak{B}_S\psi^\urcorner$ as convenient abbreviations for $^\ulcorner S$ knows $\psi^\urcorner$ and $^\ulcorner S$ believes $\psi^\urcorner$ respectively, we have:

(2.1) $B_\P[\partial,\psi]$ is true iff $\mathfrak{B}_S\psi$;

(2.2) $K_\P[\partial,\psi]$ is true iff $\mathfrak{K}_S\psi$.

However, more is required to specify the identity of the statements themselves, because any statements logically equivalent to $B_\P[\partial,\psi]$ and $K_\P[\partial,\psi]$ will have the same truth conditions. The statements must either be described in terms of their diagrams, or given structural descriptions (which is a shorthand way of describing their diagrams).

A natural proposal regarding structural descriptions for $B_\P[\partial,\psi]$ and $K_\P[\partial,\psi]$ is:

(2.3) $B_\P[\partial,\psi] = (\mathfrak{B}:\partial,\psi)$;

(2.4) $K_\P[\partial,\psi] = (\mathfrak{K}:\partial,\psi)$.

But (2.3) and (2.4) are not well-formed. $\mathfrak{B}$ and $\mathfrak{K}$ are binary concepts. In other words, they relate pairs of objects (construed broadly). In describing a proposition by filling in the blanks in '$(\mathfrak{B}:\ ,\ )$', one must fill in propositional designators. Similarly, in describing a statement, one must fill in statemental designators. The difficulty is that ψ is not a designator at all—it is a proposition. Proper descriptions of $B_\P[\partial,\psi]$ and $K_\P[\partial,\psi]$ must have the form:

(2.5) $B_\P[\partial,\psi] = (\mathfrak{B}:\partial,\partial_\psi)$;

(2.6) $K_\P[\partial,\psi] = (\mathfrak{K}:\partial,\partial_\psi)$;

where ∂_ψ is a statemental designator designating ψ. ψ itself is not a statemental designator.

To throw light on this, consider a first-person belief sentence $^\ulcorner$I believe that $P^\urcorner$. The statement I make with this sentence is $B_\P[\mathbf{I}(S),\psi]$. My sent-proposition is the proposition I must believe in order to believe what I say. This proposition has the form $(\mathfrak{B}:\iota_S,\delta)$ where δ is some propositional designator designating ψ. In thinking to myself $^\ulcorner$I believe that $P^\urcorner$, I am thinking of ψ in terms of its content.

189

In other words, I am thinking of ψ in terms of the designator $\langle\psi\rangle$. Thus my sent-proposition for $B_{\P}[\mathbf{I}(S),\psi]$ is $(\mathfrak{B}:\iota_S,\langle\psi\rangle)$. It follows that

(2.8) $B_{\P}[\mathbf{I}_S,\psi] = (\mathfrak{B}:\mathbf{I}_S,\langle\psi\rangle)$.

In general, I would propose that:

(2.9) $B_{\P}[\partial,\psi] = (\mathfrak{B}:\partial,\langle\psi\rangle)$;

(2.10) $K_{\P}[\partial,\psi] = (\mathfrak{K}:\partial,\langle\psi\rangle)$.

This embellishment of the traditional theory seems to constitute an adequate account of the doxastic sentences ⌜S believes that P⌝ and ⌜S knows that P⌝ for the special case in which P expresses a proposition.

3. Nonpropositional Doxastic Sentences

When P expresses the nonpropositional statement ϕ, let us symbolize the statements expressed by ⌜S believes that P⌝ and ⌜S knows that P⌝ as ⌜$B[\partial,\phi]$⌝ and ⌜$K[\partial,\phi]$⌝. There is no straightforward generalization of (2.9) and (2.10) which will provide analyses of these statements. We cannot even write ⌜$(\mathfrak{B}:\partial,\langle\phi\rangle)$⌝ because, on the one hand, ⌜$\langle\phi\rangle$⌝ is only defined for propositions, and on the other hand, $\mathfrak{B}$ is a relation between persons and propositions (not statements).

Let us begin our investigation of $B[\partial,\phi]$ by inquiring into its truth conditions. I shall make a simple proposal:

(3.1) $B[\partial,\phi]$ is true iff $(\exists\psi)[\psi$ is an acceptable received-proposition for ϕ for S under the circumstances of utterance & $\mathfrak{B}_S\psi]$.

In order to confirm (3.1), let us examine several different kinds of nonpropositional statements, beginning with statements involving proper names.

I suspect that most doxastic statements involving proper names use them in indirect discourse. So employed, ⌜S believes that N is F⌝ is equivalent to ⌜S believes N to be F⌝. We will discuss such indirect discourse in section five. The statement made in indirect discourse is not the statement $B[\partial,\phi]$ which we are currently attempting to describe. Let us simply stipulate that the latter is to be the statement expressed by the sentence ⌜S believes that P⌝ when this sentence is used in such a way that it involves no indirect discourse.

Although proper names most frequently occur in indirect discourse in doxastic sentences, there are also some clear cases which must be construed as direct discourse. For example, knowing that there is no such person as Bourbaki, I may nevertheless assert that Jones believes that Bourbaki is a great mathematician.[1] I am attributing to Jones a belief of the form $(\mu:\beta)$ where β is a propositional designator in terms of which he is thinking of Bourbaki. But as there is no such person as Bourbaki, what does the latter constraint on β amount to? We cannot require that β designate Bourbaki, because Bourbaki does not exist and hence no designator designates him. There must be some constraint on β, and the only one that appears plausible is that β be convergent with my sent-designator for 'Bourbaki', i.e., β is an acceptable received-designator for $\partial_{\text{`Bourbaki'}}$. Similarly, it seems that μ should be an acceptable received-concept for the attribute of being a great mathematician, in which case $(\mu:\beta)$ is an acceptable received-proposition for the statement expressed by 'Bourbaki is a great mathematician'.

Turning to a second example, consider a definite description used referentially. The village is in an uproar. A witch has been reported, and all the able-bodied menfolk are out looking for her, albeit with some trepidation. Hearing a noise from the next room, Hob screams 'The witch is in the next room', and Hob and Nob cower together in the corner. Although I know that there is no witch, I may nevertheless assert on the basis of his demeanor, 'Nob also believes that the witch is in the next room'. Letting W be the attribute of being a witch and N be the attribute of being in the next room, I am asserting $B[\partial_{\text{`Nob'}}, (N:\partial_w)]$ where ∂_w is a W-hereditary designator. In asserting this, I am attributing to Nob belief in a proposition of the form $(\eta:\delta_w)$ where η is an acceptable received-concept for N, and δ_w is the propositional designator in terms of which Nob thinks of the putative witch. What constraints must there be on δ_w? δ_w cannot designate just any old witch—it must designate the one Hob was talking about. As there aren't any witches, what can this mean except that it is convergent with Hob's use of 'the witch', and hence convergent with mine? Once again then, (3.1) appears to be correct.

We could compound examples indefinitely, but they all appear to support (3.1). It is of interest to see how (3.1) handles some well

---

[1] A group of French mathematicians published their results collectively under the name 'Bourbaki', and many people believed that those results were the work of a single person named 'Bourbaki'.

known puzzles concerning belief. The best known is that of Hesperus and Phosphorus. Although 'Hesperus' and 'Phosphorus' are used to refer to the same object, I might be able to make a true statement by saying 'Jones believes that Hesperus is Venus' and a false statement by saying 'Jones believes that Phosphorus is Venus'. The explanation for how this is possible becomes obvious given (3.1). Although 'Hesperus' and 'Phosphorus' are used to refer to the same object, they do not express the same hereditary designators. Consequently, the acceptable received-propositions for the statements expressed by 'Hesperus is Venus' and 'Phosphorus is Venus' are different. Thus (3.1) imposes different requirements for the truth of the corresponding belief statements.[2]

A more sophisticated puzzle is due to David Lewis [1981]. In discussing Kripke's version of the Hesperus/Phosphorus problem (in Kripke [1979]), Lewis considers Pierre who, although he has never been to London, has heard much about London and on that basis believes that London is pretty. Lewis then has us consider a counterfactual possible world in which Bristol rather than London is called 'London', in which Pierre's informants were all talking about Bristol, and in which Pierre's qualitative beliefs concerning London (in this world) are all true of Bristol. In this counterfactual world, these qualitative propositions would all be about Bristol. In the counterfactual world, Pierre believes the same propositions as he believes in this world, but we in this world would not describe Pierre in the counterfactual world as believing that London is pretty. Rather, Pierre would believe that Bristol is pretty. Lewis quite properly takes this as an argument against what I have termed "the traditional analysis of belief sentences". How does (3.1) fare in connection with this example? Principle (3.1) is only about simple belief sentences of the form $\ulcorner S$ believes that $P\urcorner$, and as such is not directly applicable. But let us make the natural assumption that when the sense of P is ϕ and the sense of Q is θ, then the sense of $\ulcorner$If it were true that Q then S would believe that $P\urcorner$ is $(\theta \succ B[\partial,\phi])$. The statement $(\theta \succ B[\partial,\phi])$ is true iff $B[\partial,\phi]$ would be true if θ were true. Thus we have:

(3.2)   Under circumstances in which the sense of P is ϕ and the sense of Q is θ, the statement we would make by saying

---

[2] This shows, incidentally, that proper names are not used rigidly in direct discourse belief sentences.

⌜If it were true that Q then S would believe that P⌝ is true iff, if θ were true then there would be a proposition ψ such that ψ would be an acceptable received-proposition for S for ϕ and S would believe ψ.

Applying (3.2) to Pierre, he believes a proposition ψ which is an acceptable received-proposition for ϕ in the actual world, but ψ would not be an acceptable received-proposition for ϕ in the counterfactual world in which Pierre is really thinking about Bristol. Thus (3.2) handles the puzzling case of Pierre correctly.

Principle (3.1) gives us a statement of truth conditions for $B[\partial,\phi]$, but in order to fully describe $B[\partial,\phi]$ we need an account of its diagram. It would be tempting to transcribe (3.1) directly into an account of the possible sent- and acceptable received-propositions for $B[\partial,\phi]$, taking these propositions to all have the form

(3.3) S believes some acceptable received-proposition for ϕ.

But there are two difficulties for this proposal. First, it seems unrealistic to suppose that ordinary people have the highly theoretical concept of an acceptable received-proposition, but if they don't, then (3.3) cannot be what they are thinking in using sentences of the form ⌜S believes that P⌝. It does seem, however, that ordinary people have the concept we might call that of 'accepting a statement'. The latter concept is *analysable* as 'believing an acceptable received-proposition for the statement', but ordinary people are not aware of this and so the two concepts are only logically equivalent—not identical. Employing the concept of accepting a statement, it seems reasonable to suggest that the possible sent- and acceptable received-propositions for $B[\partial,\phi]$ all have the form:

(3.4) S accepts ϕ.

If we take *Accept* to be the concept of accepting a statement, (3.4) can be made more precise as the proposal that the possible sent- and acceptable received-propositions for $B[\partial,\phi]$ are of the form $(Accept:\partial,\partial_\phi)$ where ∂_ϕ is a statemental designator designating ϕ. But this brings us to the second problem for (3.3) and (3.4). What statemental designator could ∂_ϕ be? In other words, how must the speaker and his audience be thinking about the statement ϕ? It would be nice if there were logical designators for statements as well as for propositions, but as there don't seem to be, the solution to our difficulty cannot take that form. My proposal is that the speaker and his audience must be thinking about ϕ partly in terms of the sentence P.

Consider a member S^* of the speaker's audience. When the speaker says $\ulcorner S$ believes that $P \urcorner$, S^* comes to entertain an acceptable received-proposition ψ for ϕ in connection with the sentence P. But ψ by itself cannot determine what ϕ is, because a single proposition can be an acceptable received-proposition for many different statements. Roughly, to get from the acceptable received-proposition to the statement, we must know what parts of ψ can be varied in what ways to generate other acceptable received-propositions and possible sent-propositions. It is the sentence which tells us this. Different parts of the sentence are put into correspondence with different parts of the proposition, and then the meanings of the sentence-parts determine how the proposition can be generalized.[3] This suggests that what S^* must be thinking in order to understand the speaker when the speaker says $\ulcorner S$ believes that $P \urcorner$ is something like:

(3.5)　　S accepts some statement which is a possible sense of P and which I can accept by believing ψ.

To say that ϕ is a possible sense of P is just to say that there are circumstances in which ϕ would be the sense of P. Let $(\mathscr{S}ense:\phi,P)$ be the concept expressed by $\ulcorner \phi$ is a possible sense of $P \urcorner$. To say that S^* can accept ϕ by believing ψ is just to say that, necessarily, given the present values of the dynamic parameters, if S^* believes ψ then S^* accepts ϕ. This is equivalent to saying that ψ is an acceptable received-proposition for ϕ for S^* under the present circumstances. Let $(\mathscr{A}ccBy:S^*,\phi,\psi)$ be the concept expressed by $\ulcorner S^*$ can accept ϕ by believing $\psi \urcorner$. Then the acceptable received-propositions for $B[\partial,\phi]$ for S^* are those of the form:

(3.6)　$(\vee\,\theta)[(\mathscr{A}ccept:\delta_S,\theta) \wedge (\mathscr{S}ense:\theta,\xi_P) \wedge (\mathscr{A}ccBy:1_{S^*},\theta,\langle\psi\rangle)]$

where δ_S is an acceptable received-designator for ∂ for S^*, ψ is an acceptable received-proposition for ϕ for S^*, P is a sentence whose sense (under the present circumstances) is ϕ, and ξ_P designates P. In connection with ξ_P, it does not seem that S^* can be thinking of P in terms of just any propositional designator designating it. Rather, he must be thinking of P in terms of a possible sent-designator for the sense of a quotation-name of P. Such designators characterize P in

---

[3] For the details of this, see the analysis of lexical sending in the Appendix.

terms of its appearance, either visual or auditory. Let us call such a designator a *structural designator* for *P*.

Turning to the possible sent-propositions for $B[\partial,\phi]$, they seem to be analogous. They are just those of the form of (3.6) where δ_S is a possible sent-designator for ∂ for S^*, ψ is a possible sent-proposition for ϕ for S^*, and ξ_P is a structural designator for *P*.

The preceding constitutes a description of $B[\partial,\phi]$ in terms of its diagram. We can describe the *S*-intension of $\ulcorner S$ believes that $P\urcorner$ as follows:

(3.7)   If π is a sequence of values of the pragmatic parameters and $\Delta_S(\pi) = \partial$ and $\Delta_P(\pi) = \phi$, then $\Delta_{\ulcorner S \text{ believes that } P\urcorner}(\pi) = B[\partial,\phi]$.

Principle (3.7) may reasonably be questioned in the case in which $S = \,$'*I*'. It is unclear to me whether $B[\mathbf{I}(S),\phi]$ is ever a sense of $\ulcorner$I believe that $P\urcorner$. It is clear, however, that $\ulcorner$I believe that $P\urcorner$ is often used with a different sense. To illustrate this, suppose there comes a time when all writings by or about Aristotle are lost and only one man, Isaac, retains any knowledge of Aristotle. Fortunately, before Isaac dies there is a reawakening of interest in ancient Greek science and philosophy, with the result that Isaac conveys his knowledge of Aristotle's biological studies to a select group of biologists and conveys his knowledge of Aristotle's philosophy to a select group of philosophers, but neglects to inform either group that Aristotle the biologist was the same man as Aristotle the philosopher. The philosophers tell other philosophers about Aristotle's philosophy, and the biologists tell other biologists about Aristotle's biology, thus perpetuating stories about Aristotle. After Isaac, all references to Aristotle are hereditarily parasitic on Isaac's references to Aristotle. One thing which Isaac told both groups is that Aristotle was Greek. It seems clear that Isaac was making the same statement when he told the biologists that Aristotle was Greek as when he told the philosophers that Aristotle was Greek. The biologists and philosophers were, in turn, repeating Isaac's statement when they passed this fact on to subsequent biologists and philosophers. Now let us suppose that there is one man, Jeremiah, who is both a biologist and a philosopher. He hears about Aristotle both as a biologist and as a philosopher, but he never suspects that it is the same person in both cases. Jeremiah's use of the name 'Aristotle' to refer to the philosopher is convergent with his use of 'Aristotle' to refer to the biologist. Thus in saying 'Aristotle was

Greek' with the intent to refer to the philosopher, Jeremiah is unknowingly making the same statement as if he had said that with the intent to refer to the biologist. But if Jeremiah believed the putative philosopher to be Greek and did not believe the putative biologist to be Greek, then in saying

(3.8)   I believe that Aristotle was Greek

with the intent to refer to the philosopher, Jeremiah is making a true statement, but in uttering (3.8) with the intent to refer to the biologist, Jeremiah would be making a false statement. The statemental designator $\partial_{\text{'Aristotle'}}$ is the same in either case, so it follows that he is not stating $B[\mathbf{I}(\text{Jeremiah}),(G:\partial_{\text{'Aristotle'}})]$. Unlike $B[\mathbf{I}(\text{Jeremiah}), (G;\partial_{\text{'Aristotle'}})]$, the statement Jeremiah is actually making requires for its truth that he believe a *specific* acceptable received-proposition for ϕ, namely, one involving the way in which he is actually thinking of Aristotle. Symbolizing this statement as $\ulcorner B[\mathbf{I}(S),\phi,\psi]\urcorner$ (where ψ is an acceptable received-proposition for ϕ), its truth conditions are:

(3.9) $B[\mathbf{I}(S),\phi,\psi]$ is true iff $\mathfrak{B}_S\psi$.

We can describe $B[\mathbf{I}(S),\phi,\psi]$ in terms of its diagram very simply. This statement can only be made by S, so there are no possible sent-propositions for $B[\mathbf{I}(S),\phi,\psi]$ for S^* if $S^* \neq S$. The only possible sent-proposition for $B[\mathbf{I}(S),\phi,\psi]$ for S is $(\mathfrak{B}:\iota_S,\langle\psi\rangle)$. Turning to the acceptable received-propositions, we cannot expect a member of the audience, S^*, to know precisely which proposition ψ S claims to believe. All that S^* can be required to know is that ψ is some acceptable received-proposition for ϕ. In other words, the acceptable received-propositions for $B[\mathbf{I}(S),\phi,\psi]$ are the same as for $B[\mathbf{I}(S),\phi]$.

4. Knowing What t Is

Our next main objective is to provide analyses of doxastic and epistemic sentences involving indirect discourse. A sentence of the form $\ulcorner S$ believes that t is $F\urcorner$ involves indirect discourse (relative to the singular term t) just in case the truth of the statement made by uttering it does not require S to have a belief involving an acceptable received-designator for the sense of t. Thus if Herman and I witness Jerry Ford slice a ball into the rough, I may report 'Herman believes that Jerry Ford just made an unfortunate drive' without implying that Herman believes the golfer in question to be Jerry Ford.

Indirect discourse in belief contexts has generally been supposed to be connected with another phenomenon: quantification into belief contexts. Such 'doxastic quantification' presumably requires a referentially transparent sense of 'believe', and such a referentially transparent sense of 'believe' would automatically admit of indirect discourse. Thus one of the subsidiary purposes of this chapter will be to investigate doxastic quantification.

Recent discussions of doxastic quantification have made important use of the notion of 'know what'. For example, Hintikka [1962] interpreted doxastic quantifiers as having what is called a 'restricted range feature' according to which one cannot infer ⌜Something is believed by S to be F⌝ from ⌜S believes t to be F⌝ without the additional premise ⌜S knows what (thing) t is⌝. It will be argued in section six that this is not quite right, but that 'knows what' does play an important role in understanding both doxastic quantification and indirect discourse. Thus it will be convenient to discuss 'knows what' before going on to indirect discourse and doxastic quantification.

The objective of this section is to provide an account of the meaning of ⌜S knows what t is ⌝ (in the sense of knowing what thing t is rather than what kind of thing t is) where t is a singular term. The meaning will be described by describing the statement made by uttering this sentence as a function of the senses of the singular terms S and t. If S and t are used to express the statemental designators ∂_S and ∂_t respectively, I will symbolize the statement as ⌜$KW[\partial_S,\partial_t]$⌝. The most common cases of knowing-what are cases of knowing-who. The difference between ⌜S knows what t is⌝ and ⌜S knows who t is⌝ is that in saying the latter the speaker implies that t is a person. However, for ease of constructing examples I will ignore this difference and identify the two locutions.

Perhaps the key to describing $KW[\partial_S,\partial_t]$ is to recognize that it is not a function of ∂_S and ∂_t exclusively. As Boër and Lycan [1975] remark, "It is a commonplace of epistemology that different circumstances demand different tests for knowing who someone is."[4] To know who someone is is to be able to identify him. You identify an object for some purpose. But different identificatory purposes require different ways of identifying. In general, an identification

---

[4] Although my analysis differs markedly from the Boër-Lycan analysis, it is based upon what I take to be their principal insight—that knowing-what is relative to a purpose.

is a description of the object. Different descriptions suffice for different purposes. Thus, relative to one identificatory purpose I may be said to know who t is, and relative to another I may not. For example, relative to identifying Jimmy Carter among important people, I know who Jimmy Carter is because I know that he is the expresident; but relative to picking him out from among a room full of politicians I may not know who Jimmy Carter is. This indicates that $KW[\partial_S, \partial_t]$ is a function in part of the identificatory purpose. Abstractly, we can regard an identificatory purpose ρ as selecting a class $\sigma(\rho)$ of "satisfactory descriptions". Let us add a subscript for the identificatory purpose to KW, writing $\ulcorner KW_\rho[\partial_S, \partial_t] \urcorner$.

A complete description of $KW_\rho[\partial_S, \partial_t]$ will be a description of its diagram, but let us begin with the somewhat simpler task of describing the circumstances under which this statement is true. To know who t is is to know that t satisfies a particular description in $\sigma(\rho)$. Knowledge takes a propositional object, so in order to know this one must be thinking about the referent of t in terms of a propositional designator designating that referent and that propositional designator will be a constituent of the proposition known. Then the following seems plausible:

(4.1) $KW_\rho[\partial_S, \partial_t]$ is true iff $(\exists\delta)(\exists\alpha)[\delta$ and ∂_t designate the same thing & $\alpha \in \sigma(\rho)$ & $\Re_S(\alpha:\delta)]$.

The inclusion of the variable ρ in KW makes 'knows what' indexical. This indexicality makes it difficult to test (4.1) by looking for counterexamples. We could probably avoid most counterexamples in an *ad hoc* way by adjusting $\sigma(\rho)$ properly. The argument in favor of (4.1) is that such indexical fluctuation seems to be required by the actual behavior of 'knows what'. For example, a London detective, convinced that he has encountered another victim of Jack the Ripper, might announce, 'I know who did this, but I still don't know who he is'. The only way to make sense of such an announcement is to suppose that 'knows who' is indexical and that there is an indexical variation between the two occurrences of 'knows who'. Given that, we can decipher this announcement in accordance with (4.1) as:

(4.2) $KW_\rho(\mathbf{I}(S), \partial_t) \wedge \neg KW_{\rho*}(\mathbf{I}(S), \partial_t)$.

This is not a contradiction if $\rho \neq \rho^*$, but there is no way to avoid its being a contradiction without the assumption that 'knows who' is indexical and depends upon some such parameter. This indexical variation is responsible for a great deal of seemingly mysterious behavior on the part of 'knows who' and 'knows what', and as we will see, its behavior (or misbehavior) infects doxastic quantification and other belief contexts and has been responsible for much of the confusion philosophers have felt when discussing this material. It is worth noting, however, that the indexical variations are not so great as to make things totally chaotic. (If they were, we would not use such a notion.) Although special purposes lead to a great deal of fluctuation, we generally operate on what may be called a "general information level" wherein knowing-what consists of knowing any "interesting" description. In this case, an interesting description is any concept α such that my knowing an object to exemplify α suffices to explain why my partner in conversation might want to talk about that object. Thus $\sigma(\rho)$ includes such a wide variety as 'the president', 'the author of *Waverly*', 'my brother', 'a man who owes me five dollars', etc. As we generally operate on this general information level, there is much less indexical variation than we might otherwise expect.

Principle (4.1) implies that 'knows what' is referentially transparent. For example, suppose that Jones has been talking with Senator Roberts, but I am unsure whether Jones knows that it is Senator Roberts with whom he has been talking. Jones leaves the scene, and Senator Roberts gets in his limousine and prepares to drive away. I might turn to Smith and ask, 'Does Jones know who the man in the limousine is?', intending my question to be taken in such a way that the answer is affirmative if Jones knows that he was talking to Senator Roberts. An affirmative answer would not imply that Jones knew that Senator Roberts was the man in the limousine. The description 'the man in the limousine' is just my way of referring to the man with whom Jones was talking.[5]

---

[5] Perhaps a better way of putting this is that (4.1) pertains to an indirect discourse sense of 'knows what'. It appears that there is also a direct discourse sense of 'knows what' and 'knows who'. This is most obvious when t is a definite description. For example, I may ask whether Jones knows who the oldest man in the world is, intending my question to be taken in such a way that the answer is affirmative only if Jones thinks of the oldest man in the world *as* the oldest man in the world and knows him to exemplify an appropriate identifying description. Or consider Bobby telling his teacher, 'I know who Christopher Columbus is'. I suggest that the truth conditions for the direct discourse sense can be captured by the following principle:

$_D KW_\rho[\partial_S, \partial_t]$ is true iff $(\exists \delta)\{\delta$ is a possible sent-designator for ∂_t for S & $(\exists \alpha)[\alpha \in \sigma(\rho)$ & $\mathfrak{R}_S(\alpha : \delta)]\}$.

Having described the truth conditions for $KW_\rho[\partial_S,\partial_t]$, what can we say about the statement itself? I suggest that $KW_\rho[\partial_S,\partial_t]$ has precisely the same form as our description of its truth conditions. Let $(\mathscr{P}\!\mathit{red}\!:\!\psi,\alpha,\delta)$ be the concept expressed by $\ulcorner\psi = (\alpha\!:\!\delta)\urcorner$, $(\mathscr{D}\mathit{es}\!:\!x,y)$ be the concept expressed by $\ulcorner x$ designates $y\urcorner$, and $(\mathscr{I}\!\mathit{den}\!:\!\alpha,\rho)$ be the concept expressed by $\ulcorner\alpha \in \sigma(\rho)\urcorner$ (i.e., $\ulcorner\alpha$ is an adequate description relative to the identificatory purpose $\rho\urcorner$. The statement is then:

$$(4.3) \quad (\vee\,\delta)(\vee\,\alpha)(\vee\,\psi)[\mathscr{D}\mathit{es}\!:\!\delta,\partial_t) \wedge (\mathscr{I}\!\mathit{den}\!:\!\alpha,\partial_\rho)$$
$$\wedge (\mathscr{P}\!\mathit{red}\!:\!\psi,\alpha,\delta) \wedge (\mathfrak{R}\!:\!\partial_S,\theta)].$$

The presence of ∂_ρ indicates that the statement is not just a function of ρ, but also of ∂_ρ. Thus we cannot get away with just subscripting it with ρ. We should revise our notation and write $\ulcorner KW[\partial_\rho,\partial_S,\partial_t]\urcorner$.

Before leaving the topic of 'knowing what', it is useful to define a new notion. Principle (4.1) involves the condition:

$$(4.4) \quad (\exists\alpha)[\alpha \in \sigma(\rho) \;\&\; \mathfrak{R}_S(\alpha\!:\!\delta)].$$

Let us abbreviate this as $\ulcorner KW_\rho(S,\delta)\urcorner$ and read it as $\ulcorner S$ knows what δ is$\urcorner$. It is, roughly, the condition of knowing what one is thinking about when one thinks about something in terms of δ. This condition will be found to play an important role in the subsequent analysis of doxastic locutions.

5. Believing To Be

Now let us turn to belief locutions involving indirect discourse. The most straightforward use of indirect discourse is in the locution $\ulcorner S$ believes t to be $F\urcorner$. This locution is generally used in such a way that it equivalent to $\ulcorner(\exists x)[x = t \;\&\; S$ believes x to be $F]\urcorner$ and hence is an instance of indirect discourse. The sentences $\ulcorner S$ believes of t that it is $F\urcorner$ and $\ulcorner S$ believes that t is $F\urcorner$ are also used in this way, but not invariably. Let us symbolize the indirect discourse statement which can be expressed by these sentences when the sense of S is ∂_S, the sense of t is ∂_t, and the sense of F is the attribute A, as $\ulcorner B[\partial_S,\partial_t,A]\urcorner$.

The case in which F is a nonconceptual predicate (which is, of course, the normal case) introduces special difficulties, so let us begin by considering the case in which F is a conceptual predicate, expressing a concept α. If S believes t to be F, S must be thinking of the referent of t in terms of some propositional designator δ, and then it seems reasonable to suppose that his believing t to be F consists of his believing the proposition $(\alpha:\delta)$:

(5.1) $B[\partial_S,\partial_t,\alpha]$ is true iff $(\exists\delta)[\delta$ designates the same thing as ∂_t & $\mathfrak{B}_S(\alpha:\delta)]$.

It is not difficult to see, however, that (5.1) is inadequate. For example, prominent among my beliefs about Jimmy Carter is the belief that he is the expresident. For the sake of the example, let us pretend that 'is the expresident' is a conceptual predicate expressing a concept α. Now suppose I am placed in a room with a group of politicians, one of whom is Jimmy Carter, but I do not recognize him when I see him face-to-face. Suppose he is sitting in the corner. It seems false to say that I believe the man sitting in the corner to be the expresident. But Carter *is* the man sitting in the corner, so someone who knows this could truly say of me, 'Pollock does not believe Carter to be the expresident'. This is a counterexample to (5.1). The proposed analysans is true, but the analysandum is false.

However, there is something very puzzling about denying that I believe Jimmy Carter to be the expresident. Five minutes earlier, before being taken into that room, if it were considered whether I believed Carter to be the expresident, that would have been affirmed. Furthermore, my beliefs have not changed in the interval. Are we wrong then in supposing that upon encountering Carter face-to-face, I do not believe him to be the expresident? I think it must be admitted that I do not believe the man sitting in the corner to be the expresident. But Carter *is* the man sitting in the corner, so does it not follow that I do not believe him to be the president? The only way to deny this inference is to claim that $\ulcorner S$ believes t to be $F\urcorner$ is referentially opaque. That seems to fly in the face of our common practice of quantifying into such contexts. Supposing that I actually believe the man in the corner *not* to be the expresident, it could correctly be concluded, 'There is someone in the room whom Pollock incorrectly believes not to be the expresident'. Such doxastic quantification should be illegitimate if believing-to-be contexts are referentially opaque.

I think that the correct conclusion is that before entering the room it was true to say 'Pollock believes Carter to be the expresident', but false to say that once I was in the room. This can only be possible if the sentence 'Pollock believes Carter to be the expresident' is being used to make two different statements in the two different contexts. And that seems right. Imagine yourself in the room and

201

saying, 'Pollock does not believe Carter to be the expresident', where you know that I could not supply the name 'Carter' for the man in the corner about whom you are talking. You are surely not denying what you would have been affirming five minutes earlier, before we entered the room, had you said, 'Pollock believes Carter to be the expresident'. The context makes a difference to what statement is made. What is the source of this variation?

To make a long story short, I propose that believing-to-be requires the believer to know whom (or what) he is thinking about:

(5.2) $B[\partial_S, \partial_t, \alpha]$ is true iff $(\exists \delta)[\delta$ designates the same thing as ∂_t & $KW_\rho(S,\delta)$ & $\mathfrak{B}_S(\alpha:\delta)]$.

As we have seen, knowing-what is subject to the same sort of contextual variation we have been observing. Let δ be the *de re* designator in terms of which I normally think of Jimmy Carter. Before I entered the room it would have been true to say that I knew who δ was (i.e., I knew what I was thinking of as δ). I knew that δ was the expresident (i.e., I knew the proposition $(\alpha:\delta)$), and that was enough for knowing who δ was in that context. But once in the room, it would not have been true to say that I knew who δ was. In that context, knowing who δ was would require the ability to pick him out from among the occupants of the room. Our identificatory purposes have changed. This change in the value of the paramater ρ is responsible for the strange behavior of the sentence 'Pollock believes Carter to be the president'. Before I entered the room, it would have been true to say that I knew who Carter was, because δ designated Carter. I knew who δ was by knowing $(\alpha:\delta)$, and I believed the requisite proposition involving δ, viz., $(\alpha:\delta)$. But once I was in the room it would no longer be true to say that I knew who Carter was. At that point I could employ two different designators designating the same man. One of those, δ, is the designator I have employed for thinking about Carter all along, and the second, γ, becomes available to me as a result of perceiving Carter sitting in the corner. In this context, I do not know who δ is because I cannot pick out in the room the person I was thinking of as δ. I do know who γ is (I can pick the designatum of γ out), but I do not believe $(\alpha:\gamma)$. Thus (5.2) yields the correct result that I do not believe Carter to be the expresident.

The presence of the indexical parameter ρ in the analysis of believing-to-be indicates that it is also an indexical parameter of the latter notion. It would be better to take explicit cognizance of this by building it into the symbolization: $B[\partial_\rho,\partial_S,\partial_t,\alpha]$. We can obtain further confirmation of the functioning of this parameter by considering what would have happened in the above examples had the identificatory purposes of the men in the room been different than we described them to be. In inquiring whether I knew who Carter was, they might simply have wanted to know whether I knew he was the expresident, without caring whether I could pick him out in the room. Given that identificatory purpose, it would have been true to say that I knew who δ was just by knowing that he was the expresident. In that case, it seems it would also be true to say that I believed Carter to be the expresident, and furthermore that I believed the man in the corner to be the expresident even though I did not know that he was the man my belief was about. I take this as further confirmation for analysis (5.2).

It is possible to have contexts in which we simultaneously appeal to more than one identificatory parameter. For example, we can have truths of the following form:

S believes t to be F, but does not know who t is.

In order for this to make sense, the identificatory parameter involved in 'knows who' must be different from that in 'believes to be', giving us the statement:

$$B[\partial_\rho,\partial_S,\partial_t,\alpha] \wedge \neg KW[\partial_{\rho*},\partial_S,\partial_t].$$

For example, I may believe the man in the corner to have a nice smile but not know who he is in the sense of knowing that he is the expresident. In this case, I know who γ is in the sense that I can pick him out in the room, but I do not know who he is in the sense that I do not know that he is the expresident.

Now let us relax the requirement that F expresses a concept α, taking it instead to express any attribute A. I suggest that the truth conditions for $B[\partial_\rho,\partial_S,\partial_t,A]$ can be stated as follows:

(5.3) $B[\partial_\rho,\partial_S,\partial_t,A]$ is true iff $(\exists\delta)\{\delta$ designates the same thing as ∂_t & $KW_\rho(S,\delta)$ & $(\exists\alpha)[\alpha$ is a possible sent-concept for A for S under the circumstances of the utterance & $\mathfrak{B}_S(\alpha:\delta)]\}$.

In order to generate a description of the diagram of $B[\partial_\rho,\partial_S,\partial_t,A]$ we must begin by acknowledging that just as ordinary people have the concept of accepting a statement, they also have the concept of accepting that an object exemplifies a certain attribute, or as I will put it, 'accepting an attribute of an object'. This concept is characterized by the following equivalence:

(5.4) S accepts A of x iff $(\exists\alpha)(\exists\delta)$ [δ designates x & α is an acceptable received-concept for A for S & $\mathfrak{B}_S(\alpha{:}\delta)$].

Just as in the case of accepting a statement, however, ordinary people are not aware of this equivalence and so the concept of accepting A of x is only equivalent to, and not identical with, the concept expressed by the right side of (5.4). Let us also define:

(5.5)   *S accepts A of x by believing* $(\alpha{:}\delta)$ iff:
(1) δ designates x and $\mathfrak{B}_S(\alpha{:}\delta)$; and
(2) necessarily, if (1) holds under the present circumstances, then S accepts A of x.

I will say that S accepts A of x by believing α of x iff $(\exists\delta)[S$ accepts A of x by believing $(\alpha{:}\delta)]$.

My proposal is that the sent- and received-propositions for the statement expressed by $\ulcorner S$ believes t to be $F\urcorner$ have the form expressible as:

(5.6)   There is something (1) which S accepts of t while thinking of t in a way such that he knows what he is thinking about, (2) which is a possible sense of F, and (3) which I could accept of t by believing α of x

where α is one's sent- or received-designator for A. This can be made completely precise on the model of (3.6), but I will spare the reader the details.

One further sophistication is desirable. We can construct quite complicated indirect discourse sentences and symbolize their senses using the devices we have developed. For example, the sense of

(5.7) S_0 believes S_1 to believe S_2 to believe S_3 to be F

is

(5.8) $B[\partial_\rho,\partial_0,\partial_1,B[\partial_{\rho*},x,\partial_2,B[\partial_{\rho**},y,\partial_3,A]]]$.

But we encounter a difficulty symbolizing the sense of

(5.9) S_0 believes S_1 to be such that S_2 believes S_3 to believe him $(=S_1)$ to be F.

It is natural to try:

(5.10) $B[\partial_\rho,\partial_0,\partial_1,B[\partial_{\rho*},\partial_2,\partial_3,B[\partial_{\rho**},x,y,A]]]$.

204

The difficulty with (5.10) is that there is no indication whether x is to go with ∂_3 and y with ∂_1 (which is required by (5.9)) or x with ∂_1 and y with ∂_3. In an expression of the form $\ulcorner B[\partial_\rho,\partial_1,\partial_2,(F:x,y)]\urcorner$, one of the variables x and y must be bound and the other must remain free. Let us subscript B with the bound variable in order to resolve the ambiguity. With this convention we can symbolize the sense of (5.9) as:

$$(5.11) \quad B[\partial_\rho,\partial_0,\partial_1,B_x[\partial_{\rho*},\partial_2,\partial_3,B[\partial_{\rho**},x,y,A]]].$$

I will spare the reader the details of the definition of this notation.

6. Doxastic Quantification

Now let us turn to doxastic quantification. This is expressed by English sentences of the form $\ulcorner$There is something which S believes to be $F\urcorner$ or $\ulcorner$There is someone whom S believes to be $F\urcorner$. Let us symbolize the statement expressed by $\ulcorner$There is something which S believes to be $F\urcorner$ when the sense of S is ∂_S and F expresses the attribute A as $\ulcorner(\vee x)B[\partial_S,(A:x)]\urcorner$. The most common attempt to state truth conditions for this statement has involved something like the following:

(6.1) $(\vee x)B[\partial_S,(A:x)]$ is true iff $(\exists x)(\exists t)[t$ is a singular term & ∂_t designates x & $\mathfrak{B}_S(A:\partial_t)]$.

In this formulation, $\ulcorner\mathfrak{B}_S(A:\partial_t)\urcorner$ does not really make sense, because $(A:\partial_t)$ is a statement, not a proposition. But even if we ignore this difficulty, the analysis will not work. As Kaplan [1966] pointed out, if there is a shortest spy and S believes that there is, then letting t be the definite description 'the shortest spy', it would follow that there is someone whom S believes to be the shortest spy. However, we would not ordinarily agree to that unless S had some belief about who the shortest spy is.

The difficulty is that the doxastic quantification $\ulcorner$There is someone whom S believes to be $F\urcorner$ means $\ulcorner$There is someone *in particular* whom S believes to be $F\urcorner$. S must not only believe that there is someone who is F, but believe that of a specific individual in the sense of knowing who he believes to be F. The 'knowing who' requirement is easily explicable in terms of its parallel occurrence in believing-to-be. It seems reasonable to suppose that doxastic quantification involves quantification into some referentially transparent belief context, and the obvious candidate for such a belief context is believing-to-be. If we add the variable ∂_ρ to the quantified statement and analyze doxastic quantification straightforwardly as

(6.2) $\quad (\vee x)B[\partial_\rho,\partial_S,(A:x)] = (\vee x)B[\partial_\rho,\partial_S,x,A],$

we automatically get the requisite knowing-who requirement. This yields the truth conditions:

(6.3) $\quad (\vee x)B[\partial_\rho,\partial_S,(A:x)]$ is true iff $(\exists\alpha)(\exists x)(\exists\delta)[\delta$ designates x & $KW_\rho(S,\delta)$ & $\mathfrak{B}_S(\alpha:\delta)$ & α is a possible sent-concept for A for S under the circumstances of utterance].

Analogously, we can quantify into $K[\partial_\rho,\partial_S,\partial_t,A]$ for epistemic quantification. On this proposal, doxastic and epistemic quantification become perfectly ordinary quantification into transparent belief and knowledge contexts. Thus if we use this as a basis for a doxastic or epistemic logic, at least the quantificational part of the logic will be perfectly normal, unlike Hintikka's with its restricted range feature.

Although doxastic quantification is ordinary quantification, this does not imply that it behaves in an ordinary way. Because of the presence of the knowing-who requirement, doxastic quantification is infected with all of the vagaries of 'knows who'. Consider once more the London policeman who is on the track of Jack the Ripper. He knows a great deal about him, but not his identity. A new murder is committed, and the policeman believes Jack the Ripper to have done it. Then in one sense, there is someone whom he believes to be guilty (Jack the Ripper), but in another sense, as he does not know who Jack the Ripper is, it is false that there is someone whom he believes to be guilty. I take this sort of fluctuation as further confirmation of the preceding analyses. Notice also that, just as in the case of believing-to-be, a single statement may appeal to more than one identificatory parameter, so that we may say of the London policeman that there is someone whom he believes to be guilty, but he doesn't know who that person is.

7. Reflexive Knowledge and Belief

Castañeda [1964] observed that with pairs of statements like those expressed by the sentences:

(7.1) The Editor of *Soul* believes that the Editor of *Soul* is a millionaire.

(7.2)   The Editor of *Soul* believes that he himself is a millionaire.

neither entails the other. How are such reflexive belief locutions as (7.2) to be analyzed?

It may seem unproblematic that when the sense of F is a concept α and the sense of S is ∂_S, then the sense of

(7.3) S believes that he himself is F

is:

(7.4) $(\mathfrak{B}:\partial_S,\langle(\alpha:\iota_S)\rangle)$.

However, the possible sent-propositions for (7.4) would all have the form $(\mathfrak{B}:\delta,\langle(\alpha:\iota_S)\rangle)$. $\langle(\alpha:\iota_S)\rangle$ is a propositional designator designating $(\alpha:\iota_S)$ such that, in thinking of $(\alpha:\iota_S)$ in terms of $\langle(\alpha:\iota_S)\rangle$ one thinks of it in terms of its content. But $(\alpha:\iota_S)$ is logically idiosyncratic relative to S, so no one other than S can entertain it or think of it in terms of its content. It would follow then that there are no possible sent-propositions for (7.4) for anyone other than S. Clearly, (7.4) cannot be the sense of (7.3).

In believing that S believes that he himself is F, I am thinking of S's doxastic state not in terms of the specific proposition he believes, but structurally in terms of the *kind* of doxastic state it is. S is in a state of *reflexive belief*, which can be described as follows:

(7.5) $B_{\mathrm{refl}}(S,\alpha) \equiv \mathfrak{B}_S(\alpha:\iota_S)$.

The concept of reflexive belief is one that ordinary people possess, despite their being unaware that it is analyzable as in (7.5). In other words, (7.5) *analyzes* the concept of reflexive belief, in the sense that the analyzandum is logically equivalent to the analysans, but it does not *exhibit* the concept in a sense which would require that the analyzandum be literally the same concept as the analysans. There is a concept of *reflexive knowledge* which can be analyzed analogously:

(7.6) $K_{\mathrm{refl}}(S,\alpha) \equiv \mathfrak{B}_S(\alpha:\iota_S)$.

Let us take $\mathfrak{B}_{\mathrm{refl}}$ to be the concept expressed by $\ulcorner B_{\mathrm{refl}}(x,y) \urcorner$. The statement expressed by (7.3) is then:

(7.7) $(\mathfrak{B}_{\mathrm{refl}}:\partial_S,\langle\alpha\rangle)$.

Relaxing the assumption that F expresses a concept, taking it instead to express any attribute A, let us symbolize the sense of

(7.3) as $\ulcorner B_{\text{refl}}[\partial_S, A] \urcorner$ and the sense of the analogous epistemic sentence as $\ulcorner K_{\text{refl}}[\partial_S, A] \urcorner$. It seems clear that the truth conditions of $B_{\text{refl}}[\partial_S, A]$ are given by the following:

> (7.8) $B_{\text{refl}}[\partial_S, A]$ is true iff $(\exists \alpha)[\alpha$ is a possible sent-concept for A for S under the present circumstances & $B_{\text{refl}}(S, \alpha)]$.

Principle (7.8) yields a description of the diagram of $B_{\text{refl}}[\partial_S, A]$ on the model of (3.6). The possible sent- and acceptable received-propositions are those expressible in the form:

> (7.9) There is something which (1) S accepts of himself by reflexively believing something of himself, (2) is a possible sense of F, and (3) I could accept of S by believing α of S

where α is one's sent- or received-concept for A. Again, this can be made completely precise on the model of (3.6). The diagram of $K_{\text{refl}}[\partial_S, A]$ can be described analogously.

Reflexive belief locutions more complicated than (7.3) can be constructed:

> (7.10) S^* believes that S believes that he (S) is F;

> (7.11) S^* believes that S believes that he (S^*) is F;

> (7.12) S^{**} believes that S^* believes that S believes that he (S^{**}) is F;

and so on. But the senses of all such locutions can be expressed in terms of the doxastic statements we have already investigated. (7.12) is ambiguous between direct and indirect discourse:

> (7.12a) $B[\partial_{S^*}, B_{\text{refl}}[\partial_S, A]]$,   direct discourse;

> (7.12b) $B[\partial_\rho, \partial_{S^*}, \partial_S, B_{\text{refl}}[x, A]]$,   indirect discourse.

(7.11) has only an indirect discourse reading:

> (7.11a) $B_{\text{refl}}[\partial_{S^*}, B[\partial_\rho, \partial_S, x, A]]$.

The second occurrence of 'believes' in (7.12) is ambiguous between direct and indirect discourse:

> (7.12a) $B_{\text{refl}}[\partial_{S^{**}}, B[\partial_{S^*}, B[\partial_\rho, \partial_S, x, A]]]$,   direct discourse;

> (7.12b) $B_{\text{refl}}[\partial_{S^{**}}, B_x[\partial_\rho, \partial_{S^*}, \partial_S, B[\partial_{\rho^*}, x, y, A]]]$,
> indirect discourse.

As opinions to the contrary have sometimes been expressed, it is perhaps worth pointing out that the analysis of reflexive belief locutions shows nothing about the meanings of the singular terms occurring in such sentences. Any singular term can occur within a reflexive belief locution. What is unique about such a sentence is its predicate, not its subject.

8. Knowing What Some *F* Is

Let us consider one final epistemic locution. That is the locution ⌜*S* knows what some *F* is⌝ (e.g., 'Henry knows something that Mary has in her purse'). This is a somewhat unusual locution, but it will play an important role in the analysis of questions in Chapter Twelve. When the sense of *S* is ∂_S and the sense of *F* is *A*, let us symbolize the statement expressed by ⌜*S* knows what some *F* is ⌝ as ⌜$KWS[\partial_\rho,\partial_S,A]$⌝. Our analysis of this statement should now be obvious. Its truth conditions are:

(8.1) $KWS[\partial_\rho,\partial_S,A]$ is true iff $(\exists\alpha)(\exists\delta)[KW_\rho(S,\delta)$ & α is a possible sent-concept for *A* & $\Re_S(\alpha{:}\delta)]$.

The condition ⌜*S* knows what some α is⌝ which will be employed in the analysis of questions in Chapter Twelve is defined as:

(8.2) $(\exists\delta)[KW_\rho(S,\delta)$ & $\Re_S(\alpha{:}\delta)]$.

X
Languages, Institutions, and Conventions

1. Introduction

By virtue of what does a linguistic item have a particular meaning? The standard answer is that meanings are assigned by rules of language, and these rules are conventional. But in what sense is a language governed by rules and in what sense are the rules conventional?[1] Philosophers have sought illumination by comparing languages with games. More recently, they have come to talk of languages as *institutions*.[2] In contemporary philosophical parlance, an institution is said to be a system of rules defining a practice. The rules of the institution define the various roles that one can play within the institution, and tell us what states result from playing those roles in various ways. Examples of institutions are games, buying and selling, judicial proceedings, elections, promising, and supposedly languages. It is to be hoped that the appeal to institutions can throw light on the nature of rules of language, and enable us to understand in what sense languages are conventional. However, before this enlightenment can be achieved, we must become clearer on the nature of institutions. That is the goal of the present chapter.

There is an orthodox theory about institutions, due principally to G.E.M. Anscombe [1958], John Rawls [1955], and John Searle [1969]. This theory can be stated as follows. We begin by distinguishing between two kinds of rules regarding institutions: constitutive rules and regulative rules. As Searle puts the distinction: "regulative rules regulate antecedently existing forms of behavior;

---

[1] Helpful and influential discussions of this question can be found in Lewis [1975] and Bennett [1973] and [1976].
[2] See particularly Searle [1969].

... but constitutive rules do not merely regulate, they create new forms of behavior".[3] The constitutive rules actually define the institution. They define the various roles within the institution, define what it is to perform various ceremonies of the institution, and stipulate the outcomes of those ceremonies. Let us say, precisely, that the constitutive rules of an institution are those rules whose deletion would result in a different institution. The regulative rules, on the other hand, are external to the institution. They are more like rules of etiquette governing participation in the institution. Examples of regulative rules would be, 'Don't talk when your opponent is teeing off', or 'Don't swear at the referees'. On this account, the regulative rules are pretty uninteresting. For philosophical purposes, the institution can be identified with the set of its constitutive rules.

Under various circumstances, individuals *participate* in institutions—e.g., they play games, are tried in courts of law, vote in elections, make promises, etc. What, precisely, does it mean to say that a person is participating in an institution? The orthodox account of institutions does not contain an analysis of this notion, and it is not at all obvious how to give such an analysis. The difficulty is indicated by the tremendous variation from one institution to another of the conditions under which one is participating in the institution. In the case of a game, participation normally requires an antecedent agreement (perhaps not verbally explicit) to participate. But if one is being tried in a court of law, one has no choice but to participate—antecedent agreement is not required. In the case of buying and selling, there is a presumption to the effect that if one performs certain actions in a certain setting, then one is participating in the institution, but that presumption can be overcome if, for example, the individuals involved are just pretending. The analysis of what it is to participate in an institution is a difficult problem, and it is one that has not been addressed by defenders of the orthodox theory. But without an analysis of this notion, little clarification will result from casting languages as institutions.

Paul Ziff [1960] and Jay Rosenberg [1974] have objected to the view that languages are institutions on the grounds that one can violate the rules of language with relative impunity (e.g., in mis-speaking, in metaphor, in poetry, etc.) and still be speaking the language. That should be impossible if the rules of language *define* what it is to be speaking the language. Although Ziff and Rosenberg

---

[3] Searle [1969], p. 33.

have cast this as an objection to the view that language is an institution, it is better construed as an objection to the orthodox theory about institutions. It is possible to violate the rules of virtually any institution without thereby ceasing to participate in the institution. For example, there is a rule in football which prohibits the ball carrier from stepping out of bounds during the play, but if he does so without getting caught at it the game goes on. The orthodox theory appears to embody a simplistic account of the constitutive rules of an institution. We cannot regard those rules as merely defining various moves within the institution, because such "definitive" rules could not be violated without thereby terminating participation in the institution. We need a more sophisticated theory about the nature of institutions.

There are two basic questions to be asked about institutions: (1) What kinds of rules are involved in an institution? (2) What is it to participate in an institution? Once we have answers to these questions, we can examine the relevance of institutions to language.

2. Three Kinds of Rules

Let us begin with the most fundamental of the difficulties facing the orthodox theory of institutions. According to the orthodox theory, the constitutive rules are definitive of the institution, so it should be impossible to violate the constitutive rules and still be participating in the institution. However, in most games it is possible to *cheat* in various ways, e.g., by surreptitiously fouling the opposing players in basketball, or by peeking at your opponents' hands in poker. As the rules prohibiting this cannot be regarded as definitive of anything, it might be suggested that they are not constitutive rules at all but merely regulative rules. But that is unrealistic. They are not mere rules of etiquette regarding how the game should be played. To eliminate these rules would be to profoundly alter the nature of the games. We would have two different card games if in one of them we allowed the players to see one another's hands while we prohibited it in the other. These rules must be regarded as constitutive. However, if a player violates these rules, it does not follow that the game is thereby no longer being played.

The orthodox theory overlooks a distinction between two radically different kinds of constitutive rules. On the one hand, there are rules which *cannot* be broken, for the simple reason that it makes no sense to talk about breaking them. What would it mean, for example, to talk about breaking the rule that carrying the football across the goal line counts as making a touchdown (in a certain context)? That is just a *definition* of what it is to make a touchdown. Such rules do not prescribe courses of action. Rather, they *define* various roles, stations, ceremonies, accomplishments, tools, etc., of the institution. Let us call these the *definitive rules* of the institution.

The constitutive rules of an institution typically include more than just definitive rules. There are also rules telling the participants what they are *supposed to do* under various circumstances, e.g., 'Do not jostle the opposing player when he is shooting a basket', 'Do not peek at your opponents' hands', 'Do not touch a chess piece unless you are going to move it', etc. Let us call these the *prescriptive rules* of the institution. If the institution is a game, these are (for the most part) the rules the breaking of which constitutes cheating. Institutions other than games also have prescriptive rules. In the institution of trial by jury we have the rules: 'No one who is prejudiced against the defendant is supposed to serve on the jury' and 'Jurors are not supposed to see newspaper reports of the trial while they are deliberating'. In buying and selling we have the rules: 'The buyer is supposed to pay the seller what he owes him' and 'The seller is not supposed to interfere with the buyer's control of the purchased item once the transaction is completed'. In elections we have: 'No one is supposed to vote who is not a resident of the district'. These are all rules which agents can break without thereby ceasing to participate in the institution, but which are still among the rules which constitute the nature of the institution. For example, it would completely alter the nature of the institution of jury trials if the members of the jury were permitted to be prejudiced against the defendant.

The only way to accomodate prescriptive rules on the orthodox theory of institutions is to construe them as regulative rules rather than constitutive rules. However, that would imply that we could have the very same institution without those rules. I claim, on the contrary, that these rules are essential parts of the institutions and that to eliminate them would be to profoundly alter the nature of the institutions. For example, a competitive game will contain a definitive rule defining what it is to win the game, but it will also contain the prescriptive rule 'Players are supposed to have the

213

objective of winning'.[4] Without this prescriptive rule, the definitive rule defining what it is to win does no more than attach a label (i.e., 'winning position') to a certain situation in the game. For example, consider a card game in which you acquire points by taking tricks and you win by acquiring more points than your opponent. If we replace the rule 'Players are supposed to have the objective of winning' with the rule 'Players are supposed to have the objective of losing', surely we have generated a different card game—one which might more conventionally be described by saying that you win by taking fewer tricks than your opponent. The point is that in formulating competitive games we cannot do without the rule 'Players are supposed to have the objective of winning'. That rule is partly constitutive of the game, and hence must be counted as a constitutive rule. It appears that the constitutive rules must include both definitive and prescriptive rules.

In formulating the rules for an institution, we will normally define a number of concepts. Thus in football we define the concepts of a touchdown, a game, a football, a foul, a goal line, a player, etc. These definitions fall into two categories. Some define what we can call 'participatory activity'. These rules specify what moves one must make in various circumstances in order to be playing various roles in the institution. It seems that all other definitions are essentially abbreviatory. For example, we define a football to be an object of a certain physical description.[5] Then in formulating other rules, rather than repeating that physical description over and over again, we can simply talk about footballs. These abbreviatory definitions are logically eliminable. We could, at the expense of added complexity, formulate all of our other rules without them. However, they may not be psychologically eliminable. For example, it could be the case that speakers process a language in terms of a com-

---

[4] Perhaps it will be contended that this is analytic, being simply part of what we mean by 'winning'. However, this implies that the rules defining what it is to win are more than just definitive rules—they also contain the prescriptive rule that the players are supposed to have the objective of achieving the state defined.

[5] It might be supposed instead that the proper definition of 'football' has the general form 'object suitable for playing such-and-such a role in playing football'. However, this definition makes reference to the institution of football. As such, it could not, without circularity, be included among the constitutive rules of the institution, nor could it be used to supply the meaning of 'football' (the object) as it occurs in other constitutive rules. Thus I think that the proper definition must be simply in terms of the required physical characteristics of a football.

plicated recursive definition of well-formedness together with prescriptive rules telling them what to do with well-formed expressions. Eliminating the recursive definition and incorporating the recursion directly into the prescriptive rules would give us an inaccurate description of speaker psychology.

Let us call those definitive rules defining participatory activity in an institution the *ceremonial rules* of the institution. The ceremonial rules tell us what ranges of activity can constitute participating in the institution. For example, in a football game we can distinguish between the acts by the performance of which the quarterback is playing football and the acts which occur incidentally during the game. The quarterback may wipe his sweaty brow while waiting for the ball to be snapped. He is not playing football *by* wiping his brow. On the other hand, he is playing football by throwing the ball. We have a general distinction between those acts by the performance of which one participates in an institution and those acts which one merely performs incidentally while participating in the institution. The former are those which constitute participatory activity. We can regard the ceremonial rules as telling us which acts constitute participatory activity under various circumstances. For this purpose we can represent the ceremonial rule ⌜Under circumstances of type C, one can participate in I by performing an act of type A⌝ by the ordered pair $\langle C,A \rangle$.

When we describe an institution in terms partly of its ceremonial rules $\langle C,A \rangle$, it will not do to have C include such "institutional facts" as that a touchdown is being made (unless, of course, we already have an independent noninstitutional characterization of that fact), because the rules are supposed to tell us what it is to make a touchdown. Adapting Anscombe's terminology of "brute facts", we might suppose that C has to be a *brute circumstance-type*. It is a bit problematic just how this notion is to be defined, but the requirement that C be entirely brute is probably too strong anyway. Although C should not contain institutional facts about the present, there is no apparent difficulty about allowing it to contain institutional facts about the past (e.g., the fact that a touchdown was just scored). This will create no circularity because the definitions of our institutional notions can be made recursive on the sequence of participatory acts. Furthermore, unless we allow C to include past-tense institutional facts, the analysis of participation proposed in section three will not work without being made considerably more complex.

215

X. Languages, Institutions, and Conventions

I will adopt the convention that whenever I write $\ulcorner \langle C,A \rangle \urcorner$, C ranges over circumstance-types which do not include any present-tense institutional facts, and A ranges over act-types. Then we can characterize the ceremonial rules of an institution as follows:

(2.1) $\langle C,A \rangle$ is a ceremonial rule of I iff $\Box(\forall\alpha)(\forall S)[$if α is an act of type A which it is possible for S to perform under circumstances of type C, then it is possible for S to participate in I by performing α under circumstances of type $C]$.

Note that $\langle C,A \rangle$ being a ceremonial rule does not require that whenever one does A in circumstances C one is thereby participating in I. Rather, it is required that it is *possible* to participate in I by doing A in circumstances of type C. For example, it is possible to participate in the institution of buying and selling by making certain moves in response to certain overtures from a potential buyer, but one does not automatically do so if, for example, he is performing in a play.

The prescriptive rules of an institution tell us that, under various circumstances, the participants are *supposed to* do various things, but not that they *have* to do them in order to participate.[6] There are two types of prescriptive rules. In games, if there is a prescriptive rule of the form $\ulcorner$In circumstances of type C perform an act of type $A\urcorner$, then by participating in the game under circumstances of type C one commits oneself to performing an act of type A, but typically the commitment is not *to* anyone in particular. On the other hand, by promising one incurs a commitment to a specific person—the promisee. Similarly, in buying and selling, the seller incurs a commitment *to the buyer* not to interfere with the buyer's control of the purchased item. We might call these *nondirectional* and *directional* prescriptive rules, respectively. The nondirectional prescriptive rules can be regarded as a limiting case of directional rules in which the commitment is to everyone. We can represent directional prescriptive rules by ordered triples $\langle C,A,f \rangle$ where C is a type of circumstance, A is a type of act, and f is a function from circumstances to sets of persons. The triple $\langle C,A,f \rangle$ represents the rule $\ulcorner$Under circumstances of type C you are supposed to perform an act of type A, and if you fail to do so under concrete

---

[6] For simplicity, we count *refraining from performing an act of type A* as an act type.

216

circumstances γ, then you are accountable to the members of $f(\gamma)$ ⌐.[7]
For example, the rule ⌐If you have promised to do A, then you are
supposed to do A, and if you fail to do so, then you are accountable
to whomever you have promised⌐ will be represented by a triple
$\langle C,A,f \rangle$ where C consists of your having promised to do A and f
is that function which assigns to concrete circumstances γ the set
$\{S\}$ where S is the promisee. Nondirectional rules will be those for
which $f(\gamma)$ is the set of everyone. The need for thus incorporating the
directionality of commitment into a prescriptive rule may not be
immediately apparent, but its necessity will become evident in the
next section where we undertake an analysis of participation.

Let us define:

(2.3)   An individual S *conforms to* $\langle C,A,f \rangle$ iff either S is not
        in circumstances of type C or S performs an act of type A.

It will also be convenient to define:

(2.4) S *has a directional commitment to conform to* $\langle C,A,f \rangle$ iff
        S is in some circumstance γ in which he is committed to
        conforming to $\langle C,A,f \rangle$ and if he fails to do so, he will be
        accountable to the members of $f(\gamma)$.

Corresponding to a particular institution will be the set of
prescriptive rules *of* that institution. Some of these rules may be
rules to which all of the participants are supposed to conform, but
in any reasonably complex institution there are apt to be prescriptive
rules governing some roles within the institution but not binding
the players of other roles within that institution. For example, in
the institution of trial by jury there might be some esoteric rule
$\langle C,A,f \rangle$ binding judges but not even known to the general populace.
A juror is in no way bound by that rule. Just because one is a juror
and hence is participating in the institution, it does not follow that
if one finds oneself in circumstances of type C one is supposed to do
A. In light of this we must relativize prescriptive rules to roles within
institutions, or what comes to the same thing, to ceremonial rules.
To say that $\langle C,A,f \rangle$ is a prescriptive rule of I relative to a ceremonial

[7] A concrete circumstance is what would be described by giving a total description
of a possible world, and then replacing some singular term throughout by a variable.
An individual is in the described circumstance iff he satisfies the resulting description.

rule $\langle D,B \rangle$ is to say that one does not automatically have a directional commitment to conform to $\langle C,A,f \rangle$ when he performs an act of type B under circumstances of type C, but if one is *participating in I* by doing B under circumstances of type D, then one is supposed to conform to $\langle C,A,f \rangle$ and the direction of his commitment is determined by f. Precisely:

(2.5)　$\langle C,A,f \rangle$ is a *prescriptive rule of I relative to* $\langle D,B \rangle$ iff $\langle D,B \rangle$ is a ceremonial rule of I and $\square(\forall S)$(if S is participating in I by performing an act of type B under circumstances of type D, then S has a directional commitment to conform to $\langle C,A,f \rangle$) and $\sim \square(\forall S)(S$ has a directional commitment to conform to $\langle C,A,f \rangle$ whenever he performs an act of type B under circumstances of type D).

To be contrasted with the prescriptive rules of an institution are the regulative rules which also prescribe behavior, but which are not among the rules which actually constitute the nature of the institution. Thus in chess we have: 'Do not make unnecessary noise when your opponent is thinking about his next move'. Roughly, prescriptive rules are rules regarding what the participants are *supposed to do*, whereas regulative rules concern what it would be *good to do* in participating in the institution. It is unclear whether there is really a sharp division between these two classes of rules. In section four we will see that there can be no sharp division in the case of conventional institutions.

The preceding discussion has characterized the rules of an institution in terms, in part, of what it is to participate in an institution. Conversely, given a characterization of the institution in terms of its rules, we can seek an analysis of what it is to participate in the institution. That will be the topic of the next section.

3. Participation

The basic problem concerning participation is: what is it to participate in an institution. One participates in an institution by performing various acts. These are acts which instantiate ceremonial rules. Let us call these *participatory acts*. Among the conditions required for participation must be the condition that one is performing participatory acts, but there is normally more required than that. The institution must, in some sense, be "in force". Let us call these additional conditions *participatory preconditions*. Thus one is participating in an institution iff he is performing participatory acts under the appropriate participatory preconditions.

The participatory preconditions vary tremendously from institution to institution. Most games are *voluntary institutions* in the sense that the participants must normally agree to participate. To be contrasted with voluntary institutions are social institutions like that of elections. If one performs the participatory acts in the right setting, one is automatically voting whether one intends to be voting or not. We might call these *involuntary institutions*. There are also social institutions like promising, or buying and selling, which, although closer to the involuntary institutions than the voluntary ones, are not totally involuntary. In the case of promising, if a non-English speaker is told that 'I promise to pay you five dollars' means 'Please pass the butter', and subsequently says 'I promise to pay you five dollars' in an attempt to secure the butter, he has not thereby promised despite his performing a participatory act in a normal setting. And as Anscombe points out, if we go through the motions of buying and selling in the context of a play, we are not normally participating in the institution. However, our going through the motions of buying and selling in the context of a play does not automatically preclude our participating in the institution either. Suppose that in the play, one of the characters sells a watch to another character. Coincidentally, the actor playing the second character has agreed to buy a watch from the actor playing the first character, and for convenience they conclude their transaction during the performance. In that case, in the same setting as before, they are participating in the institution. Thus there is an important voluntary element in the institution of buying and selling.

It should be noted that even in the "voluntary institutions", wherein one *normally* comes to participate only by agreeing to do so, it is possible to come to participate involuntarily. Suppose a man is an announced participant in a chess tournament. When his name is called, he sits in his assigned place and begins moving the pieces around in an unintelligent way which results in his being quickly defeated. It will do him no good to protest, "I was only pretending to play; I wasn't really playing because I had not agreed to begin playing yet." Even if the protest is in earnest, and he did not intend to be playing, he *was* playing and *did* lose.

An account of the participatory preconditions of institutions must explain this tremendous variation from institution to institution. It might seem that we could explain this by supposing that the constitutive rules of the institution define what it is to participate in that institution by simply stipulating participatory preconditions for the institution. However, it takes little reflection to see that the constitutive rules cannot simply lay down the participatory preconditions by definition. An institution, as a system of constitutive rules, is an abstract entity. There are infinitely many institutions in which no one has ever participated and whose rules have never been transcribed. If the rules of the institution could determine the participatory preconditions, then infinitely many of these 'unused' institutions would be involuntary institutions, and it would follow that we have really been participating in them all along. That is nonsense. When I put on my shoes in the morning, I am not thereby participating in some complicated game which no one has ever thought about or would ever want to think about whose winning move involves, say, being the first person to jump off the top of the Washington Monument while singing 'Yankee Doodle'. But there is such a game, and if the participatory preconditions could be laid down stipulatively by the constitutive rules, then there would be such an involuntary game. It must be concluded that the participatory preconditions are not so determined. They must have an origin external to the institution itself. The constitutive rules contribute to the determination of the participatory conditions by stipulating what acts are participatory acts of the institution, but they cannot go further and stipulate the participatory preconditions under which the performance of participatory acts actually constitutes participation.

An obvious suggestion regarding why we are not participating in the game of the preceding paragraph is that it has never been "invented". The proposal would be that although institutions, as abstract entities, exist prior to anyone's coming to think about them, they must in some sense be "constructed" or "invented" or otherwise explicitly introduced into a society before people can participate in them. But that won't solve the problem for a least two reaons. First, even if we did "invent" the involuntary game of the preceding paragraph, it would not be true that people are automatically participating in it. We could invent the game, but we could not make it involuntary. The invention consists only of the construction of the rules and does not include a stipulation of participatory preconditions. They must have a different origin. Second, it is clear that most of the institutions in which we participate are not "invented". Many games are invented, but many others grow up implicitly by being played, and most social institutions have similar implicit origins. Whether an institution is "invented" appears to be irrelevant to the nature of its participatory preconditions.

We are looking for a source for the participatory preconditions of an institution which is external to the specification of the institution itself, and this source must be such as to explain why those conditions vary so widely from institution to institution. I suggest that the source of this variation lies in the varying moral and legal roles which institutions play in our society. Consider football. When you participate in a football game, you lead the other players to depend upon you to follow the rules. By participating in the game, you commit yourself to doing this, and you thereby incur a *prima facie* obligation to do it. Normally, this obligation arises from an antecedent agreement on your part to play the game, reflecting the fact that football is a voluntary institution. But as we have seen, even in the case of a voluntary institution, one can get oneself into the position of participating without explicitly agreeing to do so. Suppose a football game is being gotten up on a vacant lot. When the organizers call out, 'Everyone who is going to play, come out here!', you wander onto the field, subsequently go through the motions of getting ready to play, and even perform participatory acts during the first few plays of the game. Suppose you do all this without saying that you are going to play, all the while thinking to yourself, 'I'm not really going to play—I am just pretending'. Despite your intentions to the contrary, you really are playing the game and you have incurred an obligation to conform to the rules. By giving the impression that you are going to conform to the rules, you have morally committed yourself to doing so, even though you have not explicitly agreed to do so. The moral commitment is what makes it true that your performance of participatory acts counts as participation. As a first approximation, I suggest that we can characterize participation in a football game roughly as follows:

(3.1) A person S is participating in a football game iff he and all of the other putative participants are performing participatory acts and are *prima facie* morally committed to conforming to the prescriptive rules of the institution relative to their respective roles.

It may be objected that it is much too pretentious to say that the players are *morally* committed to playing the game out in accordance with the rules. But I disagree. Admittedly, it is not a very strong moral commitment. It is a *prima facie* commitment, and it would easily be overturned by conflicting moral considerations, but it is a moral commitment nevertheless. In the normal case in which all of the players begin by agreeing to play, the moral commitment is that of a promise. It is a morally innocuous sort of promise, easily overturned by weightier moral considerations, but it still carries a moral commitment. To break this commitment for no reason at all would be to behave immorally, just as to break any promise for no reason is to behave immorally.

The proposal is then that the participatory preconditions of football are the conditions under which one incurs a (*prima facie*) moral commitment to obey the prescriptive rules. This must be refined a bit, but it immediately explains why, on the one hand, one normally comes to play the game only by antecedently agreeing do so, but on the other hand, in extraordinary circumstances one can come to play the game without having agreed to do so.

Next I want to propose that an analogous account works for other institutions. Consider an involuntary institution—trial by jury. Simply going through the motions of a trial is not enough to make it true that you are actually being tried. The trial must be legally sanctioned. What this amounts to is that you are legally committed, by the laws of society, to conforming to the prescriptive rules of the institution insofar as they relate to your role as the defendant. Your going through the motions (performing the participatory acts) constitutes participation in the institution iff you have such a legal commitment. Thus the participatory preconditions for being tried are the conditions under which one has a *prima facie* legal commitment to conform to the prescriptive rules of the institution. This is analogous to the case of football, although in this case the moral commitment has been replaced by a legal commitment.

Consider the institution of buying and selling. To use Anscombe's example, suppose that at my request the grocer delivers a quarter pound of potatoes to me, the posted price of the potatoes being five shillings, and upon receipt of the potatoes I hand the grocer five shillings. Under what circumstances have I purchased the potatoes? Not under *all* circumstances—we might be doing this in an amateur theatrical performance. The participatory acts involved in the purchase consists of (a) my making an offer for the potatoes, (b) the grocer accepting my offer, (c) the grocer physically transferring the potatoes to me, and (d) my physically transferring the five shillings to the grocer. On the suggested account, my purchasing the potatoes consists of my performing acts (a) and (d), the grocer performing acts (b) and (c), and our doing so under conditions in which we each have a *prima facie* legal commitment to obeying the prescriptive rules of the institution. The main prescriptive rule of this institution is the rule that once the participatory acts have been completed the seller is not supposed to interfere with the buyer's control of the purchased item (within certain legal limits) and the buyer is not supposed to interfere with the seller's control of the money paid. In our society, buying and selling is a legal institution and the commitment required for participation is legal commitment. In a less formalized society it could be a moral commitment.

The conception of institutions which emerges from these examples is that they are essentially moral and legal instruments of a certain sort, and participation consists of the performance of acts whereby one acquires certain kinds of moral and legal obligations with respect to the institution. This suggests the following simple analysis:

(3.2) S is participating in I iff there is a ceremonial rule $\langle C,A \rangle$ of I such that S is performing an act of type A under circumstances of type C and S is *prima facie* directionally committed to conforming to the prescriptive rules of I relative to $\langle C,A \rangle$.

However, one may be in circumstances of type C under which it is possible to participate in I by performing α, but also in circumstances of a narrower type C^* in which it is not possible to participate in I by performing α. If C and C^* are types of circumstances, let us say that C^* is *narrower than* C iff being in circumstances of type C^* logically entails being in circumstances of type C. Then (3.2) should be modified to read:

(3.3) S is participating in I iff there is a ceremonial rule $\langle C,A \rangle$ of I such that S is performing an act of type A under circumstances of type C and S is *prima facie* directionally committed to conforming to the prescriptive rules of I relative

223

to $\langle C,A \rangle$ and S is not in circumstances of any narrower type C^* such that $\langle C^*,A \rangle$ is not a ceremonial rule of I.[8]

The necessity for including reference to the direction of the commitment can be illustrated by looking at promising. Suppose Jones and Smith are performing roles in a play in which the character played by Jones promises to pay five dollars to the character played by Smith. Suppose that before the play, Jones promises Smith's mother that if he utters the line 'I promise to pay you five dollars' during the performance, then he will pay Smith five dollars. During the play, Jones does utter that line, thereby performing the participatory activity of promising under circumstances in which he appears to be committed to conforming to all of the prescriptive rules of promising (the principal one being that he is supposed to do what he has promised to do). Thus the analysans of (3.3) appears

---

[8] Two observations about the sense of 'committed' in (3.3) should be made to diffuse possible objections. First, there is a sense of $\ulcorner S$ is morally committed to conforming to $\langle C,A,f \rangle \urcorner$ which is equivalent to $\ulcorner S$ is morally committed to its being the case that he is conforming to $\langle C,A,f \rangle \urcorner$, but this is a very weak sense. This can be seen as follows. Let $C\bar{A}$ be the kind of circumstance which consists of being in circumstances of type C and not performing an act of type A. Necessarily, if one conforms to $\langle C,A,f \rangle$, then one conforms to $\langle C\bar{A},B,f \rangle$, regardless of what B is. Thus if one is morally committed to its being the case that he is conforming to $\langle C,A,f \rangle$, then he is morally committed to its being the case that he is conforming to $\langle C\bar{A},B,f \rangle$. But now let $\langle C,A,f \rangle$ be the rule 'Do not covet your neighbor's wife' and let $\langle C\bar{A},B,f \rangle$ be the rule 'If you covet your neighbor's wife, throw yourself in the volcano'. Clearly, being committed to conforming to the first rule does not, in any interesting sense, commit you to conforming to the second rule. It does, however, commit you to its being the case that you are conforming to the second rule. What is required by the ordinary sense of 'commitment' and lacking in the example is that if you were in circumstances of type $C\bar{A}$ then you would have a *prima facie* obligation to perform an act of type B.

There is a second possible confusion to be avoided. Let $A \cup B$ be the act type exemplified by any act which is either of type A or of type B. Necessarily, if one conforms to $\langle C,A,f \rangle$, then one conforms to $\langle C, A \cup B, f \rangle$. Furthermore, there is a temptation to say that if one is committed to conforming to $\langle C,A,f \rangle$, then one is committed to conforming to $\langle C, A \cup B, f \rangle$. I am inclined to think that there is a sense in which that is true, but that in the most important sense of 'committed to conforming', it is false. Otherwise, every act one performs would be the fulfillment of an obligation, because if one performs an act β which is of some type B, and one has an obligation to conform to $\langle C,A,f \rangle$, then by the above principle one has the obligation to conform to $\langle C, A \cup B, f \rangle$ and one is fulfilling that obligation by performing β. This is surely not an interesting sense of fulfilling an obligation. The normal sense of $\ulcorner S$ is committed (or obligated) to conform to $\langle C,A,f \rangle \urcorner$ does not license the inference from this to $\ulcorner S$ is committed (or obligated) to conform to $\langle C, A \cup B, f \rangle \urcorner$.

to be satisfied. But Jones' actions during the play do not constitute promising. The reason appears to be that although Jones is committed to paying Smith five dollars, his commitment is not to Smith. Rather, it is to Smith's mother. If we change the example and suppose Jones to have promised Smith (rather than Smith's mother) that if he utters the line 'I promise to pay you five dollars' then he will subsequently pay Smith five dollars, it is not unreasonable to say that upon uttering that line during the play Jones *does* promise Smith that he will pay him five dollars. The situation is peculiar and it is not completely obvious that this is the right thing to say, but it is not obviously wrong either, whereas it is obviously wrong to say that Jones promises in the previous case.[9] Thus the direction of the commitment makes a difference.

We have seen that two different kinds of commitment can lead to participation in an institution: moral commitment and legal commitment. We can define two kinds or modes of participation—social participation and legal participation—depending upon whether the commitment is moral or legal. It is also possible to generate "quasi-legal" modes of participation from quasi-legal rules generated within various organizations. Thus, for example, students can vote in a school election and their participatory obligations arise from the school rules. It is possible to participate in an institution in more than one of these ways.

With all of the preceding qualifications, I am reasonably confident that (3.3) formulates a necessary condition for participation. I am less confident that it formulates a sufficient condition, but its ability to withstand counterexamples is suggestive of its adequacy. The simplest way of trying to construct counterexamples to the sufficiency of the analysans is to consider the performance of participatory acts in plays. In such cases, we are not committed in the normal ways to conforming to the prescriptive rules, but we might obtain such obligations in abnormal ways and this might lead to counterexamples. In this respect, consider a play in which two characters play a game of chess in which one defeats the other by a fool's mate. The moves in the game are prescribed by the dramatist. If two actors make these moves in the context of the play, they are not playing chess (e.g., it is not true that one of them has really

---

[9] If we decide that no promise occurs in this case, this will presumably be because (unlike buying and selling, or playing chess) it is simply impossible to promise by uttering a line in a play. If so, such promising will be precluded by the ceremonial rules.

beaten the other with a fool's mate). And yet, assuming that they have an obligation to perform the play, it appears at first blush as if they are committed to conforming to the prescriptive rules of chess. The game they pretend to play is a real game (in the abstract sense in which a chess game can be repeated), and hence it appears that anyone making those moves is conforming to the rules of the game. Accordingly, if they are committed to making those moves, then they are committed to conforming to the rules. Thus (3.3) appears to yield the unfortunate conclusion that they are playing chess. However, this is illusory. We have already noted that a rule which all competitive games have in common stipulates that players are supposed to have the objective of winning. This is not to say that if they don't have the objective of winning then they are not playing—that would make it impossible to throw a game. But it does imply that if they are not making the moves of the game under circumstances in which they have a *prima facie* obligation to be trying to win, then they are not playing. No such obligation exists when the moves are made in the course of a theatrical performance, so the actors are not really playing chess.

If we make reasonable assumptions about the rules of various institutions, it is possible to handle at least a wide variety of putative counterexamples. On this basis, I shall tentatively endorse (3.3) as the analysis of participation. This is to affirm the necessity of a biconditional relating participation to participatory activity and obligations to conform to prescriptive rules. A natural rejoinder is that although this biconditional is necessary it does not constitute an analysis—when one is participating in an institution one only has obligations to conform to the prescriptive rules *because* one is participating. The participation does not consist of the possession of such obligations, because the obligations arise from the participation. But if we look at concrete examples, this appears to be false. The participatory obligations always seem to have other origins. For example, when one voluntarily agrees to play football one acquires certain obligations, but those obligations stem directly from one's antecedent agreement. Similarly, when we sit on a jury we have certain legal obligations, but they derive from the laws of the land. Those laws tell us that if our name has been chosen in a certain way then we are supposed to do such and such. The laws do not mention participation and we do not have to talk about participation in order to explain our having the legal obligations we do. The obligations do not derive from the participation.

Of course, it does not yet follow that the participation derives from the obligation. Perhaps the participation and obligation have a common origin. If this were so, we would normally expect there to be cases in which they diverge. But that does not seem to be the case. For example, consider the argument about whether a person was playing chess when he did not explicitly agree to play chess but gave the impression that he had and went through the motions of getting beaten. The argument is precisely the same as the argument about whether he committed himself to playing chess. If the moral question has no unequivocal answer, neither does the question about participation.

My primary concern has been to affirm the necessity of (3.3). This biconditional is neutral regarding what derives from what, and it is difficult to get a clear grasp on what is being asked in inquiring whether the participation derives from the obligation or the obligation derives from the participation. But some sense can be given to the claim that the participation derives from the obligation by noting that if (3.3) is necessary and there is such a thing as the naturalistic fallacy, then no compilation of nonmoral facts can be logically equivalent to the claim that one is participating in an institution. Thus no nonmoral analysis of participation is possible. In this sense, participation is an inherently moral notion.[10]

4. Conventional Institutions

It will be my contention that languages are not just institutions, but *conventional* institutions. That rules of language are conventional is almost a philosophical cliché. It is intended to provide an explanation for the origin of the particular rules we actually employ in using language, but it is not very helpful without an explanation of conventions. A great deal of recent work has been directed at the analysis of the notion of a convention. Most of this work takes its impetus from David Lewis [1969]. Lewis' objective was to give a general analysis of the notion of a convention, and then apply that to language. We could undertake detailed criticism of Lewis' analysis at this point, but a more general objection can be elicited by

---

[10] This provides the ammunition for a rebuttal of Searle's infamous derivation of 'ought' from 'is'. (See Searle [1969], Chapter 8.) Premise (1b) of the derivation says, in our terminology, that the participatory preconditions of promising are satisfied. That requires, in part, that the promiser have certain moral obligations, and hence is a moral premise.

considering what we are trying to accomplish by the appeal to conventionality.[11] Our objective is to explain the sense in which linguistic rules are conventional. One way to do that would be to give a general analysis of 'convention', but an equally good way to do it is to explain the specific sense in which languages are conventional without attempting to explain what conventions are in general. We will undertake this latter task by attempting to explain, in a slightly more general vein, the sense in which institutions can be conventional. Many of our institutions might reasonably be said to be conventional in either of two senses. The first sense in which an institution may be conventional is that its participatory preconditions are determined by social conventions. That is, social conventions may determine under what circumstances the performance of participatory activity constitutes participation. As we have seen, the participatory preconditions are the conditions under which the participants acquire suitable commitments so that their participatory activity constitutes participation. Those commitments may arise voluntarily out of their explicitly agreeing to participate, as happens in most games. But many of our institutions are in varying degrees "involuntary" so that if one performs certain acts under certain conditions one automatically acquires the requisite commitments and is participating. Thus in buying and selling, by performing certain initial acts under normal circumstances, one automatically incurs the moral obligations required for participation in the institution. The circumstances under which these obligations are incurred are established by social conventions. An institution of this sort, whose participatory preconditions are determined by convention, will henceforth be called 'conventional'.

There is also a stronger sense in which an institution can be conventional. This concerns the origin of the constitutive rules themselves. Some institutions have "inventors"—there was a historical time at which some person or group of persons explicitly compiled a list of constitutive rules for the institution (often by modifying the list of constitutive rules of an earlier institution). This describes the proximal origin of most games and many other institutions. However, some of our most important institutions were not originally introduced to us in this manner. Rather, their con-

[11] The most recent statement of Lewis' analysis is in Lewis [1975] wherein he makes significant modifications in response to suggestions in Jonathan Bennett [1973]. See also Bennett [1977], Tyler Burge [1975], and Richard Grandy [1977].

stitutive rules are themselves the result of social conventions. This applies to language *par excellence*. Living languages are not invented. They grow up by themselves as a result of our evolving social conventions. Insofar as the rules are written down, this is done in an attempt to describe the rules implicit in our conventions. The transcription of the rules is a descriptive process rather than a stipulative process. It is an attempt to describe a pre-existing phenomenon rather than to design a new pattern of behavior. Institutions of this sort, whose constitutive rules are themselves determined by convention, will be called 'strongly conventional'.

Our most important institutions are all either strongly conventional or of a strongly conventional origin. In an advanced society, the legal institutions may have explicitly codified sets of rules which serve to define the institutions in which the members of the society participate, but those institutions are generally developments out of earlier strongly conventional institutions whose rules were first descriptively transcribed and then modified. Thus it becomes of some importance to understand the nature of social conventions as they relate to institutions.

I suggest that the nature of conventional institutions has eluded philosophers through their not realizing that participation in an institution is a moral notion, and hence the conventionality of institutions is a phenomenon of conventional *morality*. They have been searching for another kind of convention—one applicable to nonmoral rules. Lewis' analysis is *only* applicable to nonmoral rules, and thus cannot help us in the analysis of what it is for an institution to be conventional. I suggest that the best way to approach the problem of conventionality for institutions is in terms of the notion of conventional obligation. There is a distinction between what we might term roughly 'important conventions' and 'unimportant conventions'. Important conventions are those which generate conventional obligations. The notion we need for the analysis of conventional institutions is that of conventional obligation, and hence the only conventions of interest to us will be important conventions.[12] Thus for the purposes of this investigation I propose

[12] Lewis' analysis attempts to straddle the distinction between important conventions and unimportant conventions by requiring that the 'belief that others conform to R gives everyone a good and decisive reason for conform to R himself'. Burge's example of the sentimental hat-tippers and Lewis' own example of conventional dress styles suggest that this is too strong a requirement for unimportant conventions. On the other hand, it is too weak to generate conventional obligations.

to restrict the use of the term 'convention' to important conventions. I will only call a rule a 'convention' when it is a rule conformance to which is required by conventional obligations. But it must be admitted that this is an artificial tightening of the notion of a convention.

How do social conventions impose moral commitments on the members of society? The most straightforward way of establishing a conventional obligation would be to literally convene all the members of society and have each member S explicitly agree to treat every other member S^* in accordance with some rule R insofar as S^* reciprocates by treating S in accordance with R. Such an explicit agreement would then commit each member of the society to conforming to rule R in dealing with other members of the society just as long as the other members also conform to rule R in dealing with him. This is the model of conventional obligation involved in the traditional social contract theory, but of course this is not what really happens in most cases of conventional obligation.

We can come closer to understanding conventional obligation by realizing that one can implicitly commit oneself to an agreement without doing so explicitly. Suppose you know that the members of some group G have committed themselves to treating anyone in accordance with rule R who agrees to reciprocate by treating them in accordance with rule R. One can incur an obligation to treat the members of G in accordance with rule R by explicitly accepting their bargain. But one can also incur such an obligation by intentionally giving the members of G the impression that one has accepted their bargain and then taking advantage of their having that impression to get them to treat oneself in accordance with rule R. It would be morally wrong to avail oneself of their commitment in this way and then, when one's own turn comes to treat them in accordance with rule R, to protest that one never agreed to do so. One has incurred an obligation. In effect, one has "implicitly accepted their bargain".[13]

I suggest that the preceding sort of situation in which one implicitly incurs an obligation provides the model on which to understand conventionality. We will make this model precise and use it to generate analyses both of 'convention' and 'conventional obliga-

---

[13] Note that this is not to explain conventions in terms of the metaphor of "implicit bargains". This is just to label a situation which we have described precisely and without metaphor.

tion'. Let us define:

(4.1) S is *personally committed* to conforming to $\langle C,A,f \rangle$ iff S intends to conform to $\langle C,A,f \rangle$ and S intends for it to be the case that in any circumstance γ in which he fails to conform to $\langle C,A,f \rangle$ he is accountable to the members of $f(\gamma)$ for having failed.

Then we might try, as a first approximation:

(4.2) R is a convention of G iff if S is any member of G (or an important subgroup of G) who is occasionally in a situation governed by R (so that he can either conform or fail to conform to R), then S is personally committed to conforming to R insofar as his doing so or not doing so affects anyone in G who in turn is personally committed to conforming to R insofar as his doing so or not doing so affects S.

However, this is too inclusive. R might be some nonconventional moral rule to which everyone automatically has a *prima facie* obligation to conform. For example, R might be 'Do not wantonly hurt others'. If the members of S are moved by the fact that they have such an obligation to conform to R, R will satisfy the analysans of (4.2), but we would not regard R as a convention of G.

This suggests that we should require that the members of G not have an automatic *prima facie* obligation to conform to R, i.e., that they not have a *prima facie* obligation to conform to R which they would have even if others did not conform to R. However, that is too strong a requirement.[14] Consider a society in which there has been a breakdown of law and order, with the result that people go about shooting one another for the fun of it. In a rare moment of sanity, the members of the society come to agree not to shoot anyone carrying a white flag. It is then a convention in this society not to shoot people carrying white flags. However, the members of G automatically have a *prima facie* obligation not to shoot people carrying white flags (because, presumably, we automatically have a *prima facie* obligation not to shoot people). Thus it is possible for R to be a convention of G even though the members of G have an automatic *prima facie* obligation to conform to R. The reason our obligation not to shoot people carrying white flags would be only

---

[14] I am indebted to Stanley Kaminsky for this observation and for the following counterexample.

conventional is apparently that the members of G are not moved by the moral obligation which they have independently of whether others shoot people carrying white flags. Their personal commitment to conform to R does not arise from that source. Thus I propose the following analysis of 'convention' (in the sense of 'important convention'):

(4.3) R is a convention of G iff if S is any member of G (or an important subgroup of G) who is occasionally in a situation governed by R (so that he can either conform or fail to conform to R), then S is personally committed to conforming to R insofar as his doing so or not doing so affects anyone in G who in turn is personally committed to conforming to R insofar as his doing so or not doing so affects S, and S's reason for thus conforming to R is at least in part not that he believes he has a *prima facie* obligation to conform to R which he would have even if others in G did not conform to R.

If the members of G have an automatic *prima facie* obligation to conform to R, their conforming to R may be partly conventional and partly nonconventional depending upon the extent to which their conformance is motivated by that automatic obligation.

Conventions in the sense of (4.3) are self-perpetuating. If a member of the society avails himself of this commitment to get other members of the society to conform to rule R, he thereby incurs a moral obligation to conform to rule R himself. Then insofar as he is motivated by moral considerations, he will acquire a personal commitment to conform to rule R. Thus in a society of reasonably moral people, once a rule becomes conventional, it will remain a convention as membership in the society changes.

The conventions of a society may logically entail other rules in the sense that if one is committed to conforming to the conventions it follows logically that one is committed to conforming to the other rules. We can define entailment between rules in a basically uninformative but unobjectionable manner as follows:

(4.4) Γ *entails* R iff, necessarily, anyone having a directional moral commitment to conform to all the rules in Γ has a directional moral commitment to conform to R.

If a rule is entailed by the conventions of a society it may not itself be a convention, but it seems reasonable to say that it is conventional to conform to that rule. Let us define:

(4.5) It is *conventional in G to conform to R* iff R is entailed by the set of conventions of G.

Now we are in a position to define the notion of conventional obligation. From the fact that it is conventional in G to conform to R it does not follow that any particular member of G has an obligation to conform to R. However, I propose that the following is a true moral principle:

(4.6) If it is conventional in G to conform to R and S knows that this is conventional and has availed himself of conventions from which R follows, then S has a *prima facie* directional obligation to conform to R insofar as his doing so or not doing so affects other members of G.

We might call this *the principle of implicit agreement*. It is the principle underlying the acquisition of conventional obligations. S incurs a *prima facie* conventional obligation to conform to R just in case he satisfies the antecedent of (4.6):

(4.7) S has a *prima facie* conventional obligation (in G) to conform to R iff it is conventional in G to conform to R and S knows that this is conventional and has availed himself of conventions which entail R.

Now let us turn to the conventionality of institutions. I propose that this is to be understood in terms of conventional obligations. Conventional institutions are those whose participatory preconditions are determined by convention. According to (3.3), participation in an institution is a moral notion involving the possession of commitments to conform to the prescriptive rules, and the participatory preconditions are the conditions under which one has those commitments. Thus to say that the participatory preconditions are determined by convention is to say that it is determined by convention when one has those commitments, i.e., those commitments are conventional. Thus the following analysis seems reasonable:

(4.8) An institution I is *conventional* iff for any ceremonial rule $\langle C,A \rangle$ of I, there is a type of circumstance C^* logically compatible with C which does not include the establishment of any new conventions and which is such that if an

233

individual performs an act instantiating $\langle C,A \rangle$ under circumstances of type C^*, then he is participating in I, and the obligations required for him to be participating are all conventional.

The conventions which establish the participatory preconditions of a conventional institution may be of either of two sorts. As in the case of most legal institutions and most games, there may be an official transcription of the constitutive rules of the institution, and the conventions may appeal directly to that transcription. On the other hand, the conventions may simply be rules telling us that under various circumstances we are supposed to do various things, and may make no reference to an official set of constitutive rules. A set of conventions of the latter sort may be just as efficacious in leading to the moral commitments required for participation in an institution. The difference is, roughly, that conventions of the first sort talk about the institution itself, whereas conventions of the second sort talk only about the particular actions that are called for under various circumstances in participating in the institution.

Let us say that an institution is *weakly conventional* iff it is conventional and there is an official transcription of its constitutive rules to which the conventions governing its participatory preconditions appeal. We defined a *strongly conventional* institution to be one whose constitutive rules are of conventional origin. This can be captured by saying that a strongly conventional institution is one in which the conventions governing the participatory preconditions do not appeal to an official transcription of any of the rules. Perhaps most of our conventional institutions have an intermediate status between being weakly conventional and being strongly conventional. For example, we have rules of correct English which originated as an attempt to partially describe English usage but which have now come to partially constitute correct English. Our current conventions regarding English appeal to those rules. However, the rules are far from being complete. The bulk of the constitutive rules of English have never been successfully transcribed and are only implicit in our social conventions governing English. Even in the case of games there are rules like 'Players are supposed to have the objective of winning' which do not appear in the rule books. These rules are common to all competitive games and are conventionally understood.

Let us say that an institution is *moderately conventional* iff it is conventional but not weakly conventional. The moderately conventional institutions are those at least some of whose constitutive rules are established by "implicit" convention. The logical mechanism by which these rules are selected by conventions is quite simple. Given the totality of our conventions and the constitutive rules of a particular institution, it is completely determinate whether that institution satisfies the analysans of (4.8). If it does, and not all of the conventions by virtue of which it satisfies that analysans make reference to transcribed rules, then it is a moderately conventional institution. In this way our social conventions select particular institutions whose constitutive rules have never been (at least completely) transcribed.

It is unlikely, however, that our social conventions will uniquely characterize the structure of our moderately conventional institutions. Because obligation admits of degrees, so must participation admit of degrees. To be participating in an institution is to be participating to at least a minimal degree. Thus if we consider two institutions which are identical except that one contains a prescriptive rule not present in the other, our social conventions might lead to our participating in both institutions but to somewhat different degrees. There is no sense to be given to the claim that one of those institutions is "really" our conventional institution and the other only a close cousin. Thus our social conventions may be inadequate to uniquely determine the prescriptive rules of our institutions. Analogously, consider two institutions I_1 and I_2 which are identical except that I_1 admits participatory acts not admitted by I_2 but contains the prescriptive rule that participants are not supposed to perform those acts. For example, in buying and selling we might have a choice between saying that certain practices are misleading and should be avoided and saying that those practices constitute outright fraud and nullify the transaction. Again, our social conventions may not be sufficient to select one of these institutions and rule out the other. In general, the best our social conventions may be able to do is select a group of related institutions in which we participate simultaneously, although to varying degrees. In time our conventions may grow sharper so as to rule out some of these institutions, but there is only one way they are ever likely to grow so sharp as to rule out all but one. That will normally require artificial legislation wherein we explicitly transcribe a set of rules which we take as defining our institutions, thus making them only weakly conventional.

5. Languages as Institutions

Now let us apply our theory of institutions to language. I claim that languages are conventional institutions. Ziff and Rosenberg, on the other hand, have objected to the view that language is rule-constituted on the grounds that one can deviate from the rules and still be using language. Both accidental and intentional deviations are possible. Regarding accidental deviations, a lecturer may misspeak and his audience may not even notice it because they know what he means. He is in violation of linguistic rules, but it would be absurd to claim that he is not making a statement. And it seems even more puzzling that a speaker can intentionally violate the rules (e.g., in metaphor) or apparently change the rules in midstream by announcing that he is going to use a word in a new way.

There are at least two reasons why the possibility of such violations does not show that languages are not rule-governed. First, Ziff and Rosenberg have fallen prey to the standard misconception of constitutive rules according to which they are all definitive rather than prescriptive. The violation of prescriptive rules does not preclude one's participating in an institution. Second, with regard to misspeaking we have already noted that a speaker can make a statement the stating of which depends upon our using a language *L* without stating *within L*. There are more ways of using linguistic institutions for communication than by participating in them.

However, the fact that we can explicitly change the rules as we go along (e.g., by redefining words) suggests that it would be better after all to say that a natural language like English is not a specific institution, but rather a *kind* of institution. Languages grow and develop, both naturally and stipulatively. When this happens, it seems likely that the constitutive rules are changing, so the institution is changing, but the language remains the same. The basis for saying that we are still using the same language is that the new institution is very closely related to the old. However, this is a minor concession. Although English may not be an institution, any particular version of English is an institution, and when we speak English we are participating in some such institution. We can express this concession by saying that language is institutional, although a specific language (e.g., English) may be a kind of institution rather than a particular institution.

If language is institutional, it follows that some linguistic rules are constitutive. Which rules are these? Preliminary to answering this, let me sketch the orthodox view of language as an institution. First come the syntactical rules. These define the notion of a syntactically correct utterance or inscription, and in our jargon would be assimilated to the ceremonial rules defining participatory activity (the ceremonies being speech acts). On the orthodox view, semantical rules are also definitive rules. They determine the product of a speech act, i.e., they stipulate what statement is made, what question is asked, what is promised, etc. This orthodox view, embodying as it does the orthodox view of institutions, is forced to classify any remaining rules as merely regulative rules. Thus, for example, rules governing Gricean implicatures must be relegated to rules of polite conversation, or some such thing.

The orthodox view seems doubtful in several respects. I think we must accept this much of it: the semantical rules determine what statement, question, promise, etc., is made when one performs a speech act. However, stating is not a ceremony created by the rules of some particular language. It is possible to state the same statement in different languages. Neither the statement nor the stating can be an artifact of a linguistic institution. Rather than being of institutional origin, these are logical notions equally applicable to all linguistic institutions. To be sure, there is an associated ceremony for a language L, viz., stating *within L*, and this is a creation of the institution L. But the concept of stating the statement is not simply the disjunction of the concepts of stating the statement in all the languages we happen to use. Rather, the concept of stating the statement is a general logical notion which imposes prior constraints on all possible languages.

A great deal of the structure of linguistic institutions is predetermined by general logical considerations dealing with statements and stating. For example, it is presumably not up to the particular language to determine whether, in successful stating, the speaker must intend to state the statement he does state. It seems likely that however this question is to be resolved, it must be resolved in the same way for all languages. Thus the amount of illumination to be gleaned from considering the institutional nature of language is limited. There are numerous logical constraints which an institution must satisfy in order to qualify as a language, and these logical constraints are not of institutional origin.

Nevertheless, although appeal to the institutional nature of language will not solve all of the problems of the philosophy of language, it does contribute significantly to the clarification of some. One of our most important observations about institutions is that in addition to definitive rules, they number prescriptive rules among their constitutive rules. This makes it possible for there to be important classes of erstwhile overlooked constitutive rules of language. For example, we are no longer automatically forced to regard the rules governing Gricean conversational implicatures as regulative rules. They may instead be prescriptive rules governing stating. And the existence of prescriptive rules will be of pre-eminent importance in the next chapter where we propose an analysis of stating.

XI
Stating

1. Stating as Participating

Two central notions of the theory of language developed in this book are those of stating a statement and sending a proposition. The main purpose of this chapter is to propose analyses of these notions. In the next chapter, related analyses will be proposed for questioning, commanding, and requesting. The basic idea behind the analysis of stating is that to state something is to commit yourself to it in a certain way. To make a statement is to offer a kind of guarantee to your audience. You are in some sense accountable for making a false statement. This basic idea is a familiar one, but it has resisted expansion into a full fledged analysis of stating. Such an analysis can be obtained from our analysis of what it is to participate in an institution.

We have distinguished between the general notion of stating and the more limited notion of stating within L. To state within L is to perform a ceremony of the institution L, i.e., it is to participate in a certain way in a linguistic institution. The participatory activity involved in stating is typically quite simple, consisting of a single "locutionary act" of uttering or writing a sentence. We follow the tradition of calling such locutionary acts *utterances*. According to our analysis of participation, such participation consists of performing an utterance under circumstances in which the "setting" is right (i.e., one is instantiating a ceremonial rule) and in which one is *prima facie* committed to conforming to those prescriptive rules of the institution which govern stating. Those rules tell us that in stating one is supposed to do or refrain from doing various things. For example, you are not supposed to state something unless you believe that it is true. Let us call these rules 'the rules of statemental obligation'. Then borrowing from our analysis of participation, we can express the bare bones of an analysis of stating within L as follows:

(1.1) S states within L iff S performs an utterance under appropriate circumstances in which he has a *prima facie* commitment to conform to the rules of statemental obligation of L.

To complete this analysis we need an account of (1) what circumstances are appropriate for stating and (2) what the rules of statemental obligation are. In the former connection we must ask what conditions are necessary for stating. For example, must the speaker have certain intentions? However, most of the weight in our analysis will be borne by the rules of statemental obligation, and the only necessary conditions to which we will be led arise out of consideration of the rules of statemental obligation.

The analysis of stating to which we will be led by our analysis of participation is a moral analysis of stating. There will be a lot of resistance to any such analysis. The main source of this resistance is twofold. First, there is the feeling that when one breaks a rule of language, surely one isn't *immoral*. That seems much too serious a description of the violation. This is the same objection as that raised earlier to the moral analysis of playing football, and the answer is the same. For example, one rule of stating will be that you are not supposed to state things which you think are false. If you go around uttering intentional falsehoods for no good reason, you really are doing something immoral. In most cases it will be a very minor breach of morality, but it is a breach nevertheless. The seriousness of your moral infraction is about on a par with that of a person who agrees to meet someone for lunch and then doesn't show up. Such an infraction isn't very important, but it cannot reasonably be denied that it is an infraction.

The other source of resistance to a moral analysis of stating lies in the feeling that stating is more objective than matters of morality. It is objectively determinate whether a statement has been made, but it may not be so objectively determinate whether a speaker has various moral obligations. It is difficult to formulate this objection precisely because the sense in which morality is nonobjective is controversial. But I think it can be seen that the same considerations which might incline us to say that morality is nonobjective should equally incline us to say that stating is nonobjective. For example, there is often a fine line between telling a joke (wherein one is not stating) and telling a lie (wherein one is stating). The dispute which might arise over whether an alleged joke was really a lie turns upon the question whether the would-be-joker said what he did under circumstances in which he could be held morally accountable for what he said being false. A sufficiently malevolent joke is often a lie. Thus moral considerations seem to be involved in important ways in stating.

The principal argument in favor of a moral analysis of stating is that it results directly from our earlier analysis of participation. It is wise to consider what alternatives there might be to a moral analysis of stating. It is likely that most philosophers will advocate seeking an analysis in terms of intending. The popularity of that general approach is conditioned largely by Grice's attempts to construct such an analysis.[1] I think it is generally agreed, however, that no successful analysis of this sort has actually been proposed.[2] Furthermore, if we reflect upon the fact that stating is a special case of participating in an institution, it seems extremely unlikely that any such analysis could ever be successful. Because language is a largely voluntary institution, it seems initially plausible to seek an analysis in terms of intending. But given the spectrum of institutions from "largely voluntary" to "largely involuntary", it seems quite unlikely that a general analysis of participation in terms of intending can be successful. An analysis of stating must be a special case of an analysis of participation, so it becomes correspondingly unlikely that there can be a successful analysis of stating in terms of intending. In light of all this, I do not think that a moral analysis of stating is as unreasonable as one might initially suppose.

Principle (1.1) approaches the analysis of $\ulcorner S$ states (something) within $L\urcorner$, but what we are really after is an analysis of the more specific notion $\ulcorner S$ states ϕ within $L\urcorner$ where ϕ is a particular statement. The rules of L determine what statements one can make by uttering different sentences under different circumstances, i.e., the rules determine the S-intensions of the sentences of L. Any rule of a linguistic institution must be either prescriptive or ceremonial. Ceremonial rules determine *whether* you are performing acts appropriate for participating, but they do not determine *how* you are participating. Different languages might have precisely the same ceremonial rules but different S-intensions, i.e., the same expressions

---

[1] See Grice [1957] and [1969].
[2] See Schiffer [1972] for a discussion of many such analyses.

might be meaningful in both languages and the same things required for stating, but the meaningful expressions might have different meanings. What determines the meaning of a sentence is what you commit yourself to when you make a statement by uttering the sentence. It is the prescriptive rules which determine what you commit yourself to, so the S-intensions of sentences must be built into the prescriptive rules of L. In uttering a sentence P in L, one states ϕ rather than θ just in case there are prescriptive rules of L which appropriately relate your utterance of P to ϕ rather than θ. If the semantics is generative (in the sense discussed in the Appendix), there may be no prescriptive rules relating P directly to ϕ, but such rules must at least be entailed (in the sense of Principle (4.4) of Chapter Ten) by general prescriptive rules of L. We will say more simply that such a rule is entailed by L. An example of the kind of rule that relates a sentence P to a statement ϕ which it can be used to state might be ⌜Do not utter P under circumstances in which the sequence of values of the pragmatic parameters is π unless you justifiably believe some possible sent-proposition for ϕ⌝. That L entails this rule and not the rule ⌜Do not utter P under circumstances in which the sequence of values of the pragmatic parameters is π unless you justifiably believe some possible sent-propostion for θ⌝ is part of what is involved in saying that the S-intension of P in L selects ϕ rather than θ under these circumstances. More generally, if the S-intension of P in L is Δ, L will entail the rule ⌜Do not utter P unless, if the sequence of values of the pragmatic parameters is π, you justifiably believe some possible sent-proposition for $\Delta(\pi)$⌝. Let us call those prescriptive rules which thus relate sentences P and S-intensions Δ, *semantical rules relating P and Δ*. Let us henceforth abbreviate 'circumstances in which the sequence of values of the pragmatic parameters is π' as 'circumstances π'. One *can* state ϕ within L by uttering P under circumstances π only if L entails semantical rules relating P and some Δ such that $\Delta(\pi) = \phi$; and one *is* stating ϕ by uttering P under those circumstances only if one has a *prima facie* obligation to conform to those semantical rules. This suggests that our analysis of ⌜S states ϕ within L⌝ should be something like:

(1.2) S states ϕ within L iff $(\exists P)(\exists \Delta)(\exists \pi)[L$ entails semantical rules relating P and Δ; S utters P under circumstances π and thereby instantiates a ceremonial rule of stating in L; $\Delta(\pi) = \phi$; and S has a *prima facie* obligation to conform to the semantical rules relating P and Δ].

To say that by uttering P under circumstances π S instantiates a ceremonial rule of L is just to say that S satisfies whatever necessary conditions there may be for stating within L by uttering P. To fill out this analysis we need an account of what those necessary conditions may be, and of what semantical rules relating P and Δ there are.

2. Semantical Rules

The most obvious semantical rule is *the rule of sincerity*, according to which one is not supposed to make a statement unless one believes that it is true. More precisely, for each declarative sentence P, if Δ is one of its S-intensions, then L will entail the rule ⌜Do not utter P under any circumstances π unless you justifiably believe some possible sent-proposition for $\Delta(\pi)$⌝. This rule is directional. Roughly, by uttering P under circumstances π you commit yourself to your audience.[3] But just which group constitutes your audience? The natural suggestion is that your audience consists of all those people who hear your spoken words or read your written words. Let us call this your *physical audience*. But as a specification of the group to whom you commit yourself, your physical audience is both too broad and too narrow. First, we often speak to particular individuals. Even though other individuals may eavesdrop on our conversation, we do not commit ourselves to them. They cannot hold us accountable for lying, making remarks which mislead them, etc. Second, we frequently intend our remarks to be disseminated beyond our physical audience, and we regard ourselves as accountable to anyone who comes to know what we have said. If a mathematician asserts that he has proven Fermat's conjecture, and does not direct his remarks to some limited audience, then his remarks can be repeated to others not in his physical audience who may nevertheless hold him accountable for those remarks. This kind of case, where we intend to be commiting ourselves to absolutely everyone and not just to our physical audience, may be the most common case of stating.

These observations suggest that the individuals to whom you commit yourself are the members of your *intended audience*. But what constitutes your intended audience? It might be supposed

[3] You can incur a commitment to its being the case that P even if you are already committed to its being the case that P. Commitments do not simply add together. That you can have two separate commitments to its being the case that P is required by the fact that subsequent occurrences might nullify the first commitment while leaving the second intact.

that your intended audience must at least include your intended physical audience. However, it is quite possible to make a statement to a particular member of a group without commiting yourself to other members of the group despite your intending for the other members of the group to hear you. For example, you might address your remarks to one person while knowing that another is eavesdropping behind the curtain, and you may fully intend for the eavesdropper to hear what you have to say. You do not thereby commit yourself to the eavesdropper. This suggests that your intended audience is simply the group with respect to whom you intend to commit yourself. Let us define:

(2.1)   *S's primary audience* relative to a statement ϕ and utterance U is that set X such that S performs U with the intention to incur thereby, with respect to the members of X, the *prima facie* commitment to its being the case that S justifiably believes some possible sent-proposition for ϕ.

The rule of sincerity relating P and Δ is then:

Do not utter P under any circumstances π unless you justifiably believe some possible sent-proposition for $\Delta(\pi)$; the direction of the commitment being to your primary audience relative to $\Delta(\pi)$ and your utterance of P.

Several other possible candidates for semantical rules are suggested by Grice's analysis of 'meaning$_{NN}$'.[4] Many roles in institutions have "standard intentions" associated with them which individuals are supposed to have in playing those roles. For example, in competitive games the players are supposed to have the objective of winning, and in buying and selling the purchaser is supposed to have the objective of securing control of the item purchased. It is plausible to suppose that in stating the speaker is supposed to have various Gricean intentions. Three possibilities suggest themselves immediately:

(1) Perhaps the speaker is supposed to be trying to bring his audience to believe what he says, i.e., to believe some acceptable received-proposition for his statement. This strikes me as right. However, it may be objected that it is too strong a requirement on the grounds that the audience might already believe that P, and the speaker might just be trying to call the fact that P to their attention

---

[4] Grice [1957] and [1969]. See also Schiffer [1972], and Bennett [1973] and [1976].

for the purpose of drawing some inference from it. Or the audience might consist of the speaker's teacher and the speaker might just be trying to show that he knows that P.[5] In such cases, it might either be denied that the speaker incurs even a *prima facie* commitment to be trying to get the members of his intended audience to believe that P, or it might be alleged that he incurs a *prima facie* commitment but that it is defeated by his knowing that the audience already believes that P. In order to avoid this controversy, I propose instead that we regard the speaker as incurring the *prima facie* conditional commitment to be trying to bring the members of his intended audience to believe what he says if they don't already. I think that this is equivalent to saying that there is a defeated *prima facie* commitment in the preceding case, but by formulating it in this way we avoid having to take a stand on that. That this conditional obligation is a statemental obligation may explain some of the appeal of the Gricean style of analysis of meaning, but notice that this is importantly different from the appeal to intentions involved in Grice's analysis. According to Grice, having the appropriate intentions is a necessary condition for meaning. The present claim is only that a necessary condition for stating is that you have a *prima facie* *obligation* to have the appropriate intentions, not that you really have those intentions. Let us call this *the Gricean rule* relating P and Δ:

> Do not utter P under any circumstances π unless you are trying to bring the members of your primary audience relative to $\Delta(\pi)$ and your utterance of P to believe some acceptable received-proposition for $\Delta(\pi)$ if they do not already.

The Gricean rule appears to be nondirectional. If you make a statement without having the required intention, and there are no other considerations which defeat your *prima facie* obligation, then you are misusing language and any member of society can take you to task for it regardless of whether he is a member of your intended audience. You just are not supposed to do that in making statements, and when you do you are guilty of a (mild) crime against society as a whole.

(2) Perhaps the speaker is supposed to be trying to bring his audience to believe that he believes that P. But consider a child

---

[5] These examples are due to Schiffer [1972], who uses them as counter-examples to Grice's analysis.

who has received all of his formal education through a computer rather than by way of a human teacher. Let us suppose that the computer communicates with the child orally. The computer has broken down and I wish to teach the child that $2 + 2 = 4$. I know that he will not believe me if I simply tell him that $2 + 2 = 4$, so instead I wire a microphone into the computer and speak to him through the computer in such a way that he thinks it is the computer telling him that $2 + 2 = 4$. It seems to me that I have stated that $2 + 2 = 4$, but there is no reason to think that I have incurred any commitment (even *prima facie*) to be trying to bring the child to believe that I believe that $2 + 2 = 4$. Thus I am inclined to doubt that there is any statemental obligation of this second sort.

(3) We might wax very Gricean and suggest that the speaker is supposed to be trying to bring his audience to believe what he says if they don't already and is supposed to intend that his audience's recognition that he is so trying will function as part of their reason for coming to believe what he says if they don't already. However, Schiffer [1972] points out that most articles in philosophy journals constitute counterexamples to the Gricean analogue of this, and they also seem to constitute counterexamples to this principle. When a philosopher gives an argument for some conclusion, he intends the audience to come to believe the conclusion on the basis of the argument. He does not usually intend for them to come to believe it partly because they know that he is trying to get them to believe it. Nor does it seem that he is *supposed* to have the latter intention. Thus this does not appear to represent a statemental obligation.

There may be some viable modifications of these principles which we should endorse, but I will not pursue that here. The fact that there does appear to be a statemental obligation to have Gricean intentions of the first sort reflects the fact that the primary purpose of stating is to instill beliefs in one's audience (insofar as they do not already have them). That is not the only purpose, and we cannot build that in as a necessary condition of stating, but it is nevertheless logically connected with the concept of stating by way of *prima facie* statemental obligations.

We can distinguish roughly between two kinds of statemental obligations. On the one hand, there are general statemental obligations which are of types common to all cases of stating irrespective of what is stated; on the other hand, there may be specific statemental obligations which are idiosyncratic to the particular statement being stated. Thus far we have only considered statemental obligations of the first sort, but it is extremely plausible to suppose that there may also be semantical rules of the second sort. For example, Grice suggests that in stating a disjunction one ordinarily implies that one does not know which disjunct is true. This suggests the existence of a prescriptive rule to the effect that one is not supposed to state a disjunction unless either one does not know which disjunct is true or one has taken adequate steps to make it clear that one's stating the disjunction should not be taken as indicative of one's not knowing which disjunct is true. If there is such a prescriptive rule, then in stating a disjunction one has the *prima facie* obligation to conform to it and that is a semantical rule governing the disjunctive statement.

It is plausible to suppose that there are a number of different kinds of semantical rules idiosyncratic to different kinds of statements. There may also be general semantical rules which we have so far overlooked. This makes it difficult to generate a testable analysis out of (1.2), because in the face of any putative counterexample there is always the possibility that we are overlooking some semantical rules. However, I suggest that we can generate a tight analysis of stating by looking at just the rule of sincerity and the Gricean rule. Let us call them the *primary semantical rules*.

3. Stating

My initial proposal, which will be modified a bit in (3.5), is:

(3.1)   *S* states ϕ within *L* iff $(\exists P)(\exists \Delta)(\exists \pi)$ [*L* entails the primary semantical rules relating *P* and Δ; $\Delta(\pi) = \phi$; *S* utters *P* under circumstances π and thereby instantiates a ceremonial rule of stating in *L*; and *S* has a *prima facie* obligation to conform to the primary semantical rules relating *P* and Δ].[6]

Next, consider the notion of stating *simpliciter* rather than stating within *L*. What is the relationship between these two notions? The obvious suggestion is that stating ϕ consists of stating ϕ within *some language or other*. This does not mean that you can only state ϕ within some recognized language. Languages are abstract structures of rules and exist independently of being invented or conceived

---

[6] The final clause in (3.1) is intended to imply that there is a primary audience.

of. If you state ϕ within L, then of course you state ϕ. Conversely, suppose you state ϕ. All that is required for your stating to be a stating within L is that your utterance is appropriate in L for stating ϕ, i.e., that the sentence you utter has the right meaning in L. But the utterance whereby you state ϕ is always appropriate for stating ϕ within some language or other (although not necessarily in any recognized language). Thus it appears that we should have:

(3.2) S states ϕ iff $(\exists L)$ S states ϕ within L.

Then from (3.1) we obtain:

(3.3) S states ϕ iff $(\exists P)(\exists \Delta)(\exists \pi)[S$ utters P under circumstances π and thereby satisfies whatever conditions are necessary in all languages for the instantiation of a ceremonial rule of stating; S has a *prima facie* obligation to conform to the primary semantical rules relating P and Δ; and $\Delta(\pi) = \phi]$.

The first condition of (3.3) is a bit vague because we have not yet explored the question of what conditions are universally necessary for stating. For example, must the speaker have certain intentions? This will be investigated in the next section.

Quite apart from the vagueness of the first clause, we can see that (3.3) is inadequate. The difficulty is that (3.3) overlooks the distinction between stating and implying. By stating ϕ, a speaker may imply θ (in a stronger sense than just stating something that entails θ) and thereby incur statemental obligations with respect to θ, but we would not agree that he has stated θ. For example, when a speaker makes a statement he often implies simple logical consequences of what he states. For example, if a speaker asserts 'George is a philosopher and no philosopher is to be trusted', he may imply that George is not to be trusted and thereby become committed (a) to its being the case that he justifiably believes that George is not to be trusted and (b) to be trying to bring his audience to believe that George is not to be trusted if they don't already. It then follows from (3.3) that the speaker has stated that George is not to be trusted, but that is not correct.

When a speaker implies θ by stating ϕ, he incurs commitments relative to θ *by* incurring commitments relative to ϕ. This suggests that in order to state ϕ by performing U, one must not only incur commitments relative to ϕ by performing U; in addition one must *not* incur those commitments *by* incurring commitments relative to other statements (by performing U). Thus I propose the following correction to (3.3):

(3.4) S states ϕ iff $(\exists P)(\exists \Delta)(\exists \pi)[S$ utters P under circumstances π and thereby satisfies whatever conditions are necessary in all languages for the instantiation of a ceremonial rule of stating; S has a *prima facie* obligation to conform to the primary semantical rules relating P and Δ; $\Delta(\pi) = \phi$; and there is no S-intension Δ^* different from Δ such that S acquires the latter obligation by acquiring the *prima facie* obligation to conform to the primary semantical rules relating P and $\Delta^*]$.

A similar modification is required for (3.1):

(3.5) S states ϕ within L iff $(\exists P)(\exists \Delta)(\exists \pi)[L$ entails the primary semantical rules relating P and Δ; S utters P under circumstances π and thereby instantiates a ceremonial rule of stating in L; $\Delta(\pi) = \phi$; S has a *prima facie* obligation to conform to the primary semantical rules relating P and Δ; and there is no S-intension Δ^* different from Δ such that S acquires the latter obligation by acquiring the *prima facie* obligation to conform to the primary semantical rules relating P and $\Delta^*]$.

Although it would be difficult to establish this without a complete inventory of semantical rules, a similar modification is presumably required for the less adventurous (1.2).

4. The Sent-Proposition

According to (3.4), one kind of necessary condition for stating is that one have a *prima facie* obligation to conform to the primary semantical rules governing stating. It is compatible with (3.4), but not required by it, to suppose that there are numerous other necessary conditions for stating. The possibilities that come most readily to mind concern various intentions which the speaker might be required to have. It follows from our discussion of the primary semantical rules that the speaker must intend to incur the commitment to his believing some possible sent-proposition for his statement. That intention is involved in the selection of the primary audience. Having that intention is a necessary condition for having the *prima facie* obligation to conform to the primary semantical rules, and hence it is a necessary condition for stating.

Are there any other intentions required for stating? Gricean intentions come naturally to mind, but the voluminous literature on this topic leaves us without any clear candidate of this sort.[7] A different kind of candidate arises from considerations of what might be called "the phenomenology of stating". It was remarked in Chapter One that ordinarily, when we make a statement, we are "putting thoughts into words". We begin with a certain proposition—normally one we believe—and we make a statement which conveys part or all of that proposition. In other words, we make a statement for which that proposition is a possible sent-proposition. We select our statement with that purpose in mind. Precisely:

(4.1) In making a statement, there is a proposition ψ such that the speaker intends for the statement he is making to be such that by justifiably believing ψ he would fulfill the obligation to be justifiably believing some possible sent-proposition for that statement.

When (4.1) is satisfied, ψ is the proposition the speaker is sending.

In Chapter One, we found ourselves unable to decide whether there must always be a sent-proposition in stating. Thus we were led to distinguish between weak stating, which does not require there to be a sent-proposition, and strong stating, which does. We then more or less arbitrarily identified stating with strong stating. However, in Chapter One we were not in a position to give analyses of weak stating or of propositional sending. That can now be rectified. I propose that weak stating be defined as follows:

(4.2) *S weakly states* ϕ iff $(\exists P)(\exists \Delta)(\exists \pi)[S$ utters P under circumstances π; $\Delta(\pi) = \phi$; S has a *prima facie* obligation to conform to the primary semantical rules relating P and Δ; and there is no S-intension Δ^* different from Δ such that S acquires the latter obligation by acquiring the *prima facie* obligation to conform to the primary semantical rules relating P and Δ^*].

(4.3) *S weakly states* ϕ *within L* iff $(\exists P)(\exists \Delta)(\exists \pi)[L$ entails the primary semantical rules relating P and Δ; S utters P

---

[7] In this connection see the discussion in Schiffer [1972]. Schiffer provides counterexamples for all the obvious candidates.

under circumstances π; $\Delta(\pi) = \phi$; S has a *prima facie* obligation to conform to the primary semantical rules relating P and Δ; and there is no S-intension Δ^* different from Δ such that S acquires the latter obligation by acquiring the *prima facie* obligation to conform to the primary semantical rules relating P and Δ^*].

In other words, there are no necessary conditions for weak stating other than that one perform an utterance and one have statemental obligations.

I further propose:

(4.4) In weakly stating ϕ by uttering P, S is *sending* ψ iff ψ is a possible sent-proposition for ϕ for S under the circumstances of the stating and S intends for the statement he is weakly stating to be such that by justifiably believing ψ he would fulfill the obligation to be justifiably believing some possible sent-proposition for that statement.

Then our stronger notion of stating is that of weakly stating and thereby sending a proposition:

(4.5) S *states* ϕ iff S weakly states ϕ and in doing so is sending some proposition.

(4.6) S *states* ϕ *within* L iff S weakly states ϕ within L and in doing so is sending some proposition.

In stating one is ordinarily sending a unique proposition. One normally starts with a proposition and seeks to express it by making a statement for which it is a possible sent-proposition. However, that does not have to be the case. For one thing, intentions are not always well defined. We can imagine a person beginning indifferently with several different propositions all of which are possible sent-propositions for his statement and intending to fulfill his obligation by justifiably believing each of them. Thus we cannot assume that the sent-proposition is unique, although it normally will be.

There has been extensive debate in the philosophy of language regarding the relative importance of the speaker's intentions and the objective setting in determining what statement is made. Our account of stating does not resolve that matter, but it does show just where the disagreement lies and what its nature is. What the speaker states is determined by what statemental obligations he incurs. Both his intentions and the objective setting figure into the determination of these statemental obligations. We have seen that a necessary condition for the speaker to state ϕ is that he have certain intentions with respect to ϕ, but despite good intentions, a speaker may fail to state ϕ if he performs an utterance which is neither conventionally appropriate nor of such a nature that his audience can tell what statement he is trying to state. The debate about the relative importance of intentions and objective setting is really a debate about what it takes to incur certain sorts of moral obligations, and it is probably characteristic of the latter question that it does not admit of a simple answer.

XII
Nondeclarative Sentences

1. Meaning and Nondeclarative Sentences

By a *declarative sentence* we mean a sentence which can be used for stating. Philosophers tend to concentrate exclusively on declarative sentences, and that has constituted the principal focus of the present investigation. It is desirable, however, to generalize our theory to apply to nondeclarative sentences too, e.g., interrogatives, imperatives, etc. That can be done without too much difficulty.

Let us begin the construction of our general account of meaning by reconsidering our identification of the meaning of a declarative sentence with its S-intension. In order to understand the meaning of a declarative sentence, one must know that it is a declarative sentence, i.e., that it can be used to make statements. I have been implicitly interpreting the assignment of an S-intension to a sentence as containing that information, but for the purpose of talking about nondeclarative sentences it is desirable to withdraw that interpretation. The reason is that most nondeclarative sentences are intimately connected with declarative sentences. For example, if P is a declarative sentence, consider the yes/no interrogative ⌜Is it true that P?⌝. Let π be a particular sequence of values of the pragmatic parameters of P, and Δ its S-intension. If $\Delta(\pi) = \phi$, then by uttering P under circumstances in which the values of the pragmatic parameters constitute the sequence π, one states ϕ. On the other hand, by uttering ⌜Is it true that P?⌝ under those same circumstances, rather than stating ϕ, one *queries* ϕ. The same statement ϕ is involved in both speech acts, but the speaker uses ϕ differently. Similarly, in saying ⌜Make it the case that P!⌝, the speaker is commanding his audience to alter the situation in such a way that ϕ becomes true; in saying ⌜Please make it the case that P⌝, the speaker is requesting his audience to alter the situation in such a way that ϕ becomes true; and in saying $\ulcorner$I promise that $P\urcorner$, the speaker is promising that ϕ is true. In each case the same statement ϕ enters into the speech act, but it is treated differently. We might reasonably say that all of these sentences have the same S-intension Δ. But if we say that these sentences all have the same S-intension, we can no longer regard the meaning of a sentence as being constituted by its S-intension, because these sentences differ in meaning. The way in which they differ in meaning is that they are used to do different things with the same statements. Let us define the *speech act potential* of a sentence to be the kind of speech act which it can be used to perform. Thus the speech act potential of P is stating, that of $\ulcorner$Is it the case that $P?\urcorner$ is questioning, that of $\ulcorner$Make it the case that $P!\urcorner$ is commanding, etc. The way in which these sentences differ in meaning is that they differ in speech act potential. This suggests that we should take the meaning of a sentence (either declarative or nondeclarative) to be constituted by an ordered pair $\langle\rho,\Delta\rangle$ where ρ is its speech act potential and Δ is its intension.[1]

The intensions of most nondeclarative sentences are S-intensions, but there are exceptions to this. So-called '*wh* interrogatives' are interrogatives formulated (in English) using 'who', 'what', 'which', 'where', 'when', 'why', 'how', 'how many', 'how much', and some other constructions equivalent to these. *Wh* interrogatives do not bear the intimate connection to declarative sentences that most other nondeclarative sentences bear. For example, the yes/no interrogative 'Did Charlie come?' is intimately connected with the declarative sentence 'Charlie came' in a way in which 'How did Charlie come?' or 'Why did Charlie come?' are not connected with any declarative sentences. The logical form of *wh* interrogatives is considerably more complicated than that of yes/no interrogatives. Consider the following examples[2]:

> What does she want?
> What is the name of that girl?
> Who is the author?
> Did she wear the red hat or the green hat?
> What four primes lie between 10 and 20?
> What is an example of a mammal?

---

[1] This is reminiscent of the treatment of nondeclarative sentences in Stenius [1967] and Lewis [1972], and takes its impetus from Hare [1952].

[2] Most of these examples are taken from Hintikka [1976].

What are several of the things she has in her purse?
What all does she have in her purse?
What are two of the things she has in her purse?
What are at least three of the things she has in her purse?
Which boys are brothers of which girls?
Who did what to whom?
Which country is Uganda?
What is the Eiffel Tower?

The first step in bringing order to this menagerie is to observe that any *wh* interrogative can be paraphrased as a 'what' interrogative. But within 'what' interrogatives we still get a variety of logical forms:

(1.1) What is the F?

(1.2) What is t?

(1.3) What is some F?

(1.4) What are all the F's?

(1.5) What are two of the F's?

(1.6) What are at least two of the F's?

(1.7) What are several of the F's?

(1.8) What are the F's and G's such that each F stands in the relation R to one of the G's?

and so on.

The second observation is that 'what' interrogatives are indexical. By uttering the same interrogative using all of the words with the same meanings, one can be seeking different information. For example, in asking 'Who is coming to dinner?', I may be attempting to ascertain the name of the guest; alternatively, I may not care about his name but be attempting to ascertain whose friend he is. There is a pragmatic parameter here reflecting the interests of the speaker. This parameter makes different answers appropriate under different circumstances. This is the same parameter as is involved in 'knowing what' locutions, as discussed in Chapter Nine.

I suggest that there are two basic forms of 'what' interrogatives—(1.2) and (1.3)—and that all of the others are reducible to these two forms. In asking ⌜What is t?⌝ (e.g., 'What is the Eiffel Tower?', or

'What is Uganda?'), one wants an appropriate description (appropriate relative to the speaker's interests) of the referent of t. In asking ⌜What is some F?⌝, one wants an appropriate description of at least one F. This much seems clear. Now consider the rest of (1.1)–(1.8). (1.1) is a special case of (1.2). Turning to (1.4), in asking ⌜What are all the F's?⌝, one wants an appropriate description of all the F's. This may take the form of a list of appropriate descriptions of the individual F's, but such a list may be impossible if there are many F's. There may even be infinitely many F's if we are asking something like 'What are all the solutions to this differential equation?'. An answer must then be an appropriate description of all of the F's jointly, or what comes to the same thing, an appropriate description of the set of all F's. This indicates that the interrogative ⌜What are all of the F's?⌝ has the same meaning as the interrogative ⌜What is the set of all of the F's?⌝, which is of the form of (1.2).

(1.5)–(1.8) can be paraphrased analogously as being about sets. ⌜What are two of the F's?⌝ has the same meaning as ⌜What is some set of two F's?⌝. ⌜What are several of the F's?⌝ has the same meaning as ⌜What is some set of several F's?⌝. Similarly, 'Who did what to whom?' means 'What is the set of all triples $\langle x,y,z \rangle$ such that x did y to z?'. And 'Did Mary wear the red hat or the green hat?' means 'What is the unique member of the set consisting of the red hat and the green hat which is such that Mary wore it?'. By thus appealing to sets, all 'what' interrogatives can be regarded as having the form of either (1.2) or (1.3). Some interrogatives are ambiguous. For example, 'What does Mary have in her purse?' can mean 'What is something which Mary has in her purse?' or 'What are a few of the things which Mary has in her purse?', or 'What are all of the things which Mary has in her purse?', or 'What is the thing which Mary has in her purse?'.[3]

Having contended that all 'what' interrogatives, and hence all *wh* interrogatives have the form of either (1.2) or (1.3), we may wonder why there are these two basic forms. Why isn't there just one basic form? The explanation seems to be this. The 'what' interrogatives are intimately connected with 'knowing what' locutions. But there

---

[3] To illustrate the latter, suppose Mary is clutching her purse protectively. I may then ask, 'What does Mary have in her purse?' in an attempt to find out what she has in her purse that is causing her to be so protective of it. This is intimately connected with the referential use of the definite description 'the thing Mary has in her purse' to refer to whatever she has in her purse which is causing her to clutch it so.

are two basic kinds of 'knowing what' locutions, one involving singular terms and the other involving predicates:

(1.9)   *S* knows what *t* is;

(1.10)   *S* knows what some *F* is.

In (1.9), *t* can be any singular term. Examples are 'Jones knows what the Eiffel tower is', 'Jones knows what Uganda is', or 'Jones knows what the name of that girl is'. Interrogatives of the form of (1.2) are transformationally related to declarative sentences of the form of (1.9), and interrogatives of the form of (1.3) are transformationally related to declarative sentences of the form of (1.10). (1.10) is a different locution from (1.9) and the two are in no way interchangeable. Analyses of both locutions were proposed in Chapter Nine.

We are left with two basic kinds of *wh* interrogatives. Let us call those of the form of (1.2) 'wh_D interrogatives', and those of the form of (1.3) 'wh_A interrogatives'. A convenient way of distinguishing between them is to regard them as having different kinds of intensions. We can regard wh_D interrogatives as having *D*-intensions, identifying the intension of ⌜What is *t*?⌝ with the *D*-intension of *t*. We can regard wh_A interrogatives as having *A*-intensions, identifying the intension of ⌜What is some *F*?⌝ with the intension of *F*. The meanings of one of these interrogatives can then be regarded as the pair $\langle query, \Delta \rangle$ where Δ is its intension. For example, we can regard the meaning of 'How did Charlie come?' as being constituted by the ordered pair $\langle query, \Delta \rangle$ where Δ is the *A*-intension of 'is a way in which Charlie came'.[4]

Unfortunately, our account of meaning must be made still more complicated. There are sentences whose meanings cannot be described in terms of single intensions. Consider conditional imperatives like:

(1.11)   If she knocks, let her in.

This cannot be identified with an imperative whose object is a conditional:

(1.12)   Make it the case that if she knocks then you let her in.

---

[4] In writing this section, I profited from reading Belnap and Steel [1976], Hintikka [1976], and Harrah [1979]. I have incorporated insights from each.

(1.12) could be satisfied by preventing her from knocking. (1.11) has the form ⌜If P then make it the case that Q⌝. Thus in describing its meaning we must say three things: (1) we must describe its speech act potential by saying that it is a conditional imperative; (2) we must give the S-intension of the antecedent; (3) we must give the S-intension of the imperative consequent. Thus its meaning can be regarded as an ordered triple $\langle \rho, \Delta_1, \Delta_2 \rangle$. Let us define in general:

(1.13) A *simple meaning* is a $(k + 1)$-tuple $\langle \rho, \Delta_1, \ldots, \Delta_k \rangle$ such that $k > 0$ and ρ is a speech act potential and $\Delta_1, \ldots, \Delta_k$ are intensions.

The meanings of most sentences can be identified with simple meanings. There are, however, mixed sentences not readily classifiable as declarative, interrogative, imperative, etc., which combine the force of several sentences of different sorts:

(1.14) John won't come today, but will he come tomorrow?

(1.15) You'll do that for me, won't you?

(1.16) Do that or I'll fire you!

(1.17) What are those ugly things and why are they on my desk?

(1.14) has the combined force of:

(1.14a) John won't come today

and

(1.14b) Will he come tomorrow?

Thus it is part declarative and part interrogative. Similarly, (1.15) is part rogative (i.e., request) and part interrogative. (1.16) is part imperative and part declarative. (1.17) is interesting in that it combines two separate interrogatives, but there is no way to incorporate them both into a single interrogative with a single simple meaning. I suggest that the meaning of such a mixed sentence be regarded as the set of simple meanings of the constituent sentences. Thus the meaning of (1.14) is the set $\{m_1, m_2\}$ where m_1 is the simple meaning of (1.14a) and m_2 is the simple meaning of (1.14b). In general:

(1.18) m is a *meaning* iff m is a simple meaning or m is a nonempty set of simple meanings.

In this way we can describe the meanings of all sentences in terms of speech act potentials and intensions.

Lexical items do not have speech act potentials in the same clear sense that sentences do. By definition, sentences are those linguistic items that can be used to perform "complete speech acts". Accordingly, there is no need to complicate our account of the meaning of a lexical item. We can continue to regard the meaning of a lexical item as being constituted by its intension.

2. Requests, Commands, and Yes/No Questions

The speech acts performed by uttering nondeclarative sentences include questioning, commanding, and requesting. Analyses of these speech acts can be modeled on our analysis of stating. Beginning with yes/no questions, let us call the sentence an *interrogative* and the speech act a *query*. A speaker performs a yes/no query (within L) by uttering a yes/no interrogative. Yes/no interrogatives have S-intensions, whose values are statements. Thus we can talk about a speaker querying a particular statement. This occurs (within L) when a speaker performs a querying by uttering a yes/no interrogative whose intension selects that statement under the circumstances of utterance. A more colloquial way of expressing $\ulcorner S$ queries $\phi\urcorner$ would be $\ulcorner S$ asks whether it is true that $\phi\urcorner$. The queried statement is the object of the speech act in the sense of Section Six of Chapter One.

Turning to requests, we will call the sentence a *rogative* and the speech act a *request*. On my view, requests and commands are two different kinds of speech acts, so we must distinguish between a sentence whose speech act potential is that of requesting (a rogative) and a sentence whose speech act potential is that of commanding. We will reserve the term 'imperative' for the latter, calling the speech act a *command*. Rogatives and imperatives have S-intensions, and correspondingly the objects of requests and commands are statements. Rogatives can be expressed in the canonical form $\ulcorner$Please make it the case that $P\urcorner$, and imperatives can be expressed in the canonical form $\ulcorner$Make it the case that $P!\urcorner$. To request ϕ or command ϕ is, more colloquially, to request or command someone to make ϕ true.

Our objective is now to give analyses of the notions of a speaker querying, requesting, or commanding a statement. The analyses of these three notions will be modeled on the analysis of stating, and will all have the same form. To avoid repeating basically the same definitions and analyses three times over, I will write all three simultaneously. The form of the analysis will be:

(2.1) $S \begin{Bmatrix} \text{queries} \\ \text{requests} \\ \text{commands} \end{Bmatrix} \phi$ within L iff $(\exists P)(\exists \Delta)(\exists \pi)[L$ entails the

primary $\begin{Bmatrix} \text{interrogative} \\ \text{rogative} \\ \text{imperative} \end{Bmatrix}$ rules relating P and Δ; S utters P

under circumstances π; $\Delta(\pi) = \phi$; S has a *prima facie*

obligation to conform to the primary $\begin{Bmatrix} \text{interrogative} \\ \text{rogative} \\ \text{imperative} \end{Bmatrix}$ rules

relating P and Δ; and there is no S-intension Δ^* different from Δ such that S acquires the latter obligation by acquiring the *prima facie* obligation to conform to the primary $\begin{Bmatrix} \text{interrogative} \\ \text{rogative} \\ \text{imperative} \end{Bmatrix}$ rules relating P and Δ^*].

To complete these analyses we need accounts of the primary interrogative, rogative, and imperative rules. The first interrogative rule is that one is supposed to want to know whether ϕ is true. The direction of commitment involved in each of these rules is to the speaker's intended audience, so let us define:

(2.2) S's primary $\begin{Bmatrix} \text{interrogative} \\ \text{rogative} \\ \text{imperative} \end{Bmatrix}$ audience relative to ϕ and U

is that set X such that S performs the utterance U with the intention to thereby incur, with respect to the members of X, the *prima facie* commitment to there being a possible sent-proposition ψ for ϕ such that S wants:

$\begin{Bmatrix} \text{to know } \psi \text{ if } \psi \text{ is true and to know } \neg\psi \text{ if } \psi \text{ is false} \\ \psi \text{ to be true} \\ \psi \text{ to be true} \end{Bmatrix}$.

The primary interrogative rules can now be described as follows:

(2.3) If P is an expression and Δ is an S-intension, *the primary interrogative rules relating P and Δ are:*
(a) Do not utter P under any circumstances π unless there is some possible sent-proposition ψ for the statement $\Delta(\pi)$

such that you want to know ψ if ψ is true and you want to know $\neg\psi$ if ψ is false; the direction of the commitment being to the primary interrogative audience relative to $\Delta(\pi)$ and the utterance of P;

(b) Do not utter P under any circumstances π unless there is some possible sent-proposition ψ for the statement $\Delta(\pi)$ such that you are trying to make it the case that some member of the primary interrogative audience relative to $\Delta(\pi)$ and the utterance of P makes a statement θ such that by believing some acceptable received-proposition for θ on the authority of that stating you will come to know ψ if ψ is true and you will come to know $\neg\psi$ if ψ is false; this rule being nondirectional.

The primary rogative rules appear to be:

(2.4)   If P is an expression and Δ is an S-intension, *the primary rogative rules relating P and Δ are:*
(a) Do not utter P under any circumstances π unless there is some possible sent-proposition ψ for the statement $\Delta(\pi)$ such that you want ψ to be true; the direction of the commitment being to the primary rogative audience relative to $\Delta(\pi)$ and the utterance of P;
(b) Do not utter P under any circumstances π unless there is some possible sent-proposition ψ for the statement $\Delta(\pi)$ such that you are trying to make it the case that some or all of the members of the primary rogative audience alter the situation in such a way that ψ becomes true; this rule being nondirectional.

It has frequently been suggested that queries are special kinds of requests.[5] On the preceding account, there is an intimate connection between queries and requests, but queries are not quite requests. To query ϕ is not the same thing as to request to be made to know whether ϕ is true, because by (2.3.b) you want to be made to know in a certain way, i.e., by being informed by the primary audience. Nor can querying ϕ be the same thing as requesting to be informed by the primary audience whether ϕ is true. There can be no such request as the latter, because the primary audience is characterized in terms of the object of the request, and so to characterize the latter in terms of the primary audience becomes circular.

[5] For example, see Belnap and Steel [1976].

The difference between a request and a command is that by issuing a command one implies that he is prepared to enforce it. This suggests:

(2.5)   If P is an expression and Δ is an S-intension, *the primary imperative rules relating P and Δ are:*
(a) the same as (2.4.a);
(b) the same as (2.4.b);
(c) Do not utter P under any circumstances π unless there is some possible sent-proposition ψ for the statement $\Delta(\pi)$ such that you want the members of the primary imperative audience to believe that if they do not try to alter the situation in such a way that ψ becomes true then you will make them regret it; this rule being nondirectional.

These analyses of querying, requesting, and commanding, make them analogues to weak stating rather than stating. We can construct definitions of the notions of sending a proposition while querying, requesting, or commanding, and then we could add to (2.1) the condition that there be a sent-proposition, if that were deemed desirable. However, I will not pursue that.

3. *Wh* Questions

I argued in Section One that there are two kinds of *wh* interrogatives—wh_A interrogatives and wh_D interrogatives. There are correspondingly two kinds of *wh* queries. Our present task is to explain what it is to perform such queries. I propose the following:

(3.1)   If $\left\{\begin{array}{l}\partial \text{ is a statemental designator}\\ A \text{ is an attribute}\end{array}\right\}$, S queries $\left\{\begin{array}{l}\partial\\ A\end{array}\right\}$ within L
iff $(\exists P)(\exists\Delta)(\exists\pi)[\Delta$ is $\left\{\begin{array}{l}\text{a } D\text{-intension}\\ \text{an } A\text{-intension}\end{array}\right\}$; L entails the primary interrogative rules relating P and Δ; S utters P under circumstances π; $\left\{\begin{array}{l}\Delta(\pi)=\partial\\ \Delta(\pi)=A\end{array}\right\}$; S has a *prima facie* obligation to conform to the primary interrogative rules relating P and Δ; and there is no $\left\{\begin{array}{l}D\text{-intension}\\ A\text{-intension}\end{array}\right\}$ Δ^* different from Δ such that S acquires the latter obligation by acquiring the *prima facie* obligation to conform to the primary interrogative rules relating P and Δ^*].

S asks a wh_A question iff he queries some attribute, and S asks a wh_D question iff he queries some statemental designator.

(3.2) If $\begin{cases}\partial \text{ is a statemental designator} \\ A \text{ is an attribute}\end{cases}$ and U an utterance, S's

primary interrogative audience relative to $\begin{Bmatrix}\partial \\ A\end{Bmatrix}$ and U is

that set X such that S performs the utterance U with the intention to thereby incur, with respect to the members of X, the *prima facie* commitment to there being a possible $\begin{cases}\text{sent-designator } \delta \text{ for } \partial \\ \text{sent-concept } \alpha \text{ for } A\end{cases}$ such that S wants $\begin{cases}\text{to know what} \\ \text{to know what}\end{cases}$ $\begin{cases}\delta \text{ is} \\ \text{some } \alpha \text{ is}\end{cases}$[6].

(3.3) If P is an expression and Δ is $\begin{cases}\text{a } D\text{-intension} \\ \text{an } A\text{-intension}\end{cases}$, *the primary interrogative rules relating P and Δ are:*

(a) Do not utter P under any circumstances π unless there is a possible $\begin{cases}\text{sent-designator } \delta \\ \text{sent-concept } \alpha\end{cases}$ for $\Delta(\pi)$ such that you want $\begin{cases}\text{to know what } \delta \text{ is} \\ \text{to know what some } \alpha \text{ is}\end{cases}$, and you justifiably believe $\begin{cases}\text{the proposition } (\mathfrak{C}:\delta) \\ \text{the proposition } (\vee x)(\alpha:x)\end{cases}$; the direction of the commitment being to the primary interrogative audience relative to $\Delta(\pi)$ and the utterance of P;

(b) Do not utter P under any circumstances π unless there is some possible $\begin{cases}\text{sent-designator } \delta \\ \text{sent-concept } \alpha\end{cases}$ for $\Delta(\pi)$ such that you are trying to make it the case that some member of the primary interrogative audience relative to $\Delta(\pi)$ and the utterance of P makes a statement θ such that by believing some acceptable received-proposition for θ on the authority of that stating you will come $\begin{cases}\text{to know what } \delta \text{ is} \\ \text{to know what some } \alpha \text{ is}\end{cases}$; this rule being nondirectional.

---

[6] In Chapter Nine, $\ulcorner S$ knows what some α is$\urcorner$ was defined as $\ulcorner(\exists \delta)[KW_\rho(S,\delta)$ & $\mathfrak{R}_S(\alpha:\delta)]\urcorner$.

Appendix:
A General Statemental Semantics

1. Introduction

I have sketched a general approach to a new kind of semantical theory—what I have called a 'statemental semantics'. The purpose of this appendix is to tidy up the logical details of the general theory. One objective is to formulate the semantics in a logically precise way. A second objective is to use the results of that precise formulation to construct a general theory of lexical sending based upon the account sketched in Chapter Three.

2. Diagrams and Intensions

In constructing a semantical theory, we begin with a language L whose sentences constitute the set Sn. Those lexical items having meanings constitute the set Lex. The set $\mathfrak{L}$ of *linguistic items* is the set $Sn \cup Lex$. A *full semantical theory for* L will be a function $\mathscr{M}$ assigning meanings to the elements of $\mathfrak{L}$.

In constructing $\mathscr{M}$ we start with the class P_0 of propositions and disjoint classes P_i $(i > 0)$ of other kinds of propositional constituents. P_1 will be the set of monadic concepts, and P_2 the set of propositional designators. In constructing diagrams for statements, attributes, statemental designators, and other categories of statemental constituents (if there are others), we begin with the dynamic parameters. These are properties of utterances, which is to say that they are functions in intension which assign the values of the parameters to utterances "in all possible worlds". Let us collect all the dynamic parameters together into an ω-sequence υ.[1,2] For each $i \in \omega$, $\mathscr{D}(\upsilon_i)$ (the domain of υ_i) is the set of all utterances.

---

[1] An ω-sequence is a function σ whose domain $\mathscr{D}(\sigma)$ is ω. If $i \in \omega$, $\sigma_i = \sigma(i)$. In other words, σ_i is the $(i + 1)st$ *element* of the sequence.

[2] This assumes that there are only countably many dynamic parameters, but this assumption is just a matter of convenience. It can be eliminated at the expense of slightly greater mathematical complexity if that becomes desirable.

265

Appendix

Diagrams are functions in intension on possible combinations of values for the dynamic parameters.[3] We can make the diagram for each statement or statemental constituent unique by making it a function on the sequence of all dynamic parameters rather than just on those dynamic parameters which are relevant to its values. A statemental constituent of *type j* will be one whose sent- and received-objects are members of P_j. Thus monadic attributes are constituents of type 1 and statemental designators are constituents of type 2. A diagram for such a constituent will be called a *diagram of type j*. For sets A and B, let ^AB be the class of all functions in extension from A into B, and for each set X, let $\mathscr{P}X$ be its power set. Then we define:

(2.1) ζ is a *diagram of type j* iff ζ is a function in intension
   & $\Box(\forall\sigma)(\forall\mathscr{S})(\sigma \in \mathscr{D}(\zeta) \supset \{\sigma$ is an ω-sequence
   & $\Diamond(\exists y)[y \in \mathscr{D}(v_0) \,\&\, (\forall i)(i \in \omega \supset v_i(y) = \sigma_i)]$
   & $[\mathscr{S}$ is the class of all people $\supset \zeta(\sigma) \in (^{\mathscr{S}}\mathscr{P}P_j \times {}^{\mathscr{S}}\mathscr{P}P_j)]\})$.

Thus diagrams for statements are diagrams of type 0, diagrams for monadic attributes of are type 1, and diagrams for statemental designators are of type 2.

The inclusion of all dynamic parameters in the arguments of every diagram makes the diagram for any statement or statemental constituent unique (relative to a particular ordering of the parameters). This removes multiplicity of diagrams as a reason for not identifying statements or statemental constituents with their diagrams. I am still inclined to resist that identification on the grounds that some statements are propositions, some attributes are concepts, etc. However, I am also inclined to regard that as unimportant, and if the reader insists that he can only understand statements and statemental constituents if they are identified with their diagrams, then I am willing to play along with him. As will become apparent, we can develop our statemental semantics without ever talking about statements and statemental constituents. We need only talk about their diagrams. Rather than taking *S*-intensions, *A*-intensions, etc., to pick out statements, attributes, etc., we can just as well have them select the corresponding diagrams. For this purpose, let us collect all the pragmatic parameters into an ω-sequence π. Like dynamic parameters, the pragmatic param-

---

[3] Some combinations may not be possible because we do not assume that the dynamic parameters are independent of one another.

eters are functions in intension on utterances. For each $i \in \omega$, $\mathscr{D}(\pi_i)$ is the set of all utterances. Then we can define:

(2.2) Δ is a *j-intension* iff Δ is a function in intension & $j \in \omega$
& $\Box(\forall\sigma)(\sigma \in \mathscr{D}(\Delta) \supset \{\sigma$ is an ω-sequence & $\Diamond(\exists y)[\, y \in \mathscr{D}(\pi_0)$
& $(\forall i)(i \in \omega \supset \pi_i(y) = \sigma_i)]$ & $\Delta(\sigma)$ is a diagram of type $j\})$.

(2.3) Δ is a *lexical intension* iff $(\exists j)[\, j > 0$ & Δ is a j-intension$]$.

For each j, let INT_j be the set of all j-intensions.

By virtue of their expanded arguments, the diagrams we have constructed here are not the same as the diagrams we constructed earlier in the book. The latter can be regarded as abbreviated diagrams:

(2.4) ζ is an *abbreviated diagram of type* $\langle j,i_0, \ldots ,i_n \rangle$ iff ζ is an
$(n + 1)$-place function in intension & $\Box(\forall\sigma)(\sigma \in \mathscr{D}(\zeta) \supset$
$\{\Diamond(\exists y)[\, y \in \mathscr{D}(v_0)$ & $v_{i_0}(y) = \sigma_0$ & $\cdots$ & $v_{i_n}(y) = \sigma_n]$ &
$(\forall\mathscr{S})[\mathscr{S}$ is the class of all people $\supset \zeta(\sigma) \in (^{\mathscr{S}}\mathscr{P}P_j \times {}^{\mathscr{S}}\mathscr{P}P_j)]\})$.

(2.5) If χ is an abbreviated diagram of type $\langle j,i_0, \ldots ,i_n \rangle$,
χ is an *abbreviation of* ζ iff ζ is a diagram of type j &
$\Box(\forall\sigma)(\forall x_0) \cdots (\forall x_n)\{[\sigma \in \mathscr{D}(\zeta)$ & $\langle x_0, \ldots ,x_n \rangle \in \mathscr{D}(\chi)$ &
$\sigma_{i_0} = x_0$ & $\cdots$ & $\sigma_{i_n} = x_n] \supset \zeta(\sigma) = \chi(x_0, \ldots ,x_n)\}$.

An abbreviated diagram uniquely determines an unabbreviated diagram, so we can describe diagrams (as we have been doing) by giving abbreviated versions of them.

We can similarly define the notion of an *abbreviated intension of type* $\langle j,i_0, \ldots ,i_n \rangle$ and describe j-intensions in terms of abbreviated versions of them. The S-intensions, A-intensions, and D-intensions discussed in earlier chapters correspond to abbreviated intensions. Unless we identify statements and statemental constituents with their diagrams, S-intensions, A-intensions, and D-intensions are still not abbreviated 0-intensions, 1-intensions, and 2-intensions, but each S-, A-, or D-intension does uniquely determine a 0-, 1-, or 2-intension respectively.

Given these resources, we can define meanings as in Chapter Twelve. It would then be natural to define a full semantical theory for L to be a function $\mathscr{M}$ such that $\mathscr{D}(\mathscr{M}) = \mathfrak{L}$ and for each $P \in \mathfrak{L}$, $\mathscr{M}(P)$ is a meaning. However, such a definition involves the familiar pretense that languages are unambiguous, assigning just one intension to each linguistic item. If we want to say something about actual languages, we must avoid that pretense. Accordingly, we should instead define:

(2.6) $\mathscr{M}$ is a *full semantical theory for* L iff $\mathscr{M}$ is a function and $\mathscr{D}(\mathscr{M}) = \mathfrak{L}$ and $(\forall w)[w \in \mathfrak{L} \supset \mathscr{M}(w)$ is a nonempty set of meanings].

3. Compositionality

Compositionality embraces two distinct but related topics. First, there is grammatical compositionality. How is it determined in what order lexical items can be strung together to form grammatical sentences? Second, there is semantical compositionality. How is the meaning of a sentence determined by the meanings of the lexical items from which it is constructed? Presumably, compositionality is governed by linguistic rules which, on the one hand, tell us how we can string lexical items together, and on the other hand, describe the meanings of the resultant structures. Let us consider what these rules must look like.

Let us begin by focusing on grammatical compositionality. It would be natural to suppose that rules of grammatical compositionality categorize lexical items in terms of their semantical character (e.g., as predicates, proper names, etc.) and then tell us which arrangements of items from different semantical categories are permitted. For example, in a simple language we might have a rule telling us that we are permitted to construct a sentence by writing a proper name following a monadic predicate, but not by writing a proper name preceding a monadic predicate. Regardless of whether real languages work in this way, it is important to realize that they do not have to. There is no reason why a language could not subdivide semantical categories into finer *grammatical categories* and treat items from the same semantical category but different grammatical categories differently. For example, there could be two arbitrarily selected classes of monadic predicates, and the rules could require that those in the first class be written before a proper name to form a sentence while those in the second class are written after a proper name to form a sentence. The point here is that rules of compositionality must treat lexical items in terms of *grammatical* categories, and if grammatical categories and semantical categories coincide within a particular language this is only a contingent fact about that particular language. It is not to be supposed that grammatical categories must somehow be justified or derived from something more basic. They *could* be arbitrary.

The rules of our language must simply *assign* grammatical categories to linguistic items. More than one grammatical category may be assigned to a single linguistic item if it is ambiguous. Formally, we can regard the rules of language as accomplishing this categorization by assigning integers to each linguistic item, and when an item is assigned the integer i, then it is of the grammatical category i. Let us define:

(3.1) $\mathfrak{G}$ is a *grammatical index* for L iff $\mathfrak{G}$ is a function and $\mathscr{D}(\mathfrak{G}) = \omega$ and $\mathfrak{L} = \bigcup_{i \in \omega} \mathfrak{G}(i)$.

For each i, $\mathfrak{G}(i)$ is the set of linguistic items of the *ith* grammatical category.

We have seen that the rules of compositionality are formulated in terms of grammatical categories, but where do the rules come from? Are they general rules governing the language of which all speakers must be apprised, or are they derivative from some more specific rules? The simplest hypothesis would be that the rules governing each lexical item tell us, among other things, how that item can be compounded with other lexical items. This is the "atomic theory" of compositionality. According to this theory, we do not require general rules of compositionality, because rules of compositionality are forthcoming from the specific features of individual lexical items. Many linguists speak as if they endorse such a theory, although it is unclear to me whether they really do. However, this kind of account cannot, ultimately, be made to work in a nontrivial way. The difficulty is that the rules governing different lexical items must be coordinated with one another. We cannot have a rule governing the use of the name 'Jim' according to which sentences are formed by writing it *after* an arbitrary monadic predicate, and a rule governing the monadic predicate 'has red hair' according to which sentences are formed by writing an arbitrary proper name *before* it (and not after it). The two rules must agree as to whether the name is to be written before or after the predicate. The basic requirement is that all lexical items in the same grammatical category must be treated in the same way by the rules of compositionality (that, after all, is the way grammatical categories are defined). We might still insist that the rules governing a particular lexical item must include the rules of compositionality for that item, but there is no sense in which this explains the origin of the rule (as if we could just conventionally lay down any rule we want for that item) because the rules must be immediately generalizable to all items in the same grammatical category. The rules are really attached to the grammatical category rather than to the individual items in it.

Although the rules of compositionality governing a lexical item are not fundamental to that item, and hence need not be included in a semantic description of that item, the grammatical category is. In describing the way in which a lexical item works in the language, we must not only describe its meaning, but also its grammatical category. Without the latter we will not know how to combine it with other lexical items to form sentences. To accomodate this let us define:

(3.2) $\mathcal{M}$ is an *indexed semantical theory for* L iff $\mathcal{M}$ is a function and $\mathcal{D}(\mathcal{M}) = \mathfrak{L}$ and $(\forall w)[w \in \mathfrak{L} \supset \mathcal{M}(w)$ is a nonempty set of pairs $\langle i,m \rangle$ such that m is a meaning and $i \in \omega]$.

An indexed semantical theory tells us both what the intensions of linguistic items are and what grammatical categories they occupy when functioning with any particular one of their intensions. An indexed semantical theory contains a grammatical index:

(3.3) If $\mathcal{M}$ is a full indexed semantical theory, $\mathfrak{G}$ is *the grammatical index derived from* $\mathcal{M}$ iff $\mathfrak{G}$ is a function & $\mathcal{D}(\mathfrak{G}) = \omega$ & for each $i \in \omega$, $\mathfrak{G}(i) = \{w | (\exists m)\langle i,m \rangle \in \mathcal{M}(w)\}$.

We have ascertained that the rules of compositionality cannot be regarded as derivative from the meanings of our lexical items. In order to understand how rules of compositionality do arise, we need the notion of a sentence matrix, which can be defined as follows. Sentences are finite sequences of symbols. Given two finite sequences $\langle x_1, \ldots, x_n \rangle$ and $\langle y_1, \ldots, y_m \rangle$, we define their *concatenate* as:

(3.4) $\langle x_1, \ldots, x_n \rangle ^\frown \langle y_1, \ldots, y_m \rangle = \langle x_1, \ldots, x_n, y_1, \ldots, y_m \rangle$.

We define:

(3.5) If ξ and σ are finite sequences, ξ *occurs within* σ iff there are finite sequences α and β such that either $\sigma = \xi$ or $\sigma = \xi ^\frown \alpha$ or $\sigma = \alpha ^\frown \xi$ or $\sigma = \alpha ^\frown \xi ^\frown \beta$.

Given any finite sequence σ, if $x_1, \ldots, x_k$ are finite sequences and $y_1, \ldots, y_k$ are distinct finite sequences occurring in σ without overlapping, let

$$Sb\begin{pmatrix} x_1, \ldots, x_k \\ y_1, \ldots, y_k \end{pmatrix} \sigma$$

be the sequence which results from simultaneously replacing each occurrence of y_1 in σ by x_1, each occurrence of y_2 in σ by x_2, etc. Let Vr be a denumerable set of variables (arbitrary symbols) distinct from any of the symbols of L. To simplify our notation, let us not distinguish between a sequence of length 1, $\langle x \rangle$, and its member x. Then we write:

(3.6) f is a k-ary *sentence matrix* of L iff there is a sentence P of L and there are linguistic items $w_1, \ldots, w_k$ (all distinct, $k > 0$) occurring in P and $x_1, \ldots, x_k$ (all distinct) in Vr such that $f = Sb\begin{pmatrix} x_1, \ldots, x_k \\ w_1, \ldots, w_k \end{pmatrix} P$.

(3.7) If P is a sentence and f is a k-ary sentence matrix, P is *of the form of f* iff there are linguistic items $w_1, \ldots, w_k$ and there are $x_1, \ldots, x_k \in Vr$ such that P

$$P = Sb\begin{pmatrix} w_1, \ldots, w_k \\ x_1, \ldots, x_k \end{pmatrix} f.$$

For example, 'The apple is red' is of the form $\ulcorner \alpha$ is $\beta \urcorner$, and 'The apple is red, and the banana is yellow' is of the form $\ulcorner \pi$, and $\rho \urcorner$, and also of the form $\ulcorner \alpha$ is β, and γ is $\delta \urcorner$.

We are including multiword items as lexical items (e.g., noun phrases). It cannot be supposed that speakers of a language process it in terms of individual rules governing each multiword lexical item. Rather, compositionality applies here too. So let us generalize the notion of a matrix to include *lexical matrices*:

(3.8) f is a *matrix of type* $\langle i, j_1, \ldots, j_k \rangle$ iff there is a linguistic item w of grammatical category i and there are distinct linguistic items $w_1, \ldots, w_k$ which are of grammatical categories $j_1, \ldots, j_k$ respectively, and there are distinct variables $x_1, \ldots, x_k \in Vr$ such that $f = Sb\begin{pmatrix} x_1, \ldots, x_k \\ w_1, \ldots, w_k \end{pmatrix} w$.

271

Appendix

For the sake of illustration, let 0 be the grammatical category of (some) complete indicative sentences, 1 be the grammatical category of (some) monadic predicates, and 2 be the grammatical category of (some) singular terms. Then $\ulcorner\alpha$ and $\beta\urcorner$ is both a matrix of type $\langle 0,0,0 \rangle$ and a matrix of type $\langle 1,1,1 \rangle$. Similarly, $\ulcorner\alpha$ is $\beta\urcorner$ is both a matrix of type $\langle 0,2,1 \rangle$ and a matrix of type $\langle 0,2,2 \rangle$.

Beginning with some simple matrices and basic lexical items, we can construct a variety of sentences. For example, consider the sentence

John won't come unless Mary asks him to come.

This can be systematically decomposed in terms of matrices and lexical items as follows:

$\ulcorner\alpha$ unless $\beta\urcorner$: $\langle$'John won't come', 'Mary asks him to come'$\rangle$

$\ulcorner\alpha$ won't $\beta\urcorner$: $\langle$'John', 'come'$\rangle$

$\ulcorner\alpha\ \beta\urcorner$: $\langle$'Mary', 'asks him to come'$\rangle$

$\ulcorner\alpha\widehat{\ }$s β to $\gamma\urcorner$: $\langle$'ask', 'him', 'come'$\rangle$

A natural supposition for a logician to make at this point would be that there is a stock of simple matrices and a stock of simple lexical items and then all linguistic items are constructed recursively by replacing variables in matrices by linguistic items of the appropriate grammatical categories, starting with the simple lexical items. This is the way we do things in logic, but natural languages are more complicated than this. For example, rather than writing 'If it were true that John comes, it would be true that Mary stays home', English allows us to write 'If John were to come, Mary would stay home'. There is an operation whereby the conditional is constructed from the sentences 'John comes' and 'Mary stays home', but the latter sentences do not become imbedded in the completed conditional as they would if this operation consisted merely of the application of a matrix to the antecedent and consequent. This same phenomenon is illustrated by tenses, singular/plural, active/passive, etc. Linguists studying transformational grammar are well familiar with it. To understand the way in which sentences are constructed out of simpler linguistic items, we need a more general notion than that of a matrix. A completely general notion can be defined as follows:

(3.9) f is a *frame of type* $\langle i,j_1,\ldots,j_k\rangle$ relative to a grammatical index $\mathfrak{G}$ iff f is a function & $\mathscr{D}(f) \subseteq (\mathfrak{G}(j_1) \times \cdots \times \mathfrak{G}(j_k))$ and $\mathscr{R}(f) \subseteq \mathfrak{G}(i)$.

(3.10) f is a *nontransformational frame of type* $\langle i,j_1,\ldots,j_k\rangle$ iff f is a frame of type $\langle i,j_1,\ldots,j_k\rangle$ and there is a matrix g of type $\langle i,j_1,\ldots,j_k\rangle$ and there are distinct variables $x_1,\ldots,x_k$ such that $(\forall w_1)\cdots(\forall w_k)[\text{if }\langle w_1,\ldots,w_k\rangle \in \mathscr{D}(f)$, then $f(w_1,\ldots,w_k) = Sb\begin{pmatrix} w_1,\ldots,w_k \\ w_1,\ldots,x_k \end{pmatrix}g]$.

(3.11) f is a *transformational frame of type* $\langle i,j_1,\ldots,j_k\rangle$ iff f is a frame of type $\langle i,j_1,\ldots,j_k\rangle$, but f is not a non-transformational frame of type $\langle i,j_1,\ldots,j_k\rangle$.

We can regard complex linguistic items as being constructed out of simpler linguistic items by the application of frames to those simpler items. The use of nontransformational frames is equivalent to the use of matrices, but our preceding observation is that transformational frames are also used. When a linguistic item is constructed by applying a transformational frame to simpler linguistic items, the latter items do not appear intact in the constructed item. They are transformed in various ways.

We can formulate a very general type of grammar as follows:

(3.12) $\langle \mathfrak{A},\mathfrak{F}\rangle$ is a *generative grammar for L relative to* $\mathfrak{G}$ iff $\mathfrak{G}$ is a grammatical index for L and $\mathfrak{A}$ is a set of pairs $\langle w,k\rangle$ such that $w \in \mathfrak{G}(k)$ and $\mathfrak{F}$ is a set of pairs $\langle f,\alpha\rangle$ such that f is a frame of type α relative to $\mathfrak{G}$.

(3.13) $\langle \mathfrak{A},\mathfrak{F}\rangle$ is a *generative grammar for L* iff $(\exists\mathfrak{G})\langle \mathfrak{A},\mathfrak{F}\rangle$ is a generative grammar for L relative to $\mathfrak{G}$.

(3.14)   If $\langle \mathfrak{A},\mathfrak{F}\rangle$ is a generative grammar, w is a *primitive linguistic item* relative to $\langle \mathfrak{A},\mathfrak{F}\rangle$ iff $(\exists i)\langle w,i\rangle \in \mathfrak{A}$, and f is a *primitive frame* relative to $\langle \mathfrak{A},\mathfrak{F}\rangle$ iff $(\exists\alpha)\langle f,\alpha\rangle \in \mathfrak{F}$.

If $\langle \mathfrak{A},\mathfrak{F}\rangle$ is a generative grammar, the set $\langle \mathfrak{A},\mathfrak{F}\rangle_n$ of pairs $\langle w,i\rangle$ where w is a linguistic item of grammatical category i generated by

n or fewer steps of grammatical construction can be defined as follows:

(3.15) $\langle \mathfrak{A},\mathfrak{F} \rangle_0 = \mathfrak{A}$;

$\langle \mathfrak{A},\mathfrak{F} \rangle_{n+1} = \langle \mathfrak{A},\mathfrak{F} \rangle_n \cup \{\langle f(w_1,\ldots,w_k),i \rangle \,|\, (\exists j_1) \cdots (\exists j_k)$
$[\langle f,\langle i,j_1,\ldots,j_k \rangle \rangle \in \mathfrak{F} \,\&\, \langle w_1,j_1 \rangle \in \langle \mathfrak{A},\mathfrak{F} \rangle_n$
$\&\cdots\&\, \langle w_k,j_k \rangle \in \langle \mathfrak{A},\mathfrak{F} \rangle_n]\}$;

$\langle \mathfrak{A},\mathfrak{F} \rangle_\omega = \bigcup_{n \in \omega} \langle \mathfrak{A},\mathfrak{F} \rangle_n.$

(3.16) If $\mathfrak{G}$ is a grammatical index for L and $\langle \mathfrak{A},\mathfrak{F} \rangle$ is a generative grammar, $\langle \mathfrak{A},\mathfrak{F} \rangle$ is *adequate relative to* $\mathfrak{G}$ iff for each $i \in \omega$, $\mathfrak{G}(i) = \{w \,|\, \langle w,i \rangle \in \langle \mathfrak{A},\mathfrak{F} \rangle_\omega \}$.

(3.17) If $\mathcal{M}$ is an indexed semantical theory and $\langle \mathfrak{A},\mathfrak{F} \rangle$ is a generative grammar, $\langle \mathfrak{A},\mathfrak{F} \rangle$ is *adequate relative to* $\mathcal{M}$ iff $\langle \mathfrak{A},\mathfrak{F} \rangle$ is adequate relative to the grammatical index derived from $\mathcal{M}$.

Let us say that $\langle \mathfrak{A},\mathfrak{F} \rangle$ is adequate *for* L just in case it generates a grammatical index for L:

(3.18) If $\langle \mathfrak{A},\mathfrak{F} \rangle$ is a generative grammar, $\langle \mathfrak{A},\mathfrak{F} \rangle$ is *adequate for* L iff $(\exists \mathfrak{G})[\mathfrak{G}$ is a grammatical index for $L \,\&\, \langle \mathfrak{A},\mathfrak{F} \rangle$ is adequate relative to $\mathfrak{G}]$.

Our notion of a generative grammar is sufficiently general to accomodate anything that might reasonably be called a generative grammar. Among those grammars which can be formulated as generative grammars are Montague grammars and transformational grammars[4], together with their variants such as what Bresnan [1978] calls 'the lexical interpretive model of transformational grammar', and the transformational extensions of Montague grammar discussed in Partee [1973]. Thus we are placing virtually no restrictions on a language by assuming that it has a generative grammar and that speakers process it in terms of some such grammar.

Now let us relate the grammar to the semantics. The simplest and most natural assumption to make is that we process our language in terms of rules which allow us to build up our sentences recursively (i.e., in terms of a generative grammar) and which assign

[4] In order to accomodate current transformational grammars, we must have a grammatical category of meaningful linguistic items which are sentence-like but not sentences to provide the base structures.

meanings to the constructed sentences as we go along. In other words, the rules assign meanings directly to the primitive linguistic items, and to each primitive frame f they assign a function which determines the meaning of $f(w_1, \ldots, w_k)$ in terms of the meanings of $w_1, \ldots, w_k$. A function of this latter sort will be called a 'semantical character'. A semantical character is any function from n-tuples of meanings to meanings. Then we define:

(3.19) $\mathcal{M}$ is a *generative semantical theory with base* $\langle \mathcal{W}, \mathcal{F} \rangle$ iff $\mathcal{F}$ is a set of frames and $\mathcal{W}$ is a set of linguistic items such that $\mathcal{D}(\mathcal{M}) = \mathcal{F} \cup \mathcal{W}$ and $(\forall w)[w \in \mathcal{W} \supset \mathcal{M}(w)$ is a nonempty set of pairs $\langle i,m \rangle$ such that $i \in \omega$ & m is a meaning] and $(\forall f)[f \in \mathcal{F} \supset \mathcal{M}(f)$ is a nonempty set of pairs $\langle \alpha, \mu \rangle$ such that f is a frame of type α & μ is a semantical character with the same number of argument places as f].

The intent here is that to each item in $\mathcal{W}$, $\mathcal{M}$ assigns a set of pairs $\langle i,m \rangle$ of grammatical categories and meanings, and to each frame in $\mathcal{F}$, $\mathcal{M}$ assigns a set of pairs of frame types and semantical characters. $\mathcal{W}$ is the class of *primitive linguistic items* and $\mathcal{F}$ is the class of *primitive frames* of $\mathcal{M}$.

A generative semantical theory generates an indexed semantical theory by extending the function inductively. Where $\mathcal{M}$ is a generative semantical theory for L, we can define the functions $\mathcal{M}_n$ inductively as follows:

(3.20)   If $P \in \mathfrak{L}$:

$\mathcal{M}_0(P) = \mathcal{M}(P)$;

$\mathcal{M}_{n+1}(P) = \mathcal{M}_n(P) \cup \{\langle i,m \rangle |$ there is an $f \in \mathcal{F}$ and a frame type $\langle i, j_1, \ldots, j_k \rangle$ and a function μ such that $\langle \langle i, j_1, \ldots, j_k \rangle, \mu \rangle \in \mathcal{M}(f)$ and there are $w_1, \ldots, w_k$ and meanings $m_1, \ldots, m_k$ such that $\langle j_1, m_1 \rangle \in \mathcal{M}_n(w_1)$ & $\cdots$ & $\langle j_k, m_k \rangle \in \mathcal{M}_n(w_k)$ and there are $x_1, \ldots, x_k \in Vr$ such that $P = f(w_1, \ldots, w_k)$ and $m = \mu(m_1, \ldots, m_k)\}$;

$\mathcal{M}_\omega(P) = \bigcup_{n \in \omega} \mathcal{M}_n(P)$.

If $\mathcal{M}$ is an adequate generative semantical theory for L, then $\mathcal{M}_\omega$ should be an indexed semantical theory for L. It could fail to be so, however, if $\mathcal{M}$ operates on too small a selection of primitive frames and primitive linguistic items. Let us define then:

(3.21) $\mathcal{M}$ is an *adequate* generative semantical theory for L iff $\mathcal{M}$ is a generative semantical theory for L and $\mathcal{M}_\omega$ is an indexed semantical theory for L.

A generative semantical theory contains a generative grammar:

(3.22) If $\mathcal{M}$ is a generative semantical theory with base $\langle \mathcal{W}, \mathcal{F} \rangle$, $\langle \mathfrak{A}, \mathfrak{F} \rangle$ is the *generative grammar contained in* $\mathcal{M}$ iff $\mathfrak{A} = \{\langle w,k \rangle \mid w \in \mathcal{W} \ \& \ (\exists m)\langle k,m \rangle \in \mathcal{M}(w)\}$ and $\mathfrak{F} = \{\langle f,\alpha \rangle \mid f \in \mathcal{F} \ \& \ (\exists \mu)\langle \alpha,\mu \rangle \in \mathcal{M}(f)\}$.

We have the following simple theorem:

(3.23) If $\mathcal{M}$ is a generative semantical theory and $\langle \mathfrak{A}, \mathfrak{F} \rangle$ is the generative grammar contained in $\mathcal{M}$, then $\mathcal{M}$ is an adequate generative semantical theory for L iff $\langle \mathfrak{A}, \mathfrak{F} \rangle$ is an adequate generative grammar for L.

My contention is now that for any natural language L, the rules in terms of which the speakers of L actually process sentences of L make more or less direct appeal to a generative semantical theory for L. Speakers clearly do not process sentences in terms of rules making direct assignments of meanings to all linguistic items. That would require infinitely many different rules. Rather, there are rules which allow speakers to compute the meaning of a sentence in terms, roughly, of the meanings of its parts. More accurately, there are rules which tell us how to recursively generate linguistic items of increasing complexity out of one another, and simultaneously tell us how the meanings of the generated items are determined by the meanings of the items from which they are generated and the means of generation. In other words, the rules determine a generative semantical theory.

Generative semantical theories involve a kind of semantical/grammatical parallelism wherein the same set of rules generates both the grammar and the semantics. As we have seen, an adequate generative semantical theory contains an adequate generative grammar. This semantical/grammatical parallelism is surely the simplest and most natural hypothesis to make about the relationship between grammar and semantics. After all, the whole point of grammar is to generate vehicles for meaning. What more natural way to do that than to generate them in a way which assigns meanings as you go along?

Most of the semantical theories of contemporary linguistics can be regarded as very simple (probably simplistic) kinds of generative semantical theories. For example, the most popular contemporary theory is that of J. J. Katz and his associates.[5] This theory assumes a transformational grammar and assigns meanings to sentences in the deep structure in accordance with a generative semantical theory. It is then assumed that transformations leave meanings intact so that the meaning of a sentence is identified with the meaning of the deep structure from which it is transformationally derived. This is equivalent, in a generative semantical theory, to taking the semantical character of all transformations to be the identity function. An obvious generalization of this theory would be to allow transformations to alter meanings and hence have more general semantical characters.

The claim is that the rules of a natural language must provide a generative semantical theory in terms of which the speakers of the language can process it. Although this seems to be uncontentious because of its extreme generality, it is nevertheless an empirical hypothesis as applied to any particular language. We might reasonably ask what evidence there is to support it. There is a simple set of observations which lend very strong support to this hypothesis. To begin with, it is obvious that there are rules assigning meanings to primitive linguistic items. But it might be denied that there are also rules assigning semantical characters to primitive frames. Frames do have semantical characters, but perhaps they have them only derivatively. Any indexed semantical theory and adequate generative grammar for L determines an assignment of semantical characters to frames. Let us define:

(3.24) If $\mathcal{M}$ is an indexed semantical theory for L, $\langle \mathfrak{A}, \mathfrak{F} \rangle$ an adequate generative grammar for L, and $\langle f, \langle i, j_1, \ldots, j_k \rangle \rangle \in \mathfrak{F}$: $\mathcal{M}_{\langle i, j_1, \ldots, j_k \rangle}[f] = \{\mu \mid \mu$ is a k-adic semantical character & $\mathcal{D}(\mu) = \{\langle m_1, \ldots, m_k \rangle \mid (\exists w_1) \cdots (\exists w_k)[\langle j_1, m_1 \rangle \in \mathcal{M}(w_1)$ & $\cdots$ & $\langle j_k, m_k \rangle \in \mathcal{M}(w_k)]\}$ & $(\forall w)(\forall w_1) \cdots (\forall w_k)(\forall m)(\forall m_1) \cdots (\forall m_k)[$if $w = f(w_1, \ldots, w_k)$ & $\langle j_1, m_1 \rangle \in \mathcal{M}(w_1)$ & $\cdots$ & $\langle j_k, m_k \rangle \in \mathcal{M}(w_k)$ & $m = \mu(m_1, \ldots, m_k)$, then $\langle i, m \rangle \in \mathcal{M}(w)]\}$.

It might be suggested, then, that the meanings of linguistic items are determined in some way independent of the assignment of

[5] See Katz and Fodor [1963], Katz and Postal [1964], and Katz [1972].

semantical characters to frames, and then the latter are derivative in accordance with (3.24) from the assignment of meanings. There are two things wrong with this proposal. First, unless $\mathcal{M}$ and $\langle \mathfrak{A}, \mathfrak{F} \rangle$ are in an appropriate sense "parallel", (3.24) will not produce an interesting assignment of semantical characters. It may even be that for every k-tuple of integers α and every frame f, $\mathcal{M}_\alpha[f] = \varnothing$. In order for (3.24) to work in a reasonable way, the structure of $\mathcal{M}$ must be such that it *can* be generated by a generative semantical theory containing the generative grammar $\langle \mathfrak{A}, \mathfrak{F} \rangle$, and there is no guarantee that that is the case.

Second, even in the ideal case in which there is a generative semantical theory $\mathcal{M}^*$ such that $\mathcal{M} = \mathcal{M}^*_\omega$ and $\langle \mathfrak{A}, \mathfrak{F} \rangle$ is the generative grammar contained in $\mathcal{M}^*$, we cannot use (3.24) to recover from $\mathcal{M}$ the semantical characters which $\mathcal{M}^*$ assigns to primitive frames. This is because the semantical characters constructed in accordance with (3.24) have domains restricted to meanings actually represented in L. If we add a new linguistic item to our language with a meaning not possessed by any linguistic item presently in the language, the semantical characters constructed in accordance with (3.24) will not be applicable to it. But if we reflect upon our understanding of simple frames like those involved in predication, conjunction, negation, quantification, etc., we know perfectly well how to apply their semantical characters to any meanings of the appropriate types, regardless of whether those meanings are represented in the language. Thus our understanding of those frames cannot be derived from a prior determination of the meanings of linguistic items. The rules in terms of which we process the language must supply semantical characters for primitive frames more or less directly. But if they do that, and they also supply us with meanings for primitive linguistic items, then they provide us with a generative semantical theory.

It is still a contingent fact that the languages we actually employ have rules which provide us with generative semantical theories. However, this fact is connected with very basic features of meaning. In Section Five I will provide analyses of lexical sending and of using a (possibly ambiguous) lexical item with a particular intension in an utterance of a sentence containing that item. It would be an extraordinarily peculiar language for which either of these notions failed to make sense. The notion of using a lexical item with a particular meaning within a sentence is fundamental to the idea that the meaning of a sentence is somehow a function of the way in which it is constructed. And as we have seen, the notion of lexical sending is central to the intensions of most singular terms and predicates. A language without the notion of lexical sending would be very different from the languages with which we are familiar and could not even have expressions with the same meanings as most of the singular terms and predicates of our language. However, the analyses of these two notions will presuppose a generative semantical theory. Furthermore, I see no way to avoid that presupposition. We will find that that presupposition appears to be involved in the very concept of either lexical sending or using a lexical item with a particular meaning. If that is correct, then the fact that our language involves a generative semantical theory has profound effects not only on the way in which meanings of complicated linguistic items are determined, but even on what kinds of meanings linguistic items can have. A language without a generative semantical theory would be totally different from anything with which we are familiar.

The appeal to generative semantical theories can also throw light on another matter. We have observed several times that there are linguistic items which are generally considered to be meaningful but which do not have intensions. Examples are 'every', 'is' (as used in predication), 'not', 'and', 'unless', 'very', and perhaps many others. The way in which these intensionless items become incorporated into sentences is through the application of frames to linguistic items that do have intensions. For example, there is a sentence frame f of type $\langle 0,0,0 \rangle$ such that $f(P,Q) = \ulcorner P \hat{~} \text{and} \hat{~} Q \urcorner$ and the semantical character μ of f is such that for any 0-intensions Δ_1 and Δ_2, if $\langle \text{state}, \Delta \rangle = \mu(\langle \text{state}, \Delta_1 \rangle, \langle \text{state}, \Delta_2 \rangle)$ and π is a sequence of values of the pragmatic parameters, then $\Delta(\pi) = (\Delta_1(\pi) \wedge \Delta_2(\pi))$. It seems reasonable to say that 'and' is meaningful only by virtue of its role in this sentence frame (and related frames dealing with the conjunction of nondeclarative sentences, predicates, etc.). If we wished, we could identify the meaning of 'and' with the semantical character of the sentence frame which introduces it. The same thing is true of 'every', 'is', 'not', 'unless', 'very', etc.

It might be objected that we have got things backwards—that the semantical character of the sentence frame derives from the meaning of 'and' rather than the meaning of 'and' deriving from the semantical character. For those sentence frames that are intimately connected with particular words or phrases, these seem to be equivalent ways of describing the same semantical phenomenon. I cannot see a substantive difference here. It is worth observing, however, that there are frames whose operation does not involve the insertion of special lexical items. The simplest example is the frame which merely concatenates linguistic items. For example, there is a frame which produces 'John runs' from 'John' and 'runs'. It is also plausible to suppose that there are primitive frames which transform the tenses of verbs, for example producing 'ran' from 'run'. The semantical characters of these frames cannot be viewed as derivative from the meanings of special lexical items, so I see no particular advantage in trying to cast other frames in that mold.

4. Semantical Occurrences

When we introduced the notion of a semantical occurrence of a linguistic item in Chapter One, we were unable to give a precise definition of that notion. We can now remedy that. The semanticality of an occurrence of w in a sentence P must be relativized to a meaning for P because, for example, the lexical items occurring within an idiom like 'Every dog has his day' do not normally have semantical occurrences, but such an idiom *can* be used literally (in which case lexical items occurring within it have semantical occurrences). Bearing this in mind, we can define:

(4.1) An occurrence of w in P is *nonsemantical relative to* $\langle i,m \rangle$ and a generative semantical theory $\mathcal{M}$ iff $\langle i,m \rangle \in \mathcal{M}_\omega(P)$ and the occurrence of w is properly contained within (i.e., contained within but not identical with) an occurrence of some w^* in P for which there are j,m^* such that $\langle j,m^* \rangle \in \mathcal{M}(w^*)$ and $(\forall \mathcal{M}^*)$(if $\mathcal{M}^*$ is a generative semantical theory and $\mathcal{M}^*$ is identical with $\mathcal{M}$ except that $\langle j,m^* \rangle \notin \mathcal{M}^*(w^*)$, then $\langle i,m \rangle \notin \mathcal{M}^*(P)$).

In other words, a nonsemantical occurrence of w in P occurs within a longer linguistic item w^* which is given its meaning directly in $\mathcal{M}$ (i.e., it is primitive) in such a way that if that assignment to w^* is deleted from $\mathcal{M}$, then P will no longer have the meaning $\langle i,m \rangle$. For example, if w occurs in P within a quotation name $\ulcorner$'w'$\urcorner$, $\mathcal{M}$ will assign a meaning directly to $\ulcorner$'w'$\urcorner$, and if that assignment is deleted from $\mathcal{M}$, then P will no longer be assigned a meaning by $\mathcal{M}$. Similarly, if w is 'peg' and it occurs within the idiom 'square peg in a round hole' which in turn occurs within P, the entire idiom will be assigned a meaning directly by $\mathcal{M}$, and if that assignment is deleted from $\mathcal{M}$, then the only meaning still assigned to P by $\mathcal{M}_\omega$ will be that in which the idiom is taken literally.

5. Lexical Sending

Our analyses of the intensions of singular terms and predicates presupposed the notion of lexical sending, but we were previously unable to do more than roughly sketch an account of that notion. Now we are in a position to give a precise definition of lexical sending. To keep the account as simple as possible, however, we will confine our attention to declarative sentences. The extension to nondeclarative sentences will be obvious, but the details are complex.

We begin with the notion of a propositional function. This is a function from n-tuples of propositions and propositional constituents to sets of propositions and propositional constitutents:

(5.1) ρ is a *propositional function of type* $\langle i, j_1, \ldots, j_k \rangle$ iff
$$\rho \in {}^{(P_{j_1} \times \cdots \times P_{j_k})}\mathscr{P}P_i.$$

We define statemental functions analogously. For each i, let $\mathfrak{S}_i$ be the set of all diagrams of type i. Then:

(5.2) σ is a *statemental function of type* $\langle i, j_1, \ldots, j_k \rangle$ iff
$$\sigma \in {}^{(\mathfrak{S}_{j_1} \times \cdots \times \mathfrak{S}_j))}\mathscr{P}\mathfrak{S}_i.$$

To simplify the discussion I will confine my attention to declarative sentences. This enables us to reconstrue semantical characters as functions from n-tuples of intensions to intensions rather than from n-tuples of meanings to meanings. Recalling that INT_j is the set of all j-intensions, let us define:

(5.3) μ is a *semantical character of type* $\langle i, j_1, \ldots, j_k \rangle$ iff
$$\mu \in {}^{(INT_{j_1} \times \cdots \times INT_{j_k})}INT_i.$$

Given this reconstrual, a semantical character induces a statemental function:

(5.4) If μ is a semantical character of type $\langle i, j_1, \ldots, j_k \rangle$, μ *induces* a statemental function σ iff σ is of type $\langle i, j_1, \ldots, j_k \rangle$ and if ζ_1 is a diagram of type j_1 & $\cdots$ & ζ_k is a diagram of type j_k, then $\sigma(\zeta_1, \ldots, \zeta_k) = \{\zeta \mid (\exists \pi)(\exists \Delta)(\exists \Delta_1) \cdots (\exists \Delta_k) [\Delta = \mu(\Delta_1, \ldots, \Delta_k)$ & π is a possible sequence of values for the pragmatic parameters & $\Delta(\pi) = \zeta$ & $\Delta_1(\pi) = \zeta_1$ & $\cdots$ & $\Delta_k(\pi) = \zeta_k]\}$.

Appendix

If f is a frame, μ its semantical character, and $P = f(w_1, \ldots, w_k)$, then σ tells us what constraints are imposed on the sense of P by a specification of the senses of $w_1, \ldots, w_k$. In many cases, the sense of P will be uniquely determined by the senses of $w_1, \ldots, w_k$. That happens, for example, when $f(\alpha, \beta) = \ulcorner \alpha \hat{\ } \text{and} \hat{\ } \beta \urcorner$. In such cases, the value of σ is always a unit set $\{\zeta\}$. But that is not always the case. For example, the sense of F does not uniquely determine the sense of $\ulcorner$ the $F \urcorner$ when the latter is used referentially.

We can also say that a statemental function induces a propositional function:

(5.5) If σ is a statemental function of type $\langle i, j_1, \ldots, j_k \rangle$ and ρ is a propositional function, σ *induces* ρ iff ρ is of type $\langle i, j_1, \ldots, j_k \rangle$ and if $\alpha_1 \in P_1 \ \& \ \cdots \ \& \ \alpha_k \in P_k$, then $\rho(\alpha_1 \ldots, \alpha_k) = \{\alpha \,|\, (\exists v)(\exists \zeta)(\exists \zeta_1) \cdots (\exists \zeta_k)(\exists \Sigma_1) \cdots (\exists \Sigma_k)(\exists S)(\exists \Omega_1) \cdots (\exists \Omega_k)$
$[\zeta \in \sigma(\zeta_1, \ldots, \zeta_k) \ \& \ v$ is a possible sequence of values for the dynamic parameters $\& \ \zeta(v) = \langle \Sigma, \Omega \rangle \ \& \ \zeta_1(v) = \langle \Sigma_1, \Omega_1 \rangle \ \& \ \cdots \ \& \ \zeta_k(v) = \langle \Sigma_k, \Omega_k \rangle \ \& \ \alpha_1 \in \Sigma_1(S) \ \& \ \cdots \ \& \ \alpha_k \in \Sigma_k(S)\}$.

Derivatively, a semantical character induces a propositional function:

(5.6) If μ is a semantical character, μ *induces* a propositional function ρ iff μ induces some statemental function which induces ρ.

Again, in many cases the propositional function induced by a semantical character will always have values of the form $\{\alpha\}$, but that is not invariably the case.

An assignment of semantical characters to primitive frames induces an assignment of semantical characters to nonprimitive frames. Nonprimitive frames are constructed recursively by functional composition from primitive frames. Let us define:

(5.7) If $\langle \mathfrak{A}, \mathfrak{F} \rangle$ is a generative grammar:

$\mathfrak{F}_0 = \mathfrak{F};$

$\mathfrak{F}_{n+1} = \mathfrak{F}_n \cup \{\langle f, \langle i, j_1, \ldots, j_k \rangle \rangle \,|\,$ there is a $\langle g, \langle i, p_1, \ldots, p_k \rangle \rangle \in \mathfrak{F}_0$ and there are $\langle f_1, \langle p_1, m_1^{(1)}, \ldots, m_{n1}^{(1)} \rangle \rangle, \ldots,$
$\langle f_k, \langle p_k, m_1^{(k)}, \ldots, m_{nk}^{(k)} \rangle \rangle$ in $\mathfrak{F}_n$ such that f is a composi-

tion of g with $f_1, \ldots, f_k$ and $\mathscr{D}(f) = \{\langle w_1, \ldots, w_k \rangle \mid \langle w_1, j_1 \rangle, \ldots, \langle w_k, j_k \rangle \in \langle \mathfrak{A}, \mathfrak{F} \rangle_\omega\}\}$;

$$\mathfrak{F}_\omega = \bigcup_{n \in \omega} \mathfrak{F}_n.$$

We have the following simple theorem:

(5.8) If $\langle \mathfrak{A}, \mathfrak{F} \rangle$ is an adequate generative grammar for L, then for any sentence P of L, there is a pair $\langle f, \langle i, j_1, \ldots, j_k \rangle \rangle \in \mathfrak{F}_\omega$ and there are $\langle j_1, w_1 \rangle, \ldots, \langle j_k, w_k \rangle \in \mathfrak{A}$ such that $P = f(w_1, \ldots, w_k)$.

The assignment of semantical characters to the primitive frames induces an assignment of semantical characters to nonprimitive frames. A nonprimitive frame f constructed at the $(n + 1)st$ level of (5.7) is constructed by the functional composition of frames already constructed, and the semantical character of f will result from composing the semantical characters of the frames out of which f is constructed. Letting $\mathscr{MF}$ be the set of triples $\langle f, \alpha, \mu \rangle$ such that $\langle f, \alpha \rangle \in \mathfrak{F}_\omega$ and μ is a semantical character induced on f, and letting $\mathscr{MF}_n$ be the set of those triples constructed by the nth stage, we have:

(5.9) $\mathscr{MF}_0 = \{\langle f, \alpha, \mu \rangle \mid \langle \alpha, \mu \rangle \in \mathscr{M}(f)\}$;

$\mathscr{MF}_{n+1} = \mathscr{MF}_n \cup \{\langle f, \langle i, j_1, \ldots, j_k \rangle, \mu \rangle \mid$ there is a $\langle g, \langle i, p_1, \ldots, p_k \rangle, \rho \rangle \in \mathscr{MF}_0$ and there are $\langle f_1, \langle p_1, m_1^{(1)}, \ldots, m_{n_1}^{(1)} \rangle, \rho_1 \rangle, \ldots, \langle f_k, \langle p_k, m_1^{(k)}, \ldots, m_{n_k}^{(k)} \rangle, \rho_k \rangle$ in $\mathscr{MF}_n$ such that f is a composition of g with $f_1, \ldots, f_k$ and $\mathscr{D}(f) = \{\langle w_1, \ldots, w_k \rangle \mid \langle w_1, j_1 \rangle, \ldots, \langle w_k, j_k \rangle \in \langle \mathfrak{A}, \mathfrak{F} \rangle_\omega\}$ and μ is the corresponding composition of ρ with $\rho_1, \ldots, \rho_k\}$;

$$\mathscr{MF} = \bigcup_{n \in \omega} \mathscr{MF}_n$$

Let us define:

(5.10) $\mathscr{M}_\alpha\{f\} = \{\mu \mid \langle f, \alpha, \mu \rangle \in \mathscr{MF}\}$.

The idea behind our analysis of lexical sending is now this. A sentence P can be viewed as the result of applying various sentence frames to various sequences of linguistic items having semantical occurrences in P. To illustrate, suppose P is the sentence:

John won't come unless Mary comes.

The linguistic items having semantical occurrences in P are 'John', 'come', 'Mary', 'comes', 'won't come', 'John won't come', and 'Mary comes'. There are sentence frames f_1–f_6 such that P is each of the following:

f_1('John', 'come', 'Mary', 'comes');
f_2('John', 'come', 'Mary comes');
f_3('John', 'won't come', 'Mary', 'comes');
f_4('John', 'won't come', 'Mary comes');
f_5('John won't come', 'Mary', 'comes');
f_6('John won't come', 'Mary comes').

Now suppose a speaker S uses P to make some statement ϕ and thereby send some proposition ψ. Our semantical theory $\mathcal{M}$ may assign more than one possible intension to P,[6] but the statement ϕ will only be appropriate to one of them, so it will determine that the sentence is being used with some intension Δ. Let ξ be the function which assigns a sent-object (i.e., a sent-designator, sent-concept, etc.) to each semantical occurrence of a linguistic item in P. Let η be the function which assigns the intension with which it is being used in P to each semantical occurrence of a linguistic item in P. The functions ξ and η must then satisfy the following condition. Given any of f_1–f_6, there is a μ in $\mathcal{M}_{\alpha_i}\{f_i\}$ such that if $P = f_i(w_1, \ldots, w_k)$, then $\Delta = \mu(\eta(w_1), \ldots, \eta(w_k))$, and if ρ is the propositional function induced by μ, then $\psi \in \rho(\xi(w_1), \ldots, \xi(w_k))$. Furthermore, ξ and η must be related in such a way that $\xi(w_j)$ is a possible sent-object for $\eta(w_j)$. More precisely, if $\eta(w_j) = \Delta$, then given the present values of the pragmatic and dynamic parameters, there corresponds to Δ and a speaker S a set $\Sigma_\Delta(S)$ of possible sent-objects for w_j, and it must be the case that $\xi(w_j) \in \Sigma_\Delta(S)$. In order to avoid circularity at this point, we must omit from consideration those pragmatic and dynamic parameters which make reference to what objects are being sent by using $w_1, \ldots, w_k$. My proposal is then that the requirement that ξ and η satisfy these conditions for each of f_1–f_6 simultaneously suffices to uniquely determine ξ and η. Should ξ and η not be uniquely determined, then no lexical sending

---

[6] As we are confining our attention to declarative sentences, we will take $\mathcal{M}$ to assign intensions rather than meanings.

takes place, in which case it will normally follow that no stating occurs. This is the idea behind our analysis of lexical sending, which is now made precise as follows:

(5.11)   If π is a sequence of values for the sequence of pragmatic or dynamic parameters, the *purification of* π is the result of deleting from π the values of any parameters which make reference to lexical sending.

(5.12) π is a *purified sequence of values* for the pragmatic or dynamic parameters iff π is the purification of some sequence of values for the pragmatic or dynamic parameters.

(5.13)   If Δ is an intention and π is a purified sequence of values for the pragmatic parameters, $(\Delta/\pi) = \{\zeta|(\exists\pi^*)[\pi^*$ is a sequence of values for the pragmatic parameters & π is the purification of π^* & $\Delta(\pi^*) = \zeta]\}$.

(5.14)   If ζ is a diagram and υ is a purified sequence of values for the dynamic parameters, $(\zeta/\upsilon) = \{\langle\Sigma,\Omega\rangle|(\exists\upsilon^*)[\upsilon^*$ is a sequence of values for the dynamic parameters & υ is the purification of υ^* & $\zeta(\upsilon^*) = \langle\Sigma,\Omega\rangle]\}$.

(5.15) $\Sigma_\Delta(S) = \{\alpha|$ if π is the purified sequence of values for the pragmatic parameters under the present circumstances and υ is the purified sequence of values for the dynamic parameters under the present circumstances, then $(\exists\zeta)(\exists\Sigma)(\exists\Omega)[\zeta \in (\Delta/\pi)$ & $\langle\Sigma,\Omega\rangle \in (\zeta/\upsilon)$ & $\alpha \in \Sigma(S)]\}$.

The function ξ is to assign sent-objects to semantical occurrences of linguistic items in P, and η is to assign intensions to those occurrences. We cannot take ξ and η to assign sent-objects and intensions to the linguistic items themselves, because that would be to suppose that every occurrence of a particular linguistic item in P is used with the same intension and to send the same object. The functions ξ and η must instead make their assignment to *occurrences* of linguistic items. This can be accomplished by arranging all linguistic items having semantical occurrences in P into a sequence $\langle w_1, \ldots, w_k \rangle$ wherein they are listed in order of occurrence in P. We will say that one occurrence of a linguistic item precedes a second iff either the first begins before the second or they begin at the same point but the first ends before the second. If a particular linguistic item has more than one semantical occurrence in P, then it will occur more than once in the sequence $\langle w_1, \ldots, w_k \rangle$. Then rather than having ξ and η make assignments to the linguistic items themselves, we can have them make assignments to occurrences by letting them assign intensions and sent-objects to the integers $1, \ldots, k$. Different assignments can thus be made to integers i and j even when $w_i = w_j$. With this in mind, we now define:

(5.16) $\langle \xi, \eta \rangle$ is a *lexical decomposition* of P relative to ψ, Δ, and $\mathcal{M}$ for S iff $P \in Sn$ and $\mathcal{M}$ is a generative semantical theory for L and $\langle 0, \Delta \rangle \in \mathcal{M}_\omega(P)$ and $\psi \in \Sigma_\Delta(S)$ and if $w_1, \ldots, w_k$ are the linguistic items having semantical occurrences in P, listed in order of occurrence in P, then:
(1) $\mathcal{D}(\xi) = \mathcal{D}(\eta) = \{1, \ldots, k\}$;
(2) for each $i \in \mathcal{D}(\xi)$, $\xi(i) \in \Sigma_{\eta(i)}(S)$;
(3) there is a unique function g such that:
  (a) $\mathcal{D}(g) = \{1, \ldots, k\}$;
  (b) for each $i \in \mathcal{D}(g)$, $\langle g(i), \eta(i) \rangle \in \mathcal{M}_\omega(w_i)$;
  (c) for every frame f and subsequence $w_{n_1}, \ldots, w_{n_m}$ of $w_1, \ldots, w_k$ such that f is of type $\langle 0, g(n_1), \ldots, g(n_m) \rangle$ and $P = f(w_{n_1}, \ldots, w_{n_m})$, there is a μ in $\mathcal{M}_{\langle 0, g(n_1), \ldots, g(n_m) \rangle}\{f\}$ such that $\Delta = \mu(\eta(n_1), \ldots, \eta(n_m))$ and if ρ is the propositional function induced by μ, then $\psi \in \rho(\xi(n_1), \ldots, \xi(n_m))$.

(5.17) S is using the *ith* semantical occurrence of w in P to *send* α in the course of using P to send ψ and state ϕ within L iff S is using P to send ψ and thereby state ϕ within L and $(\exists j)(\exists \Delta)(\exists \pi)$(the *ith* semantical occurrence of w in P is the *jth* semantical occurrence of a linguistic item in P & π is the purified sequence of values for the pragmatic parameters & Δ is the unique intension such that $[\langle 0, \Delta \rangle \in \mathcal{M}_\omega(P) \ \& \ \phi \in (\Delta/\pi)]$ and there is a unique lexical decomposition $\langle \xi, \eta \rangle$ of P relative to ψ, Δ, and $\mathcal{M}$, and $\xi(j) = \alpha$).

The basic idea behind this analysis of lexical sending is that the same assignment of sent-objects to semantical occurrences must work no matter how we decompose P into sentence frames applied to linguistic items. Such an assignment is a lexical decomposition. Should there be no unique lexical decomposition of P, no lexical sending can occur.

We can give a similar analysis of the related notion of using a (possibly ambiguous) linguistic item with a certain intension in the course of making a statement by uttering a sentence containing an occurrence of that linguistic item:

(5.18) S is *using* the *ith* semantical occurrence of w in P *with the intension* Δ in the course of using P to send ψ and state ϕ within L iff S is using P to send ψ and thereby state ϕ within L and $(\exists j)(\exists \Delta^*)(\exists \pi)$(the *ith* semantical occurrence of w in P is the *jth* semantical occurrence of a linguistic item in P & π is the purified sequence of values for the pragmatic parameters & Δ^* is the unique intension such that $[\langle 0, \Delta^* \rangle \in \mathcal{M}_\omega(P) \ \& \ \phi \in (\Delta^*/\pi)]$ and there is a unique lexical decomposition $\langle \xi, \eta \rangle$ of P relative to ψ, Δ^*, and $\mathcal{M}$, and $\eta(j) = \Delta$).

6. The Path of the Analysis

This book aims at giving an analysis of language which proceeds, ultimately, in terms of nonlinguistic and nonsemantical notions. In the Preface, I referred to such an analysis as being *vertically complete*. The analysis is complicated and the details of the analysis are apt to obscure its overall structure and make it hard to evaluate the claim to vertical completeness, so let us briefly review the general path of the analysis from nonlinguistic up through linguistic notions:

1. We characterized statements in terms of their diagrams, the latter being set-theoretic structures built out of propositions. It is not quite accurate to say that we identified statements with their diagrams, but for the purpose of our general theory of language, all reference to statements can be eliminated in favor of reference to diagrams.

2. We analyzed stating and propositional sending in terms of statemental commitments, which are moral commitments of a sort.

3. We analyzed sentence meaning in terms of S-intensions, which are functions from features of the world (the pragmatic parameters) to statements.

4. Languages are taken to be institutions comprised of constitutive rules of certain sorts. Speaking a language consists of participating in the institution, and we provided a moral analysis of what it is to participate in an institution.

5. Statemental constituents are also characterized by their diagrams.

6. We analyzed lexical meaning in terms of intensions, which are functions from pragmatic parameters to statemental constituents.

7. Lexical sending is defined in terms of participation in a language (conceived as an institution), with the rules of the language determining lexical meanings and sentence meanings.

8. Finally, accounts were proposed of the meanings of particular lexical items.

The accounts of lexical meaning proposed under (8) proceed, in part, in terms of lexical sending. Thus we seem to be threatened with circularity in (7) and (8). The circularity is avoided by the fact that the analysis of lexical sending appeals only to the *possible* sent-objects for a statemental constituent, and that is given by the diagram independently of any account of the actual sent-object. Thus if the analysis of the book is correct, the claim to vertical completeness is justified.

Bibliography

Ackerman, Diana
  1979   Proper names, propositional attitudes and non-descriptive connotations. *Philosophical Studies* 35, 55–70.
  1979a Proper names, essences, and intuitive beliefs. *Theory and Decision* 11, 5–26.
  1980   Thinking about an object: comments on Pollock. *Midwest Studies in Philosophy* 5, 501–508.
  1980a Natural kinds, concepts, and propositional attitudes. *Midwest Studies in Philosophy* 5, 469–486.

Anscombe, G. E. M.
  1958   On brute facts. *Analysis* 18, 69–72.

Belnap, Nuel, Jr., and Thomas Steel Jr.
  1976   *The Logic of Questions and Answers*. New Haven: Yale University Press.

Bennett, Jonathan
  1973   The meaning-nominalist strategy. *Foundations of Language* 10, 141–168.
  1976   *Linguistic Behavior*. Cambridge: Cambridge University Press.

Boër, Steven E., and William G. Lycan
  1975   Knowing who. *Philosophical Studies* 28, 299–344.

Bresnan, Joan
  1978   A realistic transformational grammar. In *Linguistic Theory and Psychological Reality*, edited by Morris Halle, Joan Bresnan, and George A. Miller, pp. 1–59. Cambridge Mass.: MIT Press.

Burge, Tyler
  1975   On knowledge and convention. *Philosophical Review* 84, 249–255.

Bibliography

Casteñeda, Hector-Neri
  1964   Review of Hintikka [1962]. *Journal of Symbolic Logic* 29, 132–134.
  1967   On the logic of self knowledge. *Nous* 1, 9–22.
  1968   On the logic of attributions of self-knowledge to others. *Journal of Philosophy* 65, 439–456.

Chisholm, Roderick
  1976   Knowledge and belief: 'de dicto' and 'de re'. *Philosophical Studies* 29, 1–20.
  1976a *Person and Object*. London: Allen & Unwin.

Davidson, Donald, and Gilbert Harman, eds.
  1972   *Semantics of Natural Language*. Dordrecht: Reidel.

Donnellan, Keith
  1962   Necessity and criteria. *Journal of Philosophy* 59, 647–658.
  1966   Reference and definite descriptions. *Philosophical Review* 75, 281–304.
  1972   Proper names and identifying descriptions. In Davidson and Harman, eds. [1972], 356–379.
  1974   Speaking of nothing. *Philosophical Review* 83, 3–31.
  1978   Speaker reference, descriptions, and anaphora. In *Syntax and Semantics*, vol. 9, edited by Peter Cole, pp. 47–68. New York: Academic Press.

Feyerabend, Paul K.
  1962   Explanation, reduction, and empiricism. In *Minnesota Studies in the Philosophy of Science*, edited by H. Feigl and G. Maxwell, vol. 3, pp. 28–97. Minneapolis: University of Minnesota Press.

Frege, Gottlob
  1956   The thought: a logical inquiry, translated by A. M. and Marcelle Quinton. *Mind* 65, 289–311.

Grandy, Richard
  1977   Review of Lewis [1975], *Journal of Philosophy* 74, 129–139.

Grice, H. P.
  1957   Meaning, *Philosophical Review* 66, 377–388.
  1969   Utterer's meaning and intentions. *Philosophical Review* 78, 147–177.

290

Hare, R. M.
1952   *The Language of Morals*. Oxford: Oxford University Press.

Harrah, David
1979   Review of Hintikka [1976]. *Nous* 13, 95–99.

Hintikka, Jaakko
1962   *Knowledge and Belief*. Ithaca: Cornell University Press.
1976   *The Semantics of Questions and the Questions of Semantics*. Acta Philosophica Fennica, vol. 28, no. 4. Amsterdam: North Holland Publishing Co.

Kamp, Hans
1971   Formal properties of "now". *Theoria* 37, 227–273.

Kaplan, David
1969   Quantifying in. In *Words and Objections: Essays on the Work of W. V. Quine*, edited by Donald Davidson and Jaakko Hintikka, pp. 206–242. Dordrecht: Reidel.
1975   How to Russell a Frege-Church. *Journal of Philosophy* 72, 716–729.
1977   *Demonstratives*, mimeographed.
1978   On the logic of demonstratives. *Journal of Philosophical Logic* 8, 81–98.

Katz, Jerrold
1972   *Semantic Theory*. New York: Harper and Row.

Katz, Jerrold J., and J. Fodor
1963   The structure of a semantic theory. *Language* 39, 170–210.

Katz, Jerrold J., and Paul M. Postal
1964   *An Integrated Theory of Linguistic Descriptions*. Cambridge: MIT Press.

Kim, Jaegwon
1973   Causation, nomic subsumption, and the concept of an event. *Journal of Philosophy* 70, 217–236.
1977   Perception and reference without causality. *Journal of Philosophy* 74, 606–620.

Kripke, Saul
1972   Naming and necessity. In Davidson and Harman, eds. [1972], 253–355.

291

> 1977   Speaker reference and semantic reference. *Midwest Studies in Philosophy* 2, 255–276.
>
> 1979   A puzzle about belief. In *Meaning and Use*, edited by Avishai Margalit, pp. 239–288. Dordrecht: Reidel.

Kuhn, Thomas S.
> 1962   *The Structure of Scientific Revolutions.* Foundations of the Unity of Science, vol. 2, no. 2. Chicago: University of Chicago Press.

Lambert, Karel, ed.
> 1970   *Philosophical Problems in Logic.* Dordrecht: Reidel.

Lewis, David
> 1969   *Convention: A Philosophical Study.* Cambridge, Mass.: Harvard University Press.
>
> 1972   General semantics. In Davidson and Harman, eds. [1972], 169–218.
>
> 1975   Languages and language. In *Minnesota Studies in the Philosophy of Science*, edited by Keith Gunderson, vol. 3, pp. 3–35. Minneapolis: University of Minnesota Press.
>
> 1979   Attitudes de dicto and de se. *Philosophical Review* 87, 513–543.
>
> 1981   What puzzling Pierre does not believe. *Australasian Journal of Philosophy* 59, 283–289.

Lycan, William G.
> 1975   Reply to Paul Teller, Ostensive definition revisited and revised, delivered at the APA (Western Division) meetings, Chicago, April, 1975.

McKinsey, Michael
> 1978   Names and intentionality. *Philosophical Review* 87, 171–200.

Montague, Richard
> 1963   Syntactical treatments of modality, with corollaries on reflexion principles and finite axiomatizability. *Acta Philosophica Fennica* 16, 153–167.
>
> 1970   Universal Grammar. *Theoria* 36, 373–398.
>
> 1972   Pragmatics and intensional logic. In Davidson and Harman, eds. [1972], 142–168.

1973   The proper treatment of quantification in ordinary English. In *Approaches to Natural Language: Proceedings of the 1970 Stanford Workshop on Grammar and Semantics*, edited by J. Hintikka, J. Moravcsik, and P. Suppes, pp. 221–242. Dordrecht: Reidel.

Partee, Barbara
1973   Some transformational extensions of Montague grammar. *Journal of Philosophical Logic* 2, 509–534.

Perry, John
1977   Frege's theory of demonstratives. *Philosophical Review* 86, 474–497.
1979   The problem of the essential indexical. *Nous* 13, 3–22.

Pollock, John L.
1974   *Knowledge and Justification*. Princeton: Princeton University Press.
1976   *Subjunctive Reasoning*. Dordrecht: Reidel.
1980   Thinking about an object. *Midwest Studies in Philosophy* 5, 487–500.
1981   Statements and Propositions. *Pacific Philosophical Quarterly* 62, 3–16.

Prior, A. N.
1968   Now. *Nous* 2, 101–120.

Putnam, Hilary
1962   It ain't necessarily so. *Journal of Philosophy* 59, 658–671.
1962a   The analytic and the synthetic. *Minnesota Studies in the Philosophy of Science*, edited by H. Feigl and G. Maxwell, vol. 3, pp. 358–397. Minneapolis: University of Minnesota Press.
1965   How not to talk about meaning. In *Boston Studies in the Philosophy of Science*, edited by R. Cohen and M. Wartofsky, vol. 2, pp. 205–222. Atlantic Highlands N. J.: Humanities Press.
1973   Explanation and reference. In *Conceptual Change*, edited by G. Pearce and P. Maynard, pp. 199–221. Dordrecht: Reidel.
1975   The meaning of "meaning". In *Minnesota Studies in the Philosophy of Science*, edited by K. Gunderson, vol. 7, pp. 131–193. Minneapolis: University of Minnesota Press.

Bibliography

Quine, W. V.
  1966   Quantifiers and propositional attitudes, In *The Ways of Paradox*, pp. 183–194. Minneapolis: Random House.

Rawls, John
  1955   Two concepts of rules. *Philosophical Review* 64, 3–32.

Reichenbach, Hans
  1947   *Elements of Symbolic Logic*. New York: MacMillan.

Rosenberg, Jay
  1974   *Linguistic Representation*. Dordrecht: Reidel.

Schiffer, Stephen R.
  1972   *Meaning*. Oxford: Oxford University Press.
  1978   The basis of reference. *Erkenntnis* 13, 171–206.

Schwartz, Stephen P.
  1978   Putnam on artifacts, *Philosophical Review* 87, 566–574.

Searle, John R.
  1958   Proper names. *Mind* 62, 166–173.
  1969   *Speech Acts*. Cambridge: Cambridge University Press.

Skyrms, Brian
  1978   An immaculate conception of modality. *Journal of Philosophy* 75, 368–387.

Stenius, Erik
  1967   Mood and language-game. *Synthese* 17, 254–274.

Strawson, P. F.
  1950   On referring. *Mind* 59, 320–344.

van Fraassen, Bas C.
  1977   The only necessity is verbal necessity. *Journal of Philosophy* 74, 71–85.

Zemach, Eddy M.
  1976   Putnam's theory on the reference of substance terms. *Journal of Philosophy* 73, 116–127.

Ziff, Paul
  1960   *Semantic Analysis*. Ithaca: Cornell University Press.

Index

Index

Library of Congress Cataloging in Publication Data

Pollock, John L.
   Language and thought.

   Bibliography: p.
   Includes index.
   1. Languages—Philosophy. 2. Meaning (Philosophy)
3. Language and logic. I. Title.
Pl06.P62   401   82-414
ISBN 0-691-07269-8   AACR2